WILEY SOURCEBOOKS IN AMERICAN SOCIAL THOUGHT

Edited by *David D. Hall and Daniel Walker Howe*

Daniel Walker Howe THE AMERICAN WHIGS

Staughton Lynd AMERICAN LABOR RADICALISM: TESTIMONIES AND INTERPRETATIONS

R. Laurence Moore THE EMERGENCE OF AN AMERICAN LEFT: CIVIL WAR TO WORLD WAR I

Laurence Veysey THE PERFECTIONISTS: RADICAL SOCIAL THOUGHT IN THE NORTH, 1815–1860

Donald Worster AMERICAN ENVIRONMENTALISM: THE FORMATIVE PERIOD, 1860–1915

Alan Trachtenberg LITERATURE AND SOCIETY IN TWENTIETH-CENTURY AMERICA

AMERICAN ENVIRONMENTALISM

THE FORMATIVE PERIOD, 1860–1915

Edited by
Donald Worster
Brandeis University

John Wiley & Sons, Inc.
New York • London • Sydney • Toronto

Library of Congress Cataloging in Publication Data:

Worster, Donald E   1941–   comp.
   American environmentalism.

   (Sourcebooks in American social thought)
   CONTENTS: Man and nature in an age of science:
Marsh, G.P. The pastoral vision refuted. Burroughs, J.
The ambiguous impact of science—The conservation
movement: Ward, L. [etc.]
     1. Human ecology—United States—Addresses, essays, lectures. 2. Conservation of natural resources—United States—Addresses, essays, lectures. 3. Cities and town—Planning—United States—Addresses, essays, lectures. I. Title. II. Series.
GF503.W67   1973   301.31'0973   73–85

ISBN 0–471–96100–0
ISBN 0–471–96101–9 (pbk.)
Printed in the United States of America
10–9 8 7 6 5 4 3 2 1

CONTENTS

INTRODUCTION   1

Part One MAN AND NATURE IN AN AGE OF SCIENCE

1. The Pastoral Vision Refuted
   George Perkins Marsh, The Study of Nature (1860)   13

2. The Ambiguous Impact of Science
   John Burroughs, The Summit of the Years (1913)   22

Part Two THE CONSERVATION MOVEMENT

1. Waste and Inefficiency in the Economy of Nature
   Lester Ward, The Psychic Factors of Civilization (1893)   39

2. The Engineered Landscape
   John Wesley Powell, The Lesson of Conemaugh (1889)   54

3. The Foundations of Industrial Empire in the West
   John Wesley Powell, Institutions for the Arid Lands (1890)   61

4. Natural Resources in the Welfare State
   Brenhard E. Fernow, Economics of Forestry (1902)   73

5. Conservation and the Progressive Ideology
   Gifford Pinchot, The Fight for Conservation (1910)   84

6. The End of Malthusian Scarcity
   Simon Patten, The New Basis of Civilization (1907)   96

Part Three GARDEN CITY AND SUBURB

1. The Urban Planner as a Civilizing Force
Frederick Law Olmstead, Public Parks and the Enlargement of Towns (1871)   111

2. Combating Disease and Pollution in the City
Edward Dalton, The Metropolitan Board of Health (1868)   133

3. An Early Experiment in Waste Recycling
C.A. Leas, On the Sanitary Care and Utilization of Refuse in Cities (1874)   150

4. Nature, Art, and Urbanity
Garden and Forest, Selected Articles and Editorials, 1888–1896   162

5. The Reformation of the City Dweller and His Habitat
Charles W. Eliot, The Need of Conserving the Beauty and Freedom of Nature in Modern Life (1914)   177

Part Four THE BIOCENTRIC REVOLUTION

1. Nature Versus Culture
John Muir, Wild Wool (1875)   185

2. The Revolt Against Utilitarianism
John Muir, The Yosemite (1912)   191

3. Darwinism and Moral Philosophy
Edward Evans, Ethical Relations between Man and Beast (1894)   198

4. The Emergence of an Ecological Consciousness
Nathaniel Shaler, Man and the Earth (1905)   209

5. Natural Kinship and the Land Ethic
Liberty Hyde Bailey, The Holy Earth (1915)   223

Suggestions for Further Reading   233

INTRODUCTION

The environmental images that dominated our early national consciousness received their first powerful articulation in *Letters from an American Farmer*, published in 1782, by Hector St. John de Crèvecoeur, a recent immigrant from France. America offers "a boundless field for the exertion of human industry," Crèvecoeur wrote, "a field which will not be cultivated in many ages." Unencumbered by institutional restraints on his initiative, the individual farmer could wrest from the soil the foundations of his own independence and his country's prosperity. Under these free conditions, Crèvecoeur predicted, the continent one day would show substantial cities as well as productive, self-sufficient farms where all was still "wild, woody, and uncultivated."

In contrast to this image of America as a fertile expanse to be developed by man, Crèvecoeur also perceived in American nature an unspoiled moral order. Humble conformity to this natural order would redeem a man's life from the corrupting artificiality of civilization. By following a simple, subsistence economy the American farmer could establish himself in ecological harmony with the land, recover an innocence that was lost to Europeans, and reawaken a sense of kinship with his fellow creatures. To the modern eye this latter image of the New World as another Eden, a pastoral garden, and the equally compelling vision of America as a beckoning field for laissez-faire enterprise lay in remarkable concord in Crèvecoeur's imagination. It was an unconscious amalgamation that appears repeatedly in the American experience at least until the middle of the nineteenth century.

To an immigrant arriving in New York in 1860, a century after Crèvecoeur's entry, the American landscape presented a dramatic shift from the earlier, almost wholly natural order. The population of the city had increased from less than 50,000 to almost 750,000, and in another half century its numbers would swell to 5 million. Sometime around 1915, moreover, America became in statistical fact a nation of cities and towns, over one-half of the populace being urban. In 1860

1

space was still available in the west for the prospective farmer, but within another three decades the frontier was closed, the unsettled land largely passing into the hands of corporations or remaining under government control. Where in Crèvecoeur's day stood wilderness forts, by World War I there sprawled enormous industrial cities turning out steel for skyscrapers and transcontinental railroads. And by 1914, at Henry Ford's plant outside Detroit, an automobile was manufactured every ninety minutes, a phenomenon that would become a key symbol of the almost completely artificial environment of twentieth-century America.

The years encompassed by this anthology—the period from 1860 to 1915—mark a vital transition from the more natural world of Crèvecoeur to the world of the automobile, mass consumption, and megalopolis. It was a period in which important new themes were appearing in American environmental thought. The image of the land as holding inexhaustible economic opportunity gave way to the vision of technological abundance. More striking was the fact that during these decades Crèvecoeur's other image, the pastoral ideal, began to lose credibility. Americans, intent on industrial progress and national power, generally refused to be confined to a static harmony with nature or to believe in the promise of virtue in primitive innocence. They sought new environmental models for an era characterized by cities, factories, and national political programs.

Answers to this search for more relevant models came especially from new professional groups of conservationists, engineers, city planners, architects, and scientists. Each of these groups helped to shape a set of environmental ideals demanded by an urban, industrial society. The period from 1860 to 1915 saw the emergence of these ideals, a body of thought that we can call environmentalism. That man's welfare depends crucially on his physical surroundings was a central premise of the new environmentalism. Another shared assumption was that it is better for society, through the agency of experts, to design and direct the development of the landscape rather than leave the process in the hands of untrained, self-interested men. Coordinated public planning would end what was viewed as the haphazard and exploitative practices common in the laissez-faire approach. A third dictum of the emerging environmentalism, and perhaps the most important, was the belief that science and scientific methods must become the chief foundation on which environmental plans would be built. The most significant environmental models that were articulated in the period are suggested in this introduction and in the selections from representative environmentalists that follow.

Nothing destroyed the credibility of the old pastoral vision more surely than the advance of science. The common sense and the intuitive feeling of the simple farmer seemed increasingly inadequate to a people awed by the authority of analytical reason. In contrast to Crèvecoeur's boast that the islanders of Nantucket had shaped their way of life through "native sagacity unassisted by science," Americans after the Civil War watched almost every province of their lives brought to the test of positive knowledge. "In truth," declared one leading conservationist, "America has become a nation of science. There is no industry, from agriculture to architecture, that is not shaped by research and its results; there is not one of our fifteen millions of families that does not enjoy the benefits of scientific advancement."[1]

The passage by Congress of the Land-Grant College Act in 1862 signaled the beginning of this new era of sophisticated science and its application to the environment. Henceforth large numbers of American farmers would be trained at state colleges in engineering, soil science, and agricultural chemistry. They would be taught the discoveries of Justus von Liebig and Friedrich Wöhler, two German scientists who had revolutionized chemistry by breaking down the constituents of the soil and using this knowledge to found the technology of chemical fertilizers. Consequently, for Americans of this period a golden age of unlimited agricultural productivity appeared on the horizon. It made the ideal of pastoral subsistence seem shabby and despicable, just as the accumulation of objective truths threw into disrepute older mythic responses to nature.

This era also saw the emergence of the science of ecology. By the turn of the century ecology was more than an obscure word in the dictionary (coined in 1866 by the German scientist and philosopher Ernst Haeckel); it had become a thriving research discipline, with many important studies published on the interrelationships of plants and animals. American science could boast some of the leading pioneers in the field. The new science of ecology was in a sense merely a more sophisticated version of earlier observations of the economy of nature. But now, with a better understanding of the fragility of the natural system and an increased capacity for precise measurement of environmental dynamics, science could exercise a significantly greater authority in man's dealings with nature.

Undoubtedly the most serious challenge by science to the older pastoral model came from Charles Darwin's theory of natural selection and evolution, first published in 1859. To appreciate how

[1]WJ McGee, "Fifty Years of American Science," *Atlantic Monthly*, LXXXII (September 1898), p. 320.

this theory intruded upon the pastoral idyll we must remember that for centuries men had founded their arcadian visions on the faith that nature was a moral order governed by a beneficent Providence. For instance, although Crèvecoeur noticed the conflict and suffering in nature, he persisted in believing that "the whole economy of what we proudly call the brute creation is admirable in every circumstance" and that men often can discover a better example for their moral conduct in the natural world than in a highly civilized society. By contrast, evolutionary biology dramatized, in Darwin's own words, "the dreadful but quiet war going on [in] the peaceful woods & smiling fields" of the pastoral landscape. Fifteen years after the *Origin of Species*, John Stuart Mill declared that "the order of nature, in so far as unmodified by man, is such as no being, whose attributes are justice and benevolence, would have made, with the intention that his rational creatures should follow it as an example."[2] The green breast of earth to which romantic figures like Crèvecoeur and the poet Wordsworth had repaired for a renewal of virtue was revealed to a later generation as, in truth, a battleground of violence and bloodshed. The discovery had immense import for environmental thought.

The upshot of this scientific revolution was that the pastoralist's affirmation of the superiority of nature over civilization was refuted either as a misunderstanding or a menace. It was exposed as a misunderstanding when the conventional trappings of the pastoral design—pleasant meadows and parklike groves—were perceived to be as artificial as the more formal gardens of Versailles. Arcadia had become merely another creation of man's art and technology, not categorically different from other man-made environments in requiring a triumph over natural chaos. The pastoral ideal then was simply an early stage in man's progressive endeavor to domesticate nature. Any more than this, say, any effort to return to man's primeval origins, was treated as a menace, a threat to replace the rule of reason and goodness with anarchic savagery, overturning respect for decency and commitment to a more civilized condition.

In suggesting a new environmental ideal for the post-Darwinian world, the Englishman Thomas Huxley was one of the most persuasive and influential figures for people on both sides of the Atlantic. The central theme in Huxley's late writings was the distinction, announced in 1893, between human morality and the operations of nature. "Social progress," he insisted, "means a checking of the cosmic process at every step and the substitution for it of another, which may be called the ethical process." The

[2]John Stuart Mill, "Nature," in *Three Essays on Religion* (New York, 1874), p. 25.

environmental correlative of this ethical process was—and its appearance here indicates that much of the earlier pastoralism had been discredited—a new version of the Edenic landscape. In Huxley's words, the progress of morality and civilization establishes "an earthly paradise, a true garden of Eden, in which all things should work together towards the well-being of the gardeners." For Huxley as well as for many of his contemporaries in America, the garden had become an expression, physical as well as moral, of man's empire over nature.[3]

In addition to this urge to make nature a civilized garden, many Americans shared a related hope, that an environment reformed by science and technology could provide the stimulus for a general reformation of mankind. Where Crèvecoeur's age often turned to nature as a source of regeneration, later Americans frequently began their schemes for moral improvement by reconstructing the feral landscape. Edward Bellamy, in his utopian novel *Looking Backward* (1888), supposed that so long as "the rosebush of humanity" is left to struggle for sustenance in the black, miasmatic swamp of laissez-faire nature, it forever must be a stunted, deformed growth. But transplanted to a paradise created by socialism in league with technology, the same bush would shoot forth in vigorous, fragrant beauty. Bellamy's garden, like Huxley's, was "a new world"—a reformed, redeemed nature that would make possible a new man as well.

One of the animating ideas of the post-Darwinian period was, in Bellamy's words, "an enthusiastic conception of the opportunities of our earthly existence, and the unbounded possibilities of human nature." Given the proper environment, men could be freed from the bonds of their biological past to realize their potential divinity. Progressive reformers dedicated to this goal, especially during the first decade of the twentieth century, took as their moral duty the demolition of the slum and the re-creation of the city. They also enlisted in the battle against nature: building roads and tunnels, straightening rivers, bringing water to the desert, managing the forests, activities all of which might serve to toughen the nation's spiritual fiber and establish the environment necessary for a better way of life.

Only against this background of science, progress, and reformism can the selections in this anthology be understood in their full implications. Section One makes clear the critical shift in man's

[3]Thomas Huxley and Julian Huxley, *Evolution and Ethics, 1893–1943* (London, 1947), pp. 44, 81.

perception of and relationship to the natural world experienced by Americans of the time. In Section Two the philosophy of the conservation movement is the focus. Since 1626, when the Plymouth colony established rules for the cutting of timber on public lands, there had been local efforts to bring about more prudent use of natural resources among a people wasteful and careless. But conservation as a national political movement did not begin to take form until the 1870s, and when it came of age during the administration of Theodore Roosevelt it carried a message of much more than simple economy and prudence. First, conservation was a prominent plank in the program of reform Darwinism, which predicted as the next stage in evolution man's collective, ethical mastery over the forces of nature. It was also at the center of the campaign of the late nineteenth century to introduce science, rationality, and expertise into the management of public and corporate affairs. Finally, conservation was a set of ideas wholly compatible with industrialism, so much so that the new technology even shaped the conservationist's view of nature. Thus, Roosevelt's chief conservation officer Gifford Pinchot could describe the forest as "a manufacturing plant for the production of wood." With a high sense of moral purpose Pinchot and his subordinates worked to keep the forests producing at their maximum capacity, and beyond that if science could tell them how. In short, perhaps the best concise definition of the conservation movement was Pinchot's: conservation, he declared, is "the material policy of civilization."

The scientific community raised the issue of more efficient management of nature long before the politicians made a popular crusade of it. Perhaps the single most effective effort of American scientists was the 1896 committee on forests created by the National Academy of Sciences and chaired by Charles Sprague Sargent of Harvard. In addition to completing a census of the nation's forests, the committee pointed to the need for an active program of policing and managing as well as preserving. In 1898 Gifford Pinchot, who was the youngest member of the committee and who had been trained in a French forestry school, became head of the forestry division in the Department of Agriculture. By 1905 he had successfully maneuvered the control of the public forests away from the General Land Office and into his own hands, while at the same time organizing the Forest Service to manage the trees for self-renewing production. During Roosevelt's years in office the number of acres managed by federal foresters increased enormously, and the Forest Service became one of the most active government sponsors of environmental research.

Even more important than forests to the development of conservation, both as an ideology and as a national program, was the problem of providing water resources for the west. The issue was central to western economic growth, and characteristically the conservationists spoke for maximum use of the water potential through careful planning. In 1888 John Wesley Powell, western explorer and key organizer of federal science, undertook a vast irrigation survey intended to provide a scientific guide to coordinated, large-scale regional planning. In 1902 Congress passed the landmark Newlands bill, establishing the Reclamation Service to build storage reservoirs, flood control dams, and irrigation systems. Five years later William John "WJ" McGee, whom Pinchot called "the scientific brains" of Progressive conservation, proposed an even broader multipurpose program of continental water development—an Inland Waterways Commission that would work out for the major river basins integrated plans for hydroelectric power, navigation, soil stabilization, and industrial development. But Congress balked, and the grand design went into mothballs until another Roosevelt's administration brought it out again in the form of the Tennessee Valley Authority.

During the first decade of the twentieth century the movement for conservation swelled into a national panic. In 1908 President Theodore Roosevelt summoned the nation's governors to Washington to preach to them the moral responsibility of developing wisely the natural resources and to discuss "the problem of national efficiency, the patriotic duty of insuring the safety and continuance of the Nation." But after this session of fervid oratory, the conservation movement quickly lost momentum; lethargy followed hard on the heels of anxiety. Although many of the less ambitious resource programs survived, the grander vision of a coordinated master plan for developing the American environment had all but vanished by World War I.

The movement for organized, efficient development of resources had an unmistakably urban, professional cast, directed as it was by Washington experts determined to supply an escalating industrial demand. Meanwhile, alongside the foresters and hydrologists were appearing city professionals: engineers, physicians, sanitarians, and landscape architects, some of whom are represented in Section Three of this volume. Like the conservationists, these urban designers were committed to making trained reason the indispensable agency for civilizing the environment. But even more than the conservationists, urban planners of this period failed to establish a unified approach to environmental management. For example, by the late 1850s, transportation experts were mapping out horsecar lines for the American city, and during the last decade of the century they were introducing electric trolleys, elevated trains, and outer railway belts. The rapid expansion of the nation's cities and industries seemed to require first the solution of the most pressing transportation problems, which in turn further stimulated the growth of suburbs and the dispersal of industry before other urban planners were ready or able to act. In Chicago, "the City of Push," this working at different levels of sophistication among planners, as well as popular apathy toward all but commercial values, created not a higher civilization but a new, man-made jungle. According to Rudyard Kipling, Chicago in this period was "a splendid chaos"; "having seen it," he added, "I urgently desire never to see it again."

Multipurpose, coordinated planning in the American city, to the extent that it existed during this period, developed in large measure out of the work of Frederick Law Olmsted in laying out urban parks, parkways, and residential suburbs. The landmark date here is 1858, the year Olmsted and Calvert Vaux won the design competition for New York City's Central Park. Thereafter Olmsted drafted plans for major parks in Brooklyn, Buffalo, Montreal, Chicago, and Boston. As he extended his parks out into the city by means of leafy boulevards and watercourses, they became devices for shaping the urban area as an organic whole, for creating separate but interrelated areas of commerce, industry, and residence, and for controlling the direction of metropolitan growth. In the suburban town of Riverside near Chicago, Olmsted skillfully integrated the meeting of city and country, substituting for the common street grid a system more sensitively adapted to the terrain. Through such work Olmsted, with his disciple Charles Eliot, Jr., founded a native urban tradition that led eventually to the environmental humanism of Lewis Mumford, to the Regional Planning Association of the 1920s, and to the greenbelt communities of the New Deal.

Many of the leading themes in environmental thought during this time were suggested by the phrase "garden city." Made famous after 1898 by the English planner Ebenezer Howard, the concept in a more general sense had its roots in America. Garden City, for example, was the name taken by a Long Island suburb as early as 1868; and according to a popular saying, before the Great Fire of 1871 Chicago had been "a garden city built on a wild onion marsh." Undoubtedly the image of a city or suburb liberally furnished with green trees and lawns spoke with special resonance to a people who had recently migrated from more rural surroundings. The related idea of large urban parks, which Olmsted promoted as "pastoral" landscapes, appealed to many city fathers as an opportunity to provide an antidote for the nervous tension in the business community and for the sorry conditions of the poorer classes. But the nature that the park movement succeeded in introducing into the city was, for its more thoughtful proponents, an extension of a distinctly urban consciousness. Boston's suburb of Brookline, the home of the firm of Olmsted, Olmsted, and Eliot, was perhaps the most complete expression of the garden-city ideal: a "village" inside the urban radius, with winding carriage drives, ample green spaces, and large half-timbered or shingle-style "cottages." No one could deny that here was a pastoral scene, but it was one that presupposed a high degree of professional planning and educated affluence to make nature suitable for civilized tastes.

The garden-city ideal pointed up a paradoxical but persuasive assertion in the environmental thought of the period that should serve as a warning against a strictly antinaturalistic reading of some of the conservationists and urban planners. In contrast to the primitivistic tendencies of Crèvecoeur's age, these later Americans frequently argued that a sensitivity to nature, especially in an aesthetic or moral sense, is the peculiar property of an advanced, civilized people. As humanity moves further away from the struggle for survival and secures an easier estate, they contended, men begin to respond to nature with affection and benevolence rather than with fear or greed. Supporting this belief was the fact that men such as Olmsted were among the earliest advocates of state and national wilderness parks. The National Audubon Society, established in 1905, also drew its principal support from educated circles in eastern cities.

But the older pastoral ideal was not entirely forgotten during these years. In the chief intellectual resource of the era, Darwinian science, a small number of Americans, who are represented in the last section, were discovering the materials for a revival of the essential elements in the earlier pastoralism. Unlike those who drew from the theory of natural selection a justification for remodeling nature, this party emerged with a scientific defense of the primitive environment. Man, it was pointed out, is but a single strand in the ecological web of life, bound also to his fellow creatures by the deepest bonds of genealogy, which can be dismissed only by denying an essential dimension of his identity. This elementary kinship, some maintained, requires from man a new "biocentric" understanding of his place and role on earth. The practical conclusions to which such a reading of Darwin were likely to lead could be sharply critical of the various forms of environmental humanism, including the commodity view of nature inherent in conservation and the amenity position commonly taken by urban planners. For the alternative sense of living nature as a community transcending the human social order, Darwin himself provided a precedent; he had spoken of other species as "our fellow brethren in pain, disease, death, suffering, and famine."

In the Americans John Muir and Liberty Hyde Bailey there was evident not only the same acknowledgment of kinship with nature but also other aspects of the older pastoralism, such as rambling through fields and woods in pursuit of a higher, divine virtue or tilling the soil to feed one's family a simple subsistence. But these distinctly rural elements had become less crucial to the pastoral ideal. The more important ingredients had been, and now were once more, a sense of man's primitive relatedness to nature and an endeavor to see beyond the obscuring civilization in order to recover that awareness and express it in environmental terms. Science then, though it promised to carry man to absolute empire, also pointed toward a less conspicuous, more cooperative relationship between the human species and the ecological order.

In this diverse and very complex period, one theme appears repeatedly: that henceforth scientists and other technical experts must furnish the guiding principles for man's environmental behavior. There was, however, an unsuspected snare in this new-found faith. Even if we grant that science was the reliable, objective guide that Americans wanted, the scientists themselves were not able to escape a biased reading of their data. Consequently they often spoke with confusing dissonance, more frequently on the side of an advancing humanistic civilization, but now and then on behalf of an older naturalistic pastoralism.

The authority of science, in other words, proved to be and still is today, an ambivalent guide. On the one hand it was seen as the chief means in modern times by which men transcend their origins, achieve dominion on earth, and demonstrate the special gift of reason that distinguishes the species. On the other hand science established on new foundations the ancient intuition that man is an integral part of nature and must be studied and appreciated primarily in that context. Neither the physical transformations in the environment since Crèvecoeur's day nor the perceptual revolutions in science made obsolete this fundamental tension between man's origins and future. The enduring problem in environmental thought is to reconcile the terms of that conflict.

Part One

MAN AND NATURE
IN AN AGE OF SCIENCE

1
THE PASTORAL VISION REFUTED

George Perkins Marsh
THE STUDY OF NATURE

George Perkins Marsh (1801–1882) was the author of the first important ecological study in America, Man and Nature, originally published in 1864 and recently reissued. An exhaustive technical account of how man, to his own misfortune, has disrupted the balance of nature by aggressive, thoughtless deforestation and overgrazing, the work is appropriately described by Lewis Mumford as "the fountainhead of the conservation movement." At home and abroad the book provoked a new awareness that man is not merely another species in an indestructible, enduring system; he is, said Marsh, "a free moral agent working independently of nature"—with enormous capacity for either self-advancement or self-destruction. Marsh, who wrote the work in the midst of a busy career as a Vermont lawyer and politician and later as minister to Italy, was no primitivist looking for a lost, stable harmony with nature. The progress of civilization, he argued, requires extensive alterations in the earth's order, but these must be carried out with informed care. In the following selection he attempts to dispel any fears Americans might have about the role of science as an intermediary between man and nature by appealing at once to American pride in material achievement and to romantic delight in the natural world. Despite its bombastic style the piece remains an effective answer to the lingering belief of pastoralists that a scientific, industrial society necessarily must destroy man's affection for and sensivity toward nature.

The life of man is a perpetual struggle with external Nature. Her spontaneous and unelaborated products yield him neither sufficient nor appropriate food, nor clothing, nor shelter; and all her influences, if untamed and unresisted, are hostile to his full development and

SOURCE. George Perkins Marsh, "The Study of Nature," *The Christian Examiner*, January 1860.

perfect growth, to his physical enjoyments and his higher aspirations, and even to his temporal existence. While obedience to her dictates is the law of all lower tribes of animated being, it is by rebellion against her commands and the final subjugation of her forces alone that man can achieve the nobler ends of his creation. His first conscious voluntary effort is to protect himself against her adverse influences, and the whole premeditated action of the primitive untutored son of Adam is absorbed in appropriating from her scattered stores the raw material which his rude art may convert into the means of sheltering himself from her rigors, and of prolonging an animal existence so low and so barren, that nothing but the instinctive fear of death gives it value. Thus far, the warfare on his part is of a defensive character; but as social life advances, as his relations are multiplied and ramified, the necessities of his position are felt to demand enlarged and varied means of action; he becomes conscious that he is the rightful lord, and Nature the lawful, though unwilling slave; he assumes an aggressive attitude, and thenceforward strives to subdue to his control, and subject to his uses, all her productive and all her motive powers.

His earliest leisure and opportunity for higher pursuits and more refined enjoyments, for the cultivation and exercise of all those powers and faculties that distinguish the human from the brute creation, are won by the subjugation of the inferior animals and the inanimate world by compelling unreasoning muscle and unconscious nature to perform those tasks that had otherwise employed and monopolized his entire physical energies; and the extent of his victories over Nature is a measure not only of his civilization, but of his progress in the highest walks of moral and intellectual life.

When a great philosopher characterized man as "Naturae minister et interpres," he did wrong to his high vocation. True, he can but interpret, not amend, her laws; but when he sinks to be her minister, to make those laws the rule of his life, to mould his action to her bidding, he descends from the sphere of true humanity, abdicates the sceptre and the purple with which the God of nature has invested him, and becomes a grovelling sensualist or a debased idolater. Wherever he fails to make himself her master, he can but be her slave. In this warfare there is no drawn battle. Within, the sensuous or the intellectual must triumph; without, intelligent energy or the brute forces must prevail. In fact, this struggle and this victory constitute so necessary a condition of all other great human achievement, that man rises higher in proportion to the magnitude of the physical inconveniences and wants he successfully combats and finally vanquishes. Humanity has exhibited her loftiest examples of heroism, and wisdom, and virtue, and great exploit, on those soils and in those climates where the earth, with the latent capacity of giving the most, does yet spontaneously yield the least.

Under such circumstances it is that all our powers enjoy their highest stimulus—the necessity of exerting every energy to secure the means of sustaining even animal life, combined with the certainty that the same efforts, wisely directed and perseveringly continued, will result in crowning our toils with the enjoyment of every good thing that Providence has anywhere placed within the reach of our species.

Universal tradition has planted our ancestral cradle on the highlands of that continent where all the cereal grains, all the textile vegetables, all the important fruits, all the domestic animals, in short, all the regular sources of supply of food and clothing, known to the Old World, appear to have originated; and this under skies so tempered, and on soils so constituted, that the infant life of our race was made up of lessons of industry, patience, self-denial, and self-reliance, which are necessary ingredients of all power and human virtue. The tribes which trace their origin most directly to the primitive stock, and which, in their subsequent migrations, have peopled regions marked by analogous physical conditions, have inherited the largest share of those fundamental excellences, and, if not the earliest in attaining a seeming and specious culture, have extended farthest the realm of human action, of human virtue, and of human thought.

On the other hand, where man is the spoiled child of what are called "more favored climes," where no rude winter stimulates the constructive power to the contrivance and erection of permanent and secure dwellings, where fairest flower and savory fruit and nutritious bulb reward the slightest effort with rich profusion, and an hour of toil insures a week of careless sensual enjoyment—there man, even of the noblest race, falls almost to an equality with the brute, and remains at that low level, until, as in some tropical regions, increasing numbers, and a consequently inadequate supply for the material wants of life, once more rouse his latent energies, and compel him to assert his right to be regarded as the master, not the parasitic guest, at the table of Nature.

The study of Nature's laws, therefore, a knowledge of her products and her powers, an independence of her influences, a control over her action, is an indispensable means of the first attainment and subsequent extension of high civilization and social improvement, of every form—in short, of general human progress, as well as of individual culture; and hence this study becomes one of the most obligatory duties, as well as the most imperious necessities, of our condition.

It is a marked and most important distinction between the relations of savage and of civilized man to nature, that, while the one is formed and wrought upon in mental as well as in physical characteristics by the peculiarities of his birthplace and other external natural causes, the other is more or less independent of their action, and his development is accordingly, in a corresponding degree, original and self-determined. Hence in proportion to man's advance in natural knowledge, and his consequent superiority over outward physical forces, is his emancipation from the influence of climatic and other local causes, and the more clearly does he manifest those attributes of his proper humanity which vindicate his claim to be called a being, not a thing—a special creation living indeed *in* Nature, but not a product of her unconscious action, or wholly subject to her inflexible laws.

When, by human art, the temperate and the torrid zones are made to yield substantially the same products, and supply the same material necessities of life; or when their inhabitants are familiarized with and brought to the use and enjoyment of each other's peculiar advantages, by more rapid and economical means of transport, when the mountains are pierced with roads and canals, the plains intersected with iron ways, when island and continent, and opposite shores of broad rivers and broader seas, are virtually joined by swift and sure conveyances; then local peculiarities and local interests give place to universal and truly human sympathies: men are set free from mere material influences, and, stripped of their national characteristics and their clannish prejudices, the horizon of their philanthropy is widened, they become cosmopolite in sentiment, and feel, emphatically, that the human family has a common interest, and tends to a common destiny.

Wherever such physical improvements as we have here noticed have reached, we find at least the educated and more favored classes alike in manners, in fundamental moral principle, in general intellectual attainment, in their views of the true aims and possible progress of civil society; and the superficial observer, disappointed at meeting the refinements of Europe in an Asiatic saloon, makes this apparent uniformity a cause of complaint against modern civilization, which, as he conceives, has reduced social man everywhere to one dead level of tame and unpicturesque mediocrity. But this is a wholly mistaken view of the actual moral and intellectual condition of civilized humanity. Man, no longer cramped by special and local restraints, no longer moulded by circumscribed and narrow influences, no longer trained to the exclusive imitation of national models, is in fact more freely developed, and, under whatever resemblances of outward form, is more distinctly individualized, than at that not remote period when every nation had its known and recognizable type, in which all individuality was lost. In our time, the local varieties are disappearing, as the general improvement of the race advances; and while men are specifically more alike, they are individually more distinct, more consciously independent and spontaneous in character and action.

These great moral and social changes are no doubt in large proportion to be ascribed to the extended and successful prosecution of the studies we are advocating; but these studies appeal also with irresistible force to those refined sensibilities which constitute the aesthetical part of our nature, and the man of cultivated taste finds them an indispensable auxiliary in the intelligent enjoyment of the visible world around him.

This, indeed, is not the current opinion of hasty inquirers. We are popularly told, that not only has the progress of physical knowledge promoted a materialistic and sensuous philosophy, but that it has tamed the imagination of the bard, vulgarized the phenomena of nature, and dispelled the poetry of common life. We are referred to the Greeks, as a people philosophic, intellectual, and refined to a degree surpassing all that modern civilization has produced, profoundly wise in all immaterial knowledge save that which the Revelation that was denied to them alone can teach, supereminently skilful in every branch of creative and of imitative art, and yet acquainted with only the most obvious physical facts, and with none but false and puerile theories whereby to explain the *rationale* of them. But this is, to some extent, a mistaken assumption. The difference between the physical knowledge possessed by the Greeks, as well as by some other ancient nations, and that which the moderns have accumulated, consists partly in its form and direction, not altogether in its amount. The laws of statics, for example, though doubtless differently conceived and enunciated, were as well known to the Greeks as to ourselves, and their works show as familiar an acquaintance with nature *in equilibrio* as the most substantial of modern erections. The permanence and stability of their great structures suppose a careful study and a long observation of the laws applicable to bodies at rest, and the curves of the Parthenon imply, not only the employment of a subtile and refined geometry, but a hitherto unsuspected knowledge of the principles of optics. Their most eminent metaphysicians attached high value to every then known branch of the science of number and magnitude, and their philosophy embraced physics in the most extended sense of the term. Learned artistic criticism has shown that the progress of their formative art was dependent upon the advancement of their science, and that their highest excellence in sculpture was not attained until they had reached an elevated point in pure mathematics.

But we must here observe what has not been usually sufficiently considered, that the intellectual conceptions, the moral sensibilities, and the poetic imagery of the Greeks, were narrowed and abridged precisely in the direction where their natural knowledge was most imperfect. With dynamics, the laws of force and motion, they had but a very limited acquaintance. They were ignorant of all the greatest facts and the most comprehensive laws of nature; and, though profound in geometry, they can hardly be said to have possessed an arithmetic. A people, however intellectually gifted, but unenlightened by a revealed and spirtualized religion; unacquainted with the vast periods of improved astronomy and cosmogony; without a knowledge of the magnitudes, the distances, the movements, or the velocities of the heavenly bodies, the speed of electricity or light, or even of modern military projectiles; with a numerical system totally unsuited to dealing with great quantities; with a geography that did not extend beyond the temperate zone, and in longitude embraced but a fourth part of the earth's circumference; and with a history whose earliest probable traditions scarcely went back ten centuries—such a people could elevate itself to none of the grand conceptions which give such dignity and such sublimity to the science of the stars, and even to the special physical history of our own planet; to none of the lofty imagery with which not our poetry alone, but our daily life, is ennobled; to none of those wide views of cosmopolite philanthropy which make this great globe a theatre for the exercise of a universal charity.

To us, accustomed from infancy to an arithmetical notation that enables the eye to seize at a glance the expression of the vastest quantities, and to combine, multiply, and divide those quantities with magical celerity—familiar with periods extending through myriads of centuries, with distances measured by millions of the earth's diameters, with magnitudes to which our globe is but a vanishing point, with material velocities that ten thousand times surpass the swiftest old poetic notions of the rapidity even of divine motion, with the countless legions of animated existences which the marvellous revelations of the microscope have made known to us, with the terrors of the polar iceberg and the gorgeous luxuriance of tropical vegetation—to us, thus instructed, it is difficult to imagine an intellect highly cultivated, but yet without the sublime conceptions of extended space, of prolonged duration, of rapid motion, of multiplied numbers, and of earthly grandeur and beauty and power, which modern science has made as it were a part of our mental constitution. But it is certain that these great ideas had no place in the mind of the imaginative Greek. His views of the sensible creation were as humble and as narrow as his theories of the character and attributes of the Divinity. His habitable earth was of less extent than the dominions of a modern Muscovite Czar, his language had no name for any collective number greater than ten thousand, the steeds that wheeled the chariot of the Homeric Jove moved but by leaps that human sight could measure, and his heavens themselves rested on terrestrial pinnacles. The necessarily circumscribed character of his material conceptions could not fail to react on his moral and intellectual nature; and not only the absence of sublime imagery in his poetry, but his want of an enlarged philanthropy, of a humane and enlightened policy in his foreign relations, and of elevated views of the temporal and eternal destiny of man, was, to some extent, the natural consequence of his limited notions of time and space, and number and motion. To the polished Athenian, as to the modern Chinese, every man of a foreign speech was a barbarian and an outlaw, and he conceded even to the alien Greek none of the rights of our common humanity, except as from time to time a temporary and shifting community of interest made it expedient to recognize them.

We can by no means admit, that a familiarity with the truly expounded laws of nature has any tendency to clothe sensuous things in a humbler garb, or to render more prosaic the current of human life. Wherever modern science has exploded a superstitious fable or a picturesque error, she has replaced it with a grander and even more poetical truth. In the whole range of those mythologies which are built on the apotheosis of mortal heroes, or the deification of the powers of spontaneous nature, in the cosmogonies of the ancient bards, in the warfare of the Gods and the Titans, we find no such theme for ode or anthem as the recent history of scientific research and triumph supplies in abundant profusion. Which is fitter to be celebrated in immortal song, the fiction of a Jupiter launching the forked lightning to avenge a slight offered to a favored mortal, or the true story of the sage philosopher, who, by the aid of a child's toy, forged fetters to chain the thunderbolt? . . .

In fact, the observation and knowledge of nature has vastly increased the wealth of imagery at the command of the poet, and opened to him an inexhaustible mine of the noblest illustration, in veins quite unknown to the ancient world. Verse is fast ridding itself of the flat conventionalities drawn from old mythologies and erroneous or symbolically expressed physical theories, and which, though once instinct with life, and even truth as seen from the point whence they were originally contemplated, have long ceased to have any significance or force for us, and are, if not unsightly excrescences, little better than expletives, in modern poetry. In all references to natural objects and natural processes, poetry now gives us living images in place of stereotyped and hollow phrases. The descriptive sketches of Wordsworth, or Bryant, or Robert Browning, or Tennyson, without parade of physical science or use of technical nomenclature, make us feel in every line that here indeed man is the interpreter of nature. . . .

In the genial influence of [Alexander von] Humboldt and other kindred spirits, we find the clearest exemplification of the connection between the progress of science and that of the fine arts, and especially of that new branch of imitation which owes its present character, if not its specific existence, to an increasing acquaintance and sympathy with nature, the art of landscape-painting.

With·rare exceptions, like that of the younger Pliny and some few others, the ancients, in spite of their high aesthetical culture, were, in general, much more insensible than the moderns to the charms of nature. The love of landscape and rural beauty has been increased much in proportion to our familiarity with the different branches of natural knowledge, whose objects are embraced in every extended view of the earth's surface. Cicero could travel from Rome to Cilicia, and fill his frequent epistles with selfish trifles, while scarcely bestowing a glance upon the magnificent scenery, so new and so strange to Roman eyes, through which his journey led him. For the same reason, landscape-painting cannot be said to have existed as an independent branch of the pictorial art, and it appears to have been only employed as a mode of architectural decoration.

A renowned German writer has asserted that Hackert, an artist of the last century, was the first painter who in his landscapes correctly discriminated between the different species of trees. The early painters of Germany itself might have taught the critic that this sweeping assertion was an error; but it is nevertheless true, that not only foliage, but all forms of vegetation, were rather conventional than imitative in art, until the diffusion of botanical knowledge had made specific distinctions familiar. . . .

The economic value and the lower uses of physical knowledge are too familiar, and the brilliant rewards it holds out to those who most successfully pursue it are too tempting, to make it necessary to appeal to such considerations, and we would rather urge the student to follow it for its own sake, and to seek in it inherent compensations for the toil it may cost him. The great object of accumulating the facts and mastering the principles which together compose the body of natural knowledge is, that we may learn, not how to extract a larger amount of physical good out of the resources of Nature, for this is but an incidental advantage, but how to emanicipate ourselves from her power, and make our victories over the external world a vantage-ground to the conquest of the yet more formidable and not less hostile world that lies within. . . .

2

THE AMBIGUOUS IMPACT OF SCIENCE

John Burroughs
THE SUMMIT OF THE YEARS

Despite Marsh's reassurances, Americans continued to harbor misgivings about science. The extraordinarily popular phenomenon of nature writing that appeared in the later decades of the nineteenth century testified to their bewilderment about the meaning of increasingly abstruse knowledge and their desire to read more genial interpreters of nature without altogether sacrificing objective truth. Chief among such nature essayists was John Burroughs (1837–1921). A self-educated farmboy from the Catskills, Burroughs' early works were idyllic portraits of birds and woodchucks. In the three decades prior to his death Burroughs was a kind of priest to Americans who were uneasy about their physical and intellectual environment. His own obvious confusions about the nature revealed by science were shared by a large audience of middle-class urban and suburban nature lovers, who were eagerly pursuing natural history but were painfully uncertain of what they were after. Few were as willing to do without science as they were anxious to leave behind the urban, industrial world. But how could one re-enter a pastoral life without also reverting to an earlier consciousness, somehow forgetting all that science had taught? Burroughs's reply, somewhat reluctantly given, was that one must try to accept both science and technology. There was not much choice in the matter.

How surely the race is working away from the attitude of mind toward life and nature begotten by an age of faith, into an attitude of mind toward these things begotten by an age of science! However the loss and gain may finally foot up, the movement to which I refer seems as inevitable as fate; it is along the line of the mental evolution of the race, and it can be no more checked or thwarted than can the

SOURCE. John Burroughs, *The Summit of the Years* (Boston, 1913), pp. 48–75.

winds or the tides. The disturbance of our mental and spiritual equilibrium consequent upon the change is natural enough.

The culture of the race has so long been of a non-scientific character; we have so long looked upon nature in the twilight of our feelings, of our hopes and our fears, and our religious emotions, that the clear midday light of science shocks and repels us. Our mental eyesight has not yet got used to the noonday glare. Our anthropomorphic views of creation die hard, and when they are dead we feel orphaned. The consolations which science offers do not move our hearts. At first the scientific explanation of the universe seems to shut us into a narrower and lower world. The heaven of the ideal seems suddenly clouded over, and we feel the oppression of the physical. The sacred mysteries vanish, and in their place we have difficult or unsolvable problems.

Physical science magnifies physical things. The universe of matter with its irrefragable laws looms upon our mental horizon larger than ever before, to some minds blotting out the very heavens. There are no more material things in the world than there always have been, and we are no more dependent upon them than has always been the case, but we are more intently and exclusively occupied with them, subduing them to our ever-growing physical and mental needs.

I am always inclined to defend physical science against the charge of materialism, and that it is the enemy of those who would live in the spirit; but when I do so I find I am unconsciously arguing with myself against the same half-defined imputation. I too at times feel the weary weight of the material universe as it presses upon us in a hundred ways in our mechanical and scientific age. I well understand what one of our women writers meant the other day when she spoke of the "blank wall of material things" to which modern science leads us. The feminine temperament—and the literary and artistic temperament generally—is quite likely, I think, to feel something like a blank wall shutting it in, in the results of modern physical sciences. We feel it in Herbert Spencer and Ernest Haeckel, and now and then in such lambent spirits as [Thomas] Huxley and W. K. Clifford. Matter, and the laws of matter, and the irrefragable chain of cause and effect, press hard upon us.

We feel this oppression in the whole fabric of our civilization—a civilization which, with all its manifold privileges and advantages, is probably to a large class of people the most crushing and soul-killing the race has ever seen. It practically abolishes time and space, while it fills the land with noise and hurry. It arms us with the forces of earth, air, and water, while it weakens our hold upon the sources of personal power; it lengthens life while it curtails leisure; it multiplies our wants while it lessens our capacity for simple enjoyments; it opens up the heights and depths, while it makes the life of the masses shallow; it vastly increases the machinery of education, while it does so little for real culture. "Knowledge comes but wisdom lingers," because wisdom cannot or will not come by railroad, or automobile, or aeroplane, or be hurried up by telegraph or telephone. She is more likely to come on foot, or riding on an ass, or to be drawn in a one-horse shay, than to appear in any of our chariots of fire and thunder.

With the rise of the scientific habit of mind has come the decline in great creative literature and art. With the spread of education based upon scientific principles, originality in mind and in character fades. Science tends to eliminate the local, the individual; it favors the general, the universal. It makes our minds and characters all alike; it unifies the nations, but it tames and, in a measure, denatures them. The more we live in the scientific spirit, the spirit of material knowledge, the farther we are from the spirit of true literature. The more we live upon the breath of the newspaper, the more will the mental and spiritual condition out of which come real literature and art be barred to us. The more we live in the hard, calculating business spirit, the farther are we from the spirit of the master productions; the more we surrender ourselves to the feverish haste and competition of the industrial spirit, the more the doors of the heaven of the great poems and works of art are closed to us.

Beyond a certain point in our culture, exact knowledge counts for so much less than sympathy, love, appreciation. We may know Shakespeare to an analysis of his last word or allusion, and yet miss Shakespeare entirely. We may know an animal in the light of all the many tests that laboratory experimentation throws upon it, and yet not really know it at all. We are not content to know what the animal knows naturally, we want to know what it knows unnaturally. We put it through a sort of inquisitorial torment in the laboratory, we starve it, we electrocute it, we freeze it, we burn it, we incarcerate it, we vivisect it, we press it on all sides and in all ways, to find out something about its habits or its mental processes that is usually not worth knowing.

Well, we can gain a lot of facts, such as they are, but we may lose our own souls. This spirit has invaded school and college. Our young people go to the woods with pencil and note-book in hand; they drive sharp bargains with every flower and bird and tree they meet; they want tangible assets that can be put down in black and white. Nature as a living joy, something to love, to live with, to brood over, is now, I fear, seldom thought of. It is only a mine to be worked and to be through with, a stream to be fished, a tree to be shaken, a field to be gleaned. With what desperate thoroughness the new men study the birds; and about all their studies yield is a mass of dry, unrelated facts.

In school and college our methods are more and more thorough and businesslike, more and more searching and systematic: we would go to the roots of the tree of knowledge, even if we find a dead tree on our hands. We fairly vivisect Shakespeare and Milton and Virgil. We study a dead language as if it were a fossil to be classified, and forget that the language has a live literature, which is the main concern. We study botany so hard that we miss the charm of the flower entirely; we pursue the bird with such a spirit of gain and exactitude that a stuffed specimen in the museum would do as well. Biology in the college class means dissecting cats and rats and turtles and frogs; psychology means analogous experimental work in the laboratory. Well, we know a lot that our fathers did not know; our schools and colleges are turning out young men and women with more and more facts, but, so it often seems to me, with less and less manners, less and less reverence, less and less humility, less and less steadfastness of character.

In this age of science we have heaped up great intellectual riches of the pure scientific kind. Our mental coffers are fairly bursting with our stores of knowledge of material things. But what will it profit us if we gain the whole world and lose our own soul? Must our finer spiritual faculties, whence come our love, our reverence, our humility, and our appreciation of the beauty of the world, atrophy? "Where there is no vision, the people perish." Perish for want of a clear perception of the higher values of life. Where there is no vision, no intuitive perception of the great fundamental truths of the inner spiritual world, science will not save us. In such a case our civilization is like an engine running without a headlight. Spiritual truths are spiritually discerned, material and logical truths—all the truths of the objective world—are intellectually discerned. The latter give us the keys of power and the conquest of the earth, but the former alone can save us—save us from the materialism of a scientific age.

The scientific temperament, unrelieved by a touch of the creative imagination, is undoubtedly too prone to deny the existence of everything beyond its ken. But science has its limitations, which its greatest exponents like [John] Tyndall and Huxley are frank to acknowledge.

All questions that pertain to the world within us are beyond the reach of science. Science is the commerce of the intellect with the physical or objective world; the commerce of the soul with the subjective and invisible world is entirely beyond its sphere. The very word "soul" belongs to literature and religion, and not to science. Science has no use for such a word because it stands for something which transcends its categories. Professor Tyndall confessed himself utterly unable to find any logical connection between the molecular activities of the brain-substance and the phenomenon of consciousness.

In trying to deal with such a question, he says, we are on the boundary line of the intellect where the canons of science fail us. Science denies all influence of subjective phenomena over physical processes. In the absence of the empirical fact, science would be bound to deny that a man could raise his arm by an act of volition; only "the phenomena of matter and force come within our intellectual range." There are questions of mind and there are questions of matter; philosophy deals with the former, science with the latter. The world of the unverifiable is the world of the soul, the world of the verifiable is the world of the senses. We have our spiritual being in the one and our physical being in the other, and science is utterly unable to bridge the gulf that separates them.

The physico-chemical explanation of life and of consciousness to which modern science seems more and more inclined, falls upon some minds like a shadow. In trying to explain life itself in terms of physics and chemistry, science is at the end of its tether.

The inorganic world may grind away like the great mill that it is, run by heat, gravity, chemical affinity, and the like, and we are not disturbed; but in the world of organic matter we strike a new principle, and in any interpretation of it in terms of mechanics and chemistry alone, we feel matter pressing in upon us like the four walls coming together. Why does one dislike the suggestion of machinery in relation to either our minds or our bodies? Why does the chemico-mechanical explanation of any living thing give one a chill like the touch of cold iron? It is because we feel that though life may be inseparably connected with chemical and mechanical principles, it is something more than chemistry and mechanics.

We are something more than machines, though every principle of mechanics be operative in our bodies. We are something more than bundles of instincts and reflexes and automatic adjustments, though all these things play a part in our lives. We are something more than mere animals, though we are assuredly of animal origin. The vital principle, even the psychic principle, may not be separable from matter, not even in thought, and yet it is not matter, because the matter with which it is identified behaves so differently from the matter with which it is not identified. Organic matter behaves so differently from inorganic, though subject to the same physical laws.

A stone may rot or disintegrate, but it will never ferment, because fermentation is a process of life. There is no life without chemical reactions, and yet chemical reaction is not life; there is no life without what biologists call the colloid state, and yet the colloid state is not life. Life is confined to a certain scale of temperature—beyond a certain degree up and down the scale life disappears, and yet life is not heat or motion, or moisture or chemical affinity, though inseparable from these things.

The biological view of our animal origin is an uncongenial fact, and we may struggle against it, but we cannot escape it. Science has fixed this brand upon us. "Brand," I say, but have we not always recognized our animality and known that the wolf and the tiger slumbered in us? We knew it through a figure of speech, now we know it as a concrete fact.

Carlyle turned his back upon Huxley on the streets of London because Huxley had taught that mankind had an ape-like ancestor. Why is such a thought uncongenial and repelling? No doubt it is so. There is no poetry or romance in it as there is in the Garden of Eden myth. If we could look *up* to our remote progenitors instead of *down,* if we could see them clothed in light and wisdom instead of clothed in hair and bestiality, how much more enticing and comforting the prospect would be! But we simply cannot; we must see them adown a long darkening and forbidding prospect, clothed in low animal forms and leading low animal lives—a prospect that grows more and more dim till it is lost in the abyss of geologic time.

Carlyle would have none of it! The Garden of Eden story had more beauty and dignity. That this "backward glance o'er traveled roads" repels us, is no concern of science. It repels us because we regard it from a higher and fairer estate. Go back there and look up: let the monkey see himself as man (if he were capable of it), and what would his emotions be? The prehistoric man, living in caves and clothed in skins, if we go no further back, is not a cheering person to contemplate. And his hairy, low-browed forebears in Tertiary times—can we see ourselves in them? It makes a vast difference whether we see the past as poetry, or see it as science. In the Bible, and in Whitman, we see it as poetry, in Darwin we see it as science.

"Rise after rise bow the phantoms behind me." Here Whitman, through his own creative imagination, anticipates Darwin. Carlyle probably would have been moved by such a picture of his origin as Whitman gives. It would have touched his fervid *ego.* When Haeckel or Darwin gives us an account of man's origin, it is not of my origin, or your origin; the personal element is left out, the past is not linked with the present by a flash: in other words, we see it in the light of science, and not in the light of the poetic imagination. And the light of science in such matters is the light of the broad, all-revealing noonday. It is therefore in the nature of things that the scientific view of life in some of its aspects should repel us, when it comes too near us, when it touches us personally, especially when it comes between us and our religious beliefs and aspirations.

We are not to forget that physical science is of necessity occupied with the physical side of things. And what is there in nature or in life that has not its physical side? Exclusive occupation with this side does not make the poet or the prophet or the artist or the philosopher; it makes the man of science. Such occupation, no doubt, tends to deaden our interest in the finer and higher spiritual and intellectual values. The physical side of things is not often the joyous and inspiring side. The physical side of life, the physical side of birth, of death, of sex love, the physical side of consicousness and of our mental processes, the physical or biological side of our animal origin, and so on, are not matters upon which we fondly or inspiringly dwell. The heart, which symbolizes so much to us, is only a muscle—a motor-muscle, as we may say—that acts under the influence of some physical stimulus like any other motor; the brain, which is the seat of thought and consciousness, is a mass of gray and white matter incased in the skull. Every emotion or aspiration, the highest as well as the lowest, has its physical or physiological equivalent in our own bodies.

In the light of physical science our bodies are mere machines, and every emotion of our souls is accounted for by molecular changes in the brain-substance. Life itself is explained in terms of chemico-mechanical principles. Physical science spoke in Huxley, and doubtless spoke accurately, when he said, "The soul stands related to the body as the bell of a clock to its works, and consciousness answers to the sound the bell gives out when struck." It is not a very comforting or inspiring comparison, but it is what physical science sees in the fact. And it is this side of life alone that science can deal with. Of the major part of our lives—of all our subjective experiences, our religious and aesthetic emotions, in fact the whole world of the ideal and the supersensuous—nothing can be known or explained in terms of exact science or mathematics.

To our higher sensibilities science is brutal, unhuman, unimaginative. It reveals to us an impersonal, mechanical world, where our hopes, our fears, our affections, in short our anthropomorphism, had created a personal world. Science has no fervor, no color, no dreams, no illusions, no weakness, no affections, no antagonisms, no temperament; it is not puffed up, thinketh no evil, and goes its way though all our gods totter and fall as it passes.

Science gives cold and colorless names to things. We are emotional as well as intellectual beings, but science appeals, in the first instance, to our intellects and not to our emotions. Where our religious emotions see the hand of God, science sees the sequence of efficient causes; where we fear and tremble, science is curious and inquiring.

As emotional and spiritual beings we cannot live by science alone. We can build our houses, run our farms, sail our ships, by the facts and methods of science, but as social, moral, religious, aesthetic beings, we require what science cannot give us. Our inner subjective lives are beyond its sphere.

Without soul and sentiment we cannot have literature, art, music, religion, and all that gives the charm and meaning to life; and without reason and the scientific habit of mind we cannot have exact knowledge and the mastery over the physical forces upon which our civilization is based. We must transcend physical science to reach the spiritual and grasp the final mystery of life. To science there is no mystery, there is only the inexplicable; there is no spiritual, there are laws and processes; there is no inner, there is only the outer, world. To science Goethe's exclamation, "There is a universe within thee as well," or as Jesus put it before him, "The kingdom of heaven is within you," has no meaning, because it cannot weigh and measure and systematize this inner universe. Hence, I say, if we would know the world as it stands related to our souls—to our emotional and aesthetic natures—we must look to literature and art; if we would know it as it stands related to our religious instincts and aspirations, we must look to the great teachers and prophets, poets and mystics; but if we would know it as it is in and of itself, and as it stands related to our physical life and well-being, and to our reason, we must look to science.

Science and poetry go hand in hand in this respect at least—they transform and illuminate the common, the near at hand. They show us the divine underfoot. One brings to pass what the other dreams. One brings home to our understanding what the other brings home to our emotions and aesthetic perceptions. The poets have always known there was nothing mean or commonplace; science shows this to be a fact. The poets and prophets have always known that the earth was our mother and the sun our father; science shows us how and why this is so. The poets know that beauty and mystery lurk everywhere, and they bring the fact home to our emotions, while science brings it home to our understanding. When Whitman says, "I am stuccoed with birds and quadrupeds all over," he makes a poetic or imaginative statement of Darwinism. We think science kills poetry, and it does when it kills the emotion which the poet awakens, but in many cases science awakens an emotion of its own. In astronomy, in geology, and often in chemistry, it awakens the emotion of the sublime. Poetry appeals to man, the emotional being; science appeals to him, the reasonable being. Science kills poetry when it moves the reason alone. The botanist with his pressed flower, and the collector with his skins, or his eggs and nests, are not objects the poet likes to contemplate. There are the aesthetic values of things and the scientific values. The interest of the poet is in the beauty of the flower, its human significance, and the like; that of the man of science in its structure and relations, etc.

There is one emotion of knowledge and one emotion of ignorance; that of knowledge is often the emotion of joy and faith, that of ignorance is often the emotion of fear and superstition. It would be absurd to say that men of science experienced no emotion; only it is not the emotion of sentiment, it is not usually the emotion of awe or reverence. It is the joy of discovery, the intellectual delight in the solution of new problems. Evidently the great biologist like Darwin is thrilled by the discovery of a biological law as is the poet by his happy inspirations. Think you Darwin's conception of natural selection and the descent of man required no imagination? Darwin's mind had not atrophied; his desire to know had outgrown his desire to feel. There is the enjoyment of knowledge and there is the enjoyment of beauty.

Science rarely antagonizes poetry; it takes the other road. The world has got to a point, no doubt, where it sets a greater store by knowing than by feeling, by knowledge than by sentiment; hence poetry is in the decline. The pleasures of the understanding are more to us than the pleasures of the imagination.

Science has its mysteries, but they do not awaken our emotions; it has its revelation, but it does not touch our religious sentiments; it has its beauty, but it is not the beauty that so moves us in wild, free nature; rather is it the beauty of the constructed, the artificial, or the beauty of machinery.

Let us give physical science its due. We owe to it all the exact knowledge we have of the physical universe in which we are placed and our physical relations to it. All we know of the heavens above us, with their orbs and the cosmic processes going on there; all we know of the earth beneath our feet, its structure, its composition, its physical history, science has told us. All we know of the mechanism of our own bodies, their laws and functions, the physical relation of our minds to them, science has told us. All we know of our own origin, our animal descent, science has revealed. The whole material fabric of our civilization we owe to science. Our relation to the physical side of things concerns us intimately; it is for our behoof to understand it. Practical or daily experience settles much of it for us, or up to a certain remove; beyond this, physical science settles it for us—the sources and nature of disease, the remedial forces of nature, the chemical compounds, the laws of hygiene and sanitation, the value of foods, and a thousand other things beyond the reach of our unaided experience, are in the keeping of science. We have the gift of life, and life demands that we understand things in their relation to our physical well-being.

Science has made or is making the world over for us. It has builded us a new house—builded it over our heads while we were yet living in the old, and the confusion and disruption and the wiping-out of the old features and the old associations have been, and still are, a sore trial—a much finer, more spacious and commodious house, with endless improvements and conveniences, but new, new, all bright and hard and unfamiliar, with the spirit of newness; not yet home, not yet a part of our lives, not yet sacred to memory and affection.

The question now is: Can we live as worthy and contented lives there as our fathers and grandfathers did in their ruder, humbler dwelling-place? What we owe to science on our moral and aesthetic side it would not be so easy to say, but we owe it much. It is only when we arm our faculties with the ideas and the weapons of science that we appreciate the grandeur of the voyage we are making on this planet. It is only through science that we know we are on a planet, and are heavenly voyagers at all. When we get beyond the sphere of our unaided perceptions and experience, as we so quickly do in dealing with the earth and the heavenly bodies, science alone can guide us. Our minds are lost in the vast profound till science has blazed a way for us. The feeling of being lost or baffled may give rise to other feelings of a more reverent and pious character, as was the case with the early stargazers, but we can no longer see the heavens with the old eyes, if we would. Science enables us to understand our own ignorance and limitations, and so puts us at our ease amid the splendors and mysteries of creation. We fear and tremble less, but we marvel and enjoy more. God, as our fathers conceived him, recedes, but law and order come to the front. The personal emotion fades, but the cosmic emotion brightens. We escape from the bondage of our old anthropomorphic views of creation, into the larger freedom of scientific faith.

Our civilization is so largely the result of physical science that we almost unconsciously impute all its ugly features to science.

But its ugly features can only indirectly be charged to science. They are primarily chargeable to the greed, the selfishness, the cupidity, the worldly-mindedness which has found in science the tools to further its ends. We can use our scientific knowledge to improve and beautify the earth, or we can use it to deface and exhaust it. We can use it to poison the air, corrupt the waters, blacken the face of the country, and harass our souls with loud and discordant noises, or we can use it to mitigate or abolish all these things. Mechanical science could draw the fangs of most of the engineering monsters that are devouring our souls. The howling locomotives that traverse the land, pouring out their huge black volumes of fetid carbon, and splitting our ears with their discordant noises, only need a little more science to purify their foul breaths and soften their agonizing voices. A great manufacturing town is hideous, and life in it is usually hideous, but more science, more mechanical skill, more soul in capital, and less brutality in labor would change all these things.

Science puts great weapons in men's hands for good or for evil, for war or for peace, for beauty or for ugliness, for life or for death, and how these weapons are used depends upon the motives that actuate us. Science now promises to make war so deadly that it will practically abolish it. While we preach the gospel of peace our preparations for war are so exhaustive and scientific that the military spirit will die of an overdose of its own medicine, and peace will fall of itself like a ripe fruit into our hands. A riotous, wasteful, and destructive spirit has been turned loose upon this continent, and it has used the weapons which physical science has placed in its hands in a brutal, devil-may-care sort of way, with the result that a nature fertile and bountiful, but never kind and sympathetic, has been outraged and disfigured and impoverished, rather than mellowed and subdued and humanized.

The beauty and joy of life in the Old World is a reflection from the past or pre-scientific age, to a degree of which we have little conception. In spite of our wealth of practical knowledge, and our unparalleled advantages (perhaps by very reason thereof, since humility of spirit is a flower that does not flourish amid such rank growths), life in this country is undoubtedly the ugliest and most materialistic that any country or age ever saw. Our civilization is the noisiest and most disquieting, and the pressure of the business and industrial spirit the most maddening and killing, that the race has yet experienced.

Yet for all these things science is only indirectly responsible. In the same sense is the sun responsible for the rains and storms that at times destroy us. The spirit of greed and violence, robust because it has been well-housed and fed, and triply dangerous because it is well-armed and drilled, is abroad in the land. Science gave us dynamite, but whence the spirit that uses it to wreak private revenge, or to blow up railroad bridges and newspaper and manufacturing plants? Let us be just to science. Had it never been, the complexion of our lives and the face of the earth itself would have been vastly different. Had man never attained to the power of reason, he would still have been a brute with the other beasts. It takes power to use power. Knowledge without wisdom is a dangerous thing. Science without sense may bring us to grief. We cannot vault into the saddle of the elemental forces and ride them and escape the danger of being ridden by them. We cannot have a civilization propelled by machinery without the iron of it in some form entering our souls.

With our vast stores of scientific knowledge come the same problems that come with the accumulation of worldly wealth—how to acquire the one and not lose sight of the higher spiritual values, or become intellectually hard and proud, and how to obtain the other and not mortgage our souls to the devil; in short, in both cases, how to gain the whole world and not lose our own souls. It has been done, and can be done. Although Darwin confessed toward the end of his life that he had lost his interest in art, in literature, and in music, of which he was once so fond, he never lost his intellectual humility or gentleness and sweetness of soul, or grew weary in the pursuit of truth for its own sake. He had sought to trace the footsteps of the creative energy in animal life with such singleness of purpose and such devotion to the ideal that the lesson of his life tells for the attitude of mind called religious as well as for the attitude called scientific. His yearning, patient eyes came as near seeing the veil withdrawn from the mystery of the world of animal life as has ever been given to any man to see.

Huxley, the valiant knight in the evolutionary warfare, was not a whit behind him in the disinterested pursuit of scientific truth, while he led him in his interest in truths of a more purely subjective and intellectual character. Huxley was often accused of materialism, but he indignantly resented the charge. He was a scientific idealist, and he shone like a holy crusader in following the Darwinian banner into the territory of the unbelievers.

One may question, after all, whether [the] oppression which our sensitive souls feel in the presence of the results of modern science be the fault of science or of our own lack of a certain mental robustness, or spiritual joy and vigor, that enables one to transmute and spiritualize science. Let us take courage from the examples of some of the great modern poets. Tennyson drew material, if not inspiration, from the two great physical sciences geology and astronomy, especially in his noblest long poem, "In Memoriam." Clearly they did not suggest to him a blank wall of material things. Later in his life he seems to have feared them as rivals: "Terrible Muses" he calls them, who might eclipse the crowned ones themselves, the great poets.

Our own Emerson was evidently stimulated by the result of

physical science, and often availed himself, in his later poems and essays, of its material by way of confirming or illustrating the moral law upon which he was wont to string everything in reach. Emerson, in his eagerness for illustrative material in writing his essays, reminds one of the pressure certain birds are under when building their nests—birds like the oriole, for instance. Hang pieces of colored yarn near the place where the oriole is building its nest, and the bird seizes upon them eagerly and weaves them into the structure, not mindful at all of the obvious incongruity. Emerson in the fever of composition often snatched at facts of science that he had read in books or heard in lectures, and worked them into his text in the same way, always reinforcing his sentence with them. The solvent power of his thought seemed equal to any fact of physical science.

Whitman was, if anything, still more complacent and receptive in the presence of science. He makes less direct use of its results than either of the other poets mentioned, but one feels that he has put it more completely under his feet than they, and used it as a vantage-ground from which to launch his tremendous "I say."

"I lie abstracted and hear the tale of things, and the reason of things,
They are so beautiful I nudge myself to listen."

Addressing men of science he says,

"Gentlemen, to you the first honors always;
Your facts are useful and yet they are not my dwelling;
I but enter by them to an area of my dwelling"

as all of us do who would live in a measure the life of the spirit. To Whitman the blank wall, if there was any wall, was in his area and not in his dwelling itself.

The same may be said of Henri Bergson whose recent volume, "Creative Evolution," is destined, I believe, to mark an epoch in the history of modern thought. The work has its root in modern physical science, but it blooms and bears fruit in the spirit to a degree quite unprecedented.

When we can descend upon the materialism of the physical sciences with the spiritual fervor and imaginative power of the men I have named, the blank wall of material things will become as transparent as glass itself, and the chill will give place to intellectual warmth. . . .

We must face and accept the new conditions. They will seem less hard to our children's children than to us. If the old awe and reverence must go, the old fear and superstition must go with them. The religious ages begat a whole brood of imps and furies—superstition, persecution, witchcraft, war—and they must go, have gone, or are going. The new wonder, the new admiration, the new humanism, with the new scientific view of the universe, chilling though it be, must come in. We shall write less poetry, but we ought to live saner lives; we shall tremble and worship less, but we shall be more at home in the universe. War must go, the zymotic diseases must go, hidebound creeds must go, and a wider charity and sympathy come in.

There is nothing that fuses and unifies the nations like scientific knowledge, and the rational views that it inculcates—knowledge founded upon the universal nature which is in all countries the same. Science puts the same tools in all hands, the same views in all minds; we are no longer divided by false aims, or by religions founded upon half-views or false views. The local gives place to the universal. We come to see that all people are one, and that the well-being of each is the well-being of all, and *vice versa*. Distrust gives place to confidence; jealousy gives place to fellowship. Like knowledge begets like aims; the truths of nature make the whole world kin. The individual and the picturesque will suffer, local color will fade, but the human, the democratic, the average weal, will gain.

It must be said that literature has gained in many respects in this hurrying, economic age; it has gained in point and precision what it has lost in power. We are more impatient of the sham, the make-believe, the dilatory, the merely rhetorical and oratorical. We are more impatient of the obscure, the tedious, the impotent, the superfluous, the far-fetched. We have a new and a sharpened sense for the real, the vital, the logical. The dilatory and meandering methods of even such a writer as Hawthorne tire us a little now, and the make-believe of a Dickens is well-nigh intolerable. We want a story to move rapidly, we want the essay full of point and suggestion; we find it more and more difficult to read books about books, and all writing "about-and-about" we are impatient of. We want the things itself; we want currents and counter-currents—movement and rapidity at all hazards.

We are used to seeing the wheels go round; we feel the tremendous push of our civilization all about us; we see the straight paths, despite obstacles, that the controlled physical forces make over the earth's surface; we are masters of the science of short cuts in all departments of life; and both literature and philosophy respond to these conditions. Pragmatism has come in, dogmatism has gone out; the formal, the perfunctory, the rhetorical, count for less and less; the direct, the manly, the essential, count for more and more. Science has cured us of many delusions, and it has made us the poorer by dispelling certain illusions, but it has surely made the earth a much more habitable place than it was in the prescientific ages.

Part Two

THE CONSERVATION
MOVEMENT

1

WASTE AND INEFFICIENCY
IN THE ECONOMY OF NATURE

Lester Ward
THE PSYCHIC FACTORS OF CIVILIZATION

Although he did not lend direct aid to the national conservation movement, Lester Ward (1841–1913) vibrated to the same reformist chord. Moreover, as a member of various scientific societies in Washington and as an employee in the Geological Survey, he stood for several decades at the right hand of the movement's early general John Wesley Powell; he dedicated his first book, Dynamic Sociology, to Powell, who returned the compliment with his last work. The following selection gives the essence of Ward's view of nature. His rebellion against a laissez-faire social ideal—supposedly founded on natural law—which produced conflict, suffering, and chaos, brought him ultimately to a rejection of nature as a guide in human affairs. Contradicting centuries of understanding, Ward demonstrated that nature's productive apparatus is decidedly inferior to human invention. The lesson for conservationists, also reacting against competitive individualism, was clear: nature as much as society requires intelligent directing, even restructuring, to make it an efficient and harmonious economic system. Just as Ward proposed a national academy of social scientists to study American social problems and to discover legislative solutions, so conservationists envisioned a technical corps in government to advise on the management of the nation's resources for the common welfare. So long as nature was valued primarily as an "economy," Ward's conclusion seemed inescapable: trained experts, that is, conservationists, should refashion the environment for improved and more useful productivity—to benefit man if not nature.

The word *nature* will be used [here] to denote all classes of phenomena, whether physical, vital, or even psychic, into which the intellectual or rational element does not enter, while the word *mind* will, for the sake of brevity, be employed in the somewhat popular or conven-

SOURCE. Lester Ward, *The Psychic Factors of Civilization* (Boston, 1893), pp. 240–262.

tional sense of rational or intellectual, the two terms thus mutually excluding each other, and taken together covering all possible phenomena. This broad classification will be seen to be useful and indeed necessary, although the specific object is somewhat narrower, viz., that of emphasizing the distinction between that system of economy which is based upon the actions of the human animal and that which is based upon the actions of the rational man. The former is the system of the Physiocrats, Adam Smith, Ricardo, Malthus, Herbert Spencer, and the modern individualists. The latter was foreshadowed by Auguste Comte, but has never taken any systematic shape except in *Dynamic Sociology* with which the present work naturally connects itself. Although its distorted image is reflected in numerous more or less obnoxious forms from the mirror of modern public opinion, its real character is quite unfamiliar to the greater number even of the best informed persons.

Comte recognized the influence of mind in society and placed psychology in its proper position in his hierarchy of the sciences, but he refused to regard it as a distinct science, and treated it under the name of "transcendental biology." Nevertheless, in his discussions he gave considerable weight to it, and laid stress on the elements of prevision and the control of social phenomena. Spencer, on the contrary, while he treated psychology at length and assigned it the same position, viz., between biology and sociology, failed to make it in any proper sense the basis of either his sociology or his ethics, both of which are made to rest squarely upon biology. His psychology, therefore, which indeed, was written before his biology, and largely from the standpoint of metaphysics, stands isolated and useless in his system of synthetic philosophy.

It was early observed that astronomical and physical phenomena were uniform and invariable, and it was also perceived that the actions of animals, though much more complicated, follow fixed laws which could be understood and taken advantage of by man. That the simplest human actions, such as those of children, were equally uniform and determinable was scarcely more than the result of observation. Nothing was more natural than the generalization that the acts of adults do not differ generically from those of children, and the wider generalization that all human activities and all social phenomena are as rigidly subject to natural law as are the activities of children and animals and the movements of terrestrial and celestial bodies, was but an additional short step. The early political economists seized upon this specious bit of reasoning and made it the cornerstone of their science, formulating from it their great laws of trade, industry, population, and wealth.

It is curious that this altogether sound abstract principle, the indispensable foundation of all economic and social science, should have led to the greatest and most fundamental of all economic errors, an error which has found its way into the heart of modern scientific philosophy, widely influencing public opinion, and offering a stubborn resistance to all efforts to dislodge it. This error consists in practically ignoring the existence of a rational faculty in man, which, while it does not render his actions any less subject to natural laws, so enormously complicates them that they can no longer be brought within the simple formulas that suffice in the calculus of mere animal motives. This element creeps stealthily in between the child and the adult, and all unnoticed puts the best laid schemes of economists and philosophers altogether aglee. A great psychic factor has been left out of the account, the intellectual or rational factor, the cause, origin, and nature of which were considered in Part II. From what was there said it must appear that this factor is so stupendous that there is no room for astonishment in contemplating the magnitude of the error which its omission has caused.

Although the question is primarily a psychological one, still, it is, as we now perceive, also an economic one, and it will be profitable to consider it now from this latter point of view. There are two distinct kinds of economics which may be called biological economics and psychological economics, or the economics of life and the economics of mind. The word economics is here used in its narrow or primary sense. The question is one of economy, and it is of the first importance to contrast sharply these two kinds of economy, the economy that prevails in the animal world, in the domain of life, in organic nature generally, with the economy that prevails in the human sphere, in the realm of mind, in the domain of reason.

Every one is now, since Darwin, familiar with the general nature of animal economics. It is the survival of the fittest in the struggle for existence. It is the mere physics of life, the pure unmodified and undirected psychic forces . . . working themselves out in nature. Just as in the physical world and the great clash of mechanical forces the superior prevail and produce the observed results, so in this animal physics it is superior force that counts and might is ever uppermost. The animal forces are their instincts, appetites, wants—in short, their desires. These are ever seeking satisfaction and only lack of strength can prevent them from attaining it.

It was formerly supposed that organic nature was economical of its energies. The facts of adaptation, while they gave rise to the theological error of special creation, gave rise at the same time to the biological error of natural economy. In the first place it was supposed that the adaptation was always perfect. This was repeatedly asserted and much dwelt upon in early ante-evolution days. It is still widely believed with the modification that while a changing environment constantly disturbs the equilibrium, natural selection as constantly tends to restore it. [August] Weismann, in the authorized translation of his Essays, allows the statement to stand that "each existing species shows the purpose of its being in every detail of its structure, and in its perfect adaptation to the conditions under which it lives. But it is only adapted so far as is actually necessary, only so far as to make it fittest to survive, and not a step further." But even this much cannot now be admitted, since, as will be hereafter explained, the struggle for existence consumes the organic energy and dwarfs all beings that engage in it. The notion of perfect economy naturally goes along with that of perfect adaptation. Nature was regarded as the great economist from whom man was to copy. Biologists, of course, now know better than this, and yet it continues to be reaffirmed by popular writers. Even Mr. Spencer has failed to strike out of his revised edition of *Social Statics* (1892) the remark of the original edition (1850) that "with a perfect economy, Nature turns all forces to account."

It is indeed true that nature creates nothing that is necessarily useless, that everything produced has a possible utility. This follows from the genetic method of evolution. Everything that exists is pushed into existence by a *vis a tergo*. This is the efficient cause, and nature works only through efficient causes. The universal life force is perpetually creating new forms, and these must be adapted to their environment, otherwise they cannot even be brought into being. But this adaptation need only reach the minimum stage. If it is sufficient to insure continuance the end is attained, though higher degrees are always being aimed at. The means, however, through which this adaptation is accomplished are not the most economical means conceivable. They often seem to be the least economical conceivable. They are just those that all the circumstances of the case combine to produce. Provided the end be accomplished the character of the means is wholly immaterial from a purely biological standpoint.

The extravagance of these means has become a common subject of discussion, and the facts that have accumulated are of a surprising character. A few of these were enumerated in *Dynamic Sociology* . . . but any number of other cases might be adduced. Thus in a lecture on the herring by Professor Huxley, after giving 10,000 as probably an underestimate of the number of ripe eggs shed in spawning by a moderate-sized female herring, he remarks: "Suppose that every mature female herring lays 10,000 eggs, that the fish are not interfered with by man, and that their numbers remain approximately the same year after year, it follows that 9,998 of the progeny of every female must be destroyed before they reach maturity. For if more than two out of the 10,000 escape destruction, the number of herrings will be proportionately increased."

Darwin, as all know, was so struck with the redundant fertility of the organic world and the necessary destruction involved that he made it the starting point of all his investigations. One of his earliest observations is recorded in a footnote in his *Journal of Researches*, as follows: "I was surprised to find, on counting the eggs of a large white Doris [kind of sea-slug] how extraordinarily numerous they were. From two to five eggs (each three-thousandths of an inch in diameter) were contained in a spherical little case. These were arranged two deep in transverse rows forming a ribbon. The ribbon adhered by its edge to the rock in an oval spire. One which I found, measured nearly twenty inches in length and half in breadth. By counting how many balls were contained in a tenth of an inch in the row, and how many rows in an equal length of the ribbon, on the most moderate computation there were six hundred thousand eggs. Yet this Doris was certainly not very common: although I was often searching under the stones, I saw only seven individuals. *No fallacy is more common with naturalists, than that the numbers of an individual species depend on its powers of propagation.*"

These, of course, are much more moderate cases than many that have been cited. According to M. Quatrefages two successive generations of a single plant-louse [plant-lice are parthenogenetic] would cover eight acres. The vegetable kingdom is equally full of examples. A large chestnut tree in June probably contains as much as a ton of pollen. Considering the size of a pollen-grain the number on such a tree would be next to inconceivable. Certain pines are almost equally prolific of their male spores, and these pine pollen-grains are very light so as to be wafted on the wind to immense distances. The "showers of sulphur" that are sometimes reported to have fallen in the states bordering on the great lakes have proved to consist of such pollen-grains that continuous south winds had borne from the great forests of the long-leaved pine that border the Gulf of Mexico. Many herbs, as orchids, the broom-rape, etc., produce minute seeds in vast quantities, and some of these are rare plants. Burst a puff-ball and there arises from it a cloud that fills the air for some distance around. This cloud consists of an almost infinite number of exceedingly minute spores, each of which, should it by the rarest chance fall upon a favorable spot, is capable of reproducing the fungus to which it belongs.

The defenders of natural economy who are acquainted with such facts excuse them on the ground of their necessity. They say that it is the only way in which organic life can progress. Thus Professor Grant Allen, in treating the origin of fruits, remarks: "Those plants which merely cast their naked embryos adrift upon the world to shift for themselves in the fierce struggle of stout and hardy competitors must necessarily waste their energies in the production of an immense number of seeds. In fact, calculations have been made which show that a single scarlet corn-poppy produces in one year no less than 50,000 embryos; and some other species actually exceed this enormous figure." The late Professor E. L. Youmans, the leading American disciple of Herbert Spencer, and an uncompromising individualist, once used the following language: "Nature seems to have been no more economical of her mental than of her material resources. There is a prodigality in her ways which a narrow philosophy cannot comprehend. Of her profusion of flowers, but few issue in fruit; of her myriads of eggs, but few are hatched; of her numerous tribes of life appearing in the remote past, multitudes are extinct; and, of the achievements of her intellect, the great mass is lost in oblivion. But, through all her seeming waste, Nature has, nevertheless, a grand economy. She gives the widest chances, under a system which favors the best; the failures are rejected and the fittest survive." Spencer himself hints at an explanation of this wide-spread state of things when he says: "Those complex influences underlying the higher orders of natural phenomena, but more especially those underlying the organic world, work in subordination to the law of probabilities. A plant, for instance, produces thousands of seeds. The greater part of these are destroyed by creatures which live upon them, or fall into places where they cannot germinate. Of the young plants produced by those which do germinate, many are smothered by their neighbors; others are blighted by insects, or eaten up by animals; and, *in the average of cases*, only one of them produces a perfect specimen of its species which, escaping all dangers, brings to maturity seeds enough to continue the race. Thus it is with every kind of creature." And he goes on to show that civilization has developed in substantially the same way, ignoring, however, the psychologic factor.

A few writers have taken a somewhat less optimistic view. Dr. Asa Gray remarks: "The waste of being is enormous, far beyond the common apprehension. Seeds, eggs, and other germs, are designed to be plants and animals, but not one of a thousand or of a million achieves its destiny. Those that fall into fitting places and in fitting numbers find beneficent provision, and, if they were to wake to consciousness, might argue design from the adaptation of their surroundings to their well-being. But what of the vast majority that perish? As of the light of the sun, sent forth in all directions, only a minute portion is intercepted by the earth or other planets where some of it may be utilized for present or future life, so of potential organisms, or organisms begun, no larger proportion attain the presumed end of their creation." And he immediately proceeds to quote to the same effect from the article he has been considering in the *Westminster Review:* "When we find, as we have seen above, that the sowing is a scattering at random, and that, for one being provided for and living, ten thousand perish unprovided for, we must allow that the existing order would be accounted as the worst disorder in any human sphere of action."

The last sentence quoted from this reviewer is precisely to our present point. No one denies that all this waste in the inorganic world is necessary, because neither man nor mind is responsible for it. No one either will contest that in the long run this method has actually resulted in what we recognize as general organic progress, although it is well established that retrogression may result as easily as progression, and certainly has resulted to a great extent. But the algebraic sum is what we have, and if there was a beginning in some primordial form, as most biologists suppose, that sum is quite a plus. Nor will any one object to having nature's method fully explained and exposed, and thoroughly taught as a great truth of science. It is only when it is held up as a model to be followed by man and all are forbidden to "meddle" with its operations that it becomes necessary to protest. I shall endeavor still further to show that it is wholly at variance with anything that a rational being would ever conceive of, and that if a being supposed to be rational were to adopt it he would be looked upon as insane.

Amid all this literature, only a small part of which can be noticed here, there has not been, so far as I am aware, any attempt to formulate the true law of biologic economics. Much has been said of the law of parsimony, which is a very subordinate one sometimes called into exercise. But of the great law of prodigality, which is universal, no adequate definition has yet been offered. We have seen that from its genetic character the organic force is incapable of producing any necessarily useless form. Its products, while they only rarely possess an actual value, nevertheless must all possess a potential value. This part of the law may therefore be expressed by the formula that *every creation of organic nature has within it the possibility of success.* Thus far the biologic law is economical. But, as we have seen, only the minutest fraction of that which is created becomes an *actual* success. The definition must therefore have another member to cover this part. Mr. Spencer, as quoted above, suggested that it involved the doctrine of probabilities. This does not seem precisely to express it. It is more correct to call it a process of trial and error. The fundamental principle may be called *the necessity for certainty,* or *the paramount importance of certainty,* while the process consists in *the multiplication of chances.* There seems to be no limit in nature to the degree of energy that may be put forth in the direction of securing certainty. The chances of survival, though they may seem to be abundant, will be multiplied a thousand fold in order that certainty may be made a thousand times certain. The complete law of biologic economics may therefore be expressed in the following form:

1. All organic energy results in potential utility.
2. Actual utility is secured through the indefinite multiplication of efforts.

It thus appears that in biology, while nothing takes place which does not secure some advantage, however slight, the amount of energy expended in gaining this advantage bears no fixed proportion to the value of the result. Nature acts on the assumption that her resources are inexhaustible, and while she never buys a wholly useless article she usually pays an extravagant price for it. The expressions *natural selection* and *survival of the fittest* both contain the significant implication that the bulk of things are not selected, and that only the select few who prove fit survive, while all else perishes. The first member of the biologic law of economy may be characterized by the term *practical.* The second member may in like manner be characterized by the term *prodigal.* Nature is therefore at once the most practical and the most prodigal of all economists; practical in that she never makes anything which has not the elements of utility, prodigal in that she spares no expense in accomplishing even the smallest result.

Nature may be said to be engaged in creating every conceivable form. Every one is familiar with the wonderful variety in the actual forms of vegetable and animal life. But these, innumerable as they are, only represent nature's successes. Intermediate between them there must be imagined an infinite number of failures—conceivable forms in the production of which the organic energy has expended itself in vain, and which really represent a much greater expenditure than that which has been required to create all that exists. Again, among the successful forms there are all degrees of success. There are the vigorous and robust, rejoicing in a full measure of vitality and marching forward toward the possession of the earth; and there are the weak and languishing, which the former class is gradually crowding out of existence. Between these there are all the intermediate grades. But even the successful are only temporarily so. Like human empires they have their rise and fall, and the path of natural history, like that of human history, is strewn with the remains of fallen dynasties and the ruins of extinct races.

This law may be illustrated in physics as well as in biotics. If the expenditure of energy be designated as the *cost* of any given result, then it may be said in general that *nature tends to exaggerate the cost of whatever is produced.* Thus, it may be assumed that the most economical way in which a river can flow would be in a straight line from its source to its mouth. But even if it were to begin in this way it would soon become irregular, sinuous, and crooked, and then more and more crooked, until at length the distance traversed by every drop of water would be at least doubled. This physical law which has been called "the rythm of motion" and rests on the "instability of the homogeneous," prevails also in the organic world. The tendency is everywhere to exaggerate the irregularities of normal development. This is often carried so far as to result in the production of abnormalities that cause their own extinction. Such were doubtless the strange dragons of Mesozoic time, the perhaps stranger mammals of early Tertiary time, the still more recent mastodon and mammoth, the moa and apteryx, and other wingless birds, while the living elephant and other overgrown creatures must also doubtless soon disappear. In the vegetable kingdom the coal flora is full of examples, as is also the less known flora of the Trias and Jura, and we still have many waning types, such as the maidenhair tree and the mammoth and redwood trees, whose paleontological record shows that they are just passing off the stage. Many other living plants, either through parasitism, as the Rafflesia, or through extreme specialization, as many orchids and yuccas, further exemplify this law. Such monstrosities inevitably perish with the slightest alteration in their material surroundings. The progress of organic development has thus been to a large extent the successive creation of types that have contained within themselves the elements of their own destruction—that have, as it were, broken down with their own weight. New ones of course have succeeded them, adapted for the time being to their environment, but destined in turn to outgrow their conditions and perish from the same cause. This rhythmical character of organic progress is therefore essentially self-defeating, the only progress taking place, if any, being the marginal increment resulting from the excess of the pluses over the minuses. This is the characteristic of all genetic progress. Teleo-logical progress takes place according to an entirely different law, involving a true economy of energy.

In this sketch of natural or biologic economics I have not gone into the physical explanation of the reason for the difference between it and what I shall now distinguish as human or rational economics, as set forth in *Dynamic Sociology* . . ., viz., that in the former effects are only just equal to causes. The organic force is applied directly to the object to be transformed, and the forms to be created are molded into the required shape by an infinite number of minute impacts, the sum of which is represented by the transformation effected. No advantage is taken of any mechanical principle whereby the effect is made to exceed the energy expended, as was shown in the last chapter to be the normal characteristic of all intellectual action. There is, it is true, a certain class of facts in which natural selection imitates ration-al design so closely in its ultimate products that it was formerly supposed, and is still supposed by many, that they must be the result of intelligent direction. Sharp teeth and claws, for example, are simi-lar to edged and pointed tools or weapons, and take advantage of the principle of the inclined plane in the form represented by the wedge, and this may in some cases be carried so far as to involve the principle of the screw, as in certain spirally arranged seed-vessels that bore into the ground to plant their seeds. . . . It is also a fact that in the arrangement of muscles and the passage of tendons through their cartilaginous sheaths the principle of the lever and fulcrum is utilized to a greater or less extent. All such cases, however, constitute excep-tions to the law of biologic economy, and only serve to show how instinctively all men recognize the distinction, from the surprise and interest felt at seeing nature do anything that seems to involve ration-al economy. That distinction is, that the latter is teleological and deals with final causes, while the former is genetic and deals with efficient causes. This means that while organic forms are merely pushed into existence by the pelting of atoms from behind, and are fortuitous, or literally chance products, human creations are con-ceived in advance by the mind, designed with skill for definite purposes, and wrought by the aid of a variety of mechanical principles, such as those mentioned above, by which means the energy expended is small, usually trifling, in proportion to the result accomplished. The inventive faculty of man is the primary application of reason. No other animal possesses it, not even to the extent of wielding a weapon that is not a part of its organic structure. The beaver, indeed, builds dams by felling trees, but its tools are its teeth, and no further advantage is taken than that which results from the way the muscles are attached to its jaws. The warfare of animals is waged literally with tooth and nail, with horn and hoof, with claw and spur, with tusk and trunk, with fang and sting—always with organic, never with mechanical weapons. And whatever work is done by animals is always done with tools that nature has provided through a long course of development, none of which takes advantage of any principle of physics further than as already stated.

It is in rational man, therefore, that the first application of anything worthy of the name of economy is made. Nature has no economy. Only through foresight and design can anything be done economically. Rivers thus constructed (canals, millraces, irrigating ditches, etc.) are straight, or as nearly so as true economy requires, and Professor [Giovanni] Schiaparelli's inference, from the supposed existence upon the planet Mars of extensive water ways stretching across its disk in right lines, that it is inhabited by rational beings, is generally felt to be a legitimate one, if the facts are as alleged. Everything that is done under the direction of the intellect is as economical as the degree of intelligence will permit. All failures to attain this maximum economy are due to ignorance—to lack of acquaintance with the conditions of the problem. The degree of economy therefore for the same degree of intellectual penetration will be exactly proportioned to the amount of knowledge possessed.

Nature's way of sowing seed is to leave it to the wind, the water, the birds and animals. The greater part falls in a mass close to the parent plant and is shaded out or choked to death by its own abundance. Only the few seeds that chance to be transported by one agency or another to some favorable spot and further happen to be covered up, can grow. The most of those that germinate never attain maturity on account of hostile surroundings, and only the rarest accidents of fortune live long enough to continue the race. To meet this enormous waste correspondingly enormous quantities of seed are produced. Such is nature's economy. How different the economy of a rational being! He prepares the ground, clearing it of its vegetable competitors, then he carefully plants the seeds at the proper intervals so that they shall not crowd one another, and after they have sprouted he keeps off their enemies, whether vegetable or animal, supplies water if needed, even supplies the lacking chemical constituents of the soil, if he knows what they are, and thus secures, as nearly as possible, the vigorous growth and fruition of every seed planted. This is the economy of mind.

A closer analysis shows that the fundamental distinction between

the animal and the human method is that *the environment transforms the animal, while man transforms the environment.* This proposition holds literally from whatever standpoint it be contemplated.
It is, indeed, the full expression of the fact above stated, that the tools
of animals are organic, while those of man are mechanical. But if we
contrast these two methods from the present standpoint, which is
that of economics, we see at once the immense superiority of the
human, or psychological, over the animal or biological method. The
economy is of two kinds, economy of time and economy of energy. It
has taken much longer to develop any one of the organic appliances of
animals, whether for supplying its wants or fighting its enemies, than
the entire period during which man has possessed any arts, even the
simplest. And yet such appliances, however complete or effective,
have not sufficed to enable any species possessing them greatly to
expand its territorial range, or to migrate far from the region to which
it was originally adapted. Man, on the other hand, without acquiring
any new organic adaptations, by the manufacture of tools, weapons,
clothing, habitations, etc., by subjecting the animal and vegetable
kingdoms to his service, and by the power of "looking before and
after"—in short, by the aid of reason—has taken possession of the
whole earth, and is the only animal whose habitat is not circumscribed. This, as just remarked, he has accomplished in a comparatively brief period, i. e., wholly since Tertiary time, and chiefly since the
glacial epoch.

   The economy of energy is fully as great as that of time, and may be
regarded as the cause of the latter. It is the result of *art.* It has been
seen that the mechanical products of rational design necessarily utilize some economic principle through which the muscular force necessary to be exerted is less for any given result accomplished than it
would otherwise be. In the great majority of cases the result could not
be produced at all without the aid of the proper implement or mechanism for producing it, and this becomes more and more the case as
machinery gains upon hand labor. The sum total of all such devices
forms the basis of the mechanic arts. Few realize how completely
civilization depends upon art in this sense. The utter helplessness of
man without the arts is well illustrated in DeFoe's Robinson Crusoe,
but the author saw clearly that in order to enable his hero to survive at
all, even in a tropical climate where nature's productions were
exuberant, he must provide himself from stores of the wrecked vessel
with a considerable supply of tools and other artificial applicances.
What was true of Robinson Crusoe, thus circumstanced, is much
more true of the great majority of mankind who inhabit what we call

temperate climates, i. e., climates in which the temperature some-times falls ten or twenty degrees below the freezing point, and where for several months each year all vegetative functions cease. One winter without art would suffice to sweep the entire population north or south of the thirtieth parallel off the face of the earth.

We are so much accustomed to the terms *labor* and *production* that we rarely stop to think what they really mean. Neither of these terms has any place in animal economics. All labor consists in an artificial transformation of man's environment. Nature *produces* nothing in the politico-economic sense of the word. Production consists in artifi-cally altering the form of natural objects. The clothes we wear are derived chiefly from the sheep, the ox, the silk-worm, and a few other animals, the cotton plant, flax, hemp, and a few other plants; but between the latest stage at which nature leaves these latter and the final form in which they are ready for use there are many transforma-tions requiring much art and great labor. The houses that man inhab-its once consisted chiefly of trees, clay, and beds of solid rock. These, too, have been transformed by labor performed with tools and machi-nery. In like manner the entire cycle of human achievement might be gone through. It would be found everywhere the same.

The arts taken in their ensemble constitute material civilization, and it is this that chiefly distinguishes man from the rest of nature. It is due exclusively to his mind, to the rational or intellectual faculty. That is, it is an exclusively psychological distinction. Civilization, which is human development beyond the animal stage, goes forward under the economics of mind, while animal development takes place under the economics of life. The difference between these two kinds of economics is fundamental. They are not merely dissimilar, they are the direct opposites of each other. The psychologic law tends to reverse the biologic law. This latter law may be briefly defined as *the survival of the best adapted structures.* Those structures which yield most readily to changes in the environment persist. It has therefore been aptly called "survival of the plastic." The environment, though ever changing, does not change to conform to the structures but in the contrary direction, always rendering the partly adapted structures less adapted, and the only organic progress possible is that which accrues through changes of structure that tend to enable organic beings to cope with sterner and ever harder conditions. In any and every case it is the environment that works the changes and the organism that undergoes them.

But the most important factor in the environment of any species is its organic environment. The hardest pressure that is brought to bear upon it comes from the living things in the midst of which it lives, and though paradoxical, it is those beings which most resemble it that crowd it most severely. The least advantage gained by one species from a favorable change of structure tends to make it spread and infringe upon others, and soon to acquire, if not strenuously resisted, a complete monopoly of all things that are required for its support. Any other species that consumes the same elements must, unless equally vigorous, be crowded out. This is the true meaning of the survival of the fittest. It is essentially a process of *competition*, but it is competition in its purest form, wholly unmixed with either moral or intellectual elements, which is never the case with competition in human society.

The prevailing idea is wholly false which claims that it is the fittest possible that survive in this struggle. The effect of competition is to prevent any form from attaining its maximum development, and to maintain a certain comparatively low level of development for all forms that succeed in surviving. This is a normal result of the rhythmic character of all purely natural, i.e., not rational or teleological, phenomena, as explained a few pages back. The greater part of what is gained in the flood tide is lost in the ebb. Wherever competition is wholly removed, as through the agency of man in the interest of any one form, great strides are immediately made by the form thus protected, and it soon outstrips all those that depend upon competition for their motive to advancement. Such has been the case with the cereals and fruit trees, and with domestic animals, in fact, with all the forms of life that man has excepted from the biologic law and subjected to the law of mind. The supposed tendency of such forms to revert to their original wild state, about which so much has been said, is simply their inability when remanded to their pristine competitive struggle to maintain the high position which they had acquired during their halcyon days of exemption from that struggle, which they can no more do than they can attain that position while subjected to it. Competition, therefore, not only involves the enormous waste which has been described, but it prevents the maximum development, since the best that can be attained under its influence is far inferior to that which is easily attained by the artificial, i.e., the rational and intelligent, removal of that influence.

Hard as it seems to be for modern philosophers to understand this, it was one of the first truths that dawned upon the human intellect. Consciously or unconsciously it was felt from the very outset that the mission of mind was to grapple with the law of competition and as far as possible to resist and defeat it. This iron law of nature, as it may be appropriately called (Ricardo's "iron law of wages" is only one manifestation of it), was everywhere found to lie athwart the path of human progress, and the whole upward struggle of rational man, whether physical, social or moral, has been with this tyrant of nature—the law of competition. And in so far as he has progressed at all beyond the purely animal stage he has done so through triumphing little by little over this law and gaining somewhat the mastery in this struggle. In the physical world he has accomplished this so far as he has been able through invention, from which have resulted the arts and material civilization. Every implement or utensil, every mechanical device, every object of design, skill, and labor, every artificial thing that serves a human purpose, is a triumph of mind over the physical forces of nature in ceaseless and aimless competition. The cultivation and improvement of economic plants and the domestication of useful animals involve the direct control of biologic forces and the exemption of these forms of life from the operation of the great organic law which dwarfs their native powers of development. All human institutions—religion, government, law, marriage, custom—together with innumerable other modes of regulating social, industrial, and commercial life, are, broadly viewed, only so many ways of meeting and checkmating the principle of competition as it manifests itself in society. And finally, the ethical code and the moral law of enlightened man are nothing else than the means adopted by reason, intelligence, and refined sensibility for suppressing and crushing out the animal nature of man—for chaining the competitive egoism that all men have inherited from their animal ancestors.

One important fact has thus far been left out of view. Man, it is true, is a rational being, but he is also still an animal. He has struggled manfully against the iron law of nature, but he is far from having overcome it. He has met with wonderful success in this direction in his dealings with it in the physical world; he has laid a firm hand upon it in the domain of organic life; by the aid of well ordained institutions he has dealt it heavy blows in its social aspects; and the suicidal tendency which it exhibits when operating upon dense masses of people has enlisted against it with telling effect the counter-law of ethics. But all this has fallen far short of completely eradicating the deep-seated principle that lies at the foundation of animal economics. Aside from these few directions in which he has succeeded in partially supplanting the competitive economics of life by the cooperative economics of mind, he is still as completely under the dominion of the former as is any other organic being.

2

THE ENGINEERED LANDSCAPE

John Wesley Powell
THE LESSON OF CONEMAUGH

In the spring of 1889 an unusually heavy rainfall caused a sudden rise in the Conemaugh River in western Pennsylvania. Under the pressure of the swollen river an inadequate earthen dam suddenly gave way, and the surging floodwaters killed more than two thousand people in the steel-making center of Johnstown. Many Americans saw in this tragedy a warning against technology in general and reservoir builders in particular; had men not presumed to reconstruct the land, they argued, the calamity might have been avoided. John Wesley Powell (1834–1902) entered the dispute to defend the work of environmental engineers and to divert attention from their critics by summoning Americans once more to the prospect of a golden future. Powell first attracted national attention in 1869 and 1871 with his expeditions down the as yet unexplored river canyons of the Colorado—intrepid feats for a man who had lost an arm in the Civil War. In 1872 he appeared in Washington and within a decade had assumed the directorship of the Bureau of Ethnology and the Geological Survey, for the founding of which he was chiefly responsible. In this selection, as the federal government's leading scientist-engineer he warns against letting a single mishap dampen popular enthusiasm for the work of hydrologists and conservationists in harnessing the rivers of America "running to waste."

The experiences of civilization teach many lessons that go unheeded until some great disaster comes as an object-lesson to recall to men's minds things known but half-forgotten. The Conemaugh disaster belongs to this category. For more than four thousand years civilized men have been constructing reservoirs in which to store water for various purposes. The conditions to be fulfilled in their construction are well known, for the lesson has been enforced upon mankind from the dawn of civilization to the present time by disasters too many to be enumerated.

SOURCE. John Wesley Powell, "The Lesson of Conemaugh," *North American Review*, August 1889.

Hydraulic engineering is the oldest scientific art. No other can compare with it in this respect, except that of architecture in its application to the building of temples and pyramids; but scientific engineering is even older than scientific architecture. Everywhere throughout the world civilization began in arid lands, and hydraulic engineering was the first great problem to be solved; and for this reason it was solved at an early time, and well solved. Something has been added through the years, but not much. In our own times these problems have come to be of far greater importance than they were in antiquity, and the civilized world has now reached the dawn of a day of hydraulic engineering of such magnitude that all the works hitherto accomplished are insignificant compared to those now to be planned and executed. Let the significance of this statement be briefly set forth.

One of the purposes for which hydraulic engineering has been prosecuted in late civilization is the utilization of powers otherwise running to waste. For a time a check has been given to this form of development by the introduction of steam, but at present the great transition in modern industries is from the employment of muscular power to the employment of the physical powers of nature, and it is probable that the resort to water-power will rapidly increase in the immediate future. It certainly will if the dream of modern electrical science is realized, so that water-power can be economically converted into electric power and transported from place to place. If this is done—and its accomplishment is hardly to be considered utopian—all our highland streams will immediately become of value as powers, and dams and reservoirs must be constructed in far greater numbers than in the past.

Modern sanitary science condemns well water for domestic purposes in cities, towns, and villages. Disease is at the bottom of a well; health in the waters of the heavens; and the people must have this pure water. The demand for highland waters for such purposes is rapidly increasing. The speedy development of city and town life under the new industrial conditions makes this one of the most important uses to which water can be applied. Wherever the houses of men are clustered reservoirs or systems of reservoirs must be built. Nothing can be more certain than that the storage of water for this purpose will greatly and quickly increase throughout the United States.

Along the course of every river there is a flood-plain of greater or less width. This is the plane established by the sediment washed from the hills and upper country and deposited along the course of the river outside of its low-water channel, but within the area covered by water at the time of greatest floods. These greatest floods are infrequent, and are not coincident with the annual floods, but much higher. The plane of the ordinary flood is much lower than this great flood-plain, which is established by the maximum floods, occurring ten, twenty, or even fifty years apart. Such flood-plains are the most fertile lands, and always tempt the agriculturist. Yet torrents sweep over them from time to time, destroying property in vast amounts, and even life. In lands already highly cultivated, densely populated, and of great value, protection from floods has come to be an important problem. One, and only one, method of protection is possible: the flood waters must be stored and allowed to find their way to the sea during times of low water. The preservation of lands in this manner accomplishes another end, as the navigable streams are improved thereby. Great floods destroy low-water channels by blocking them with natural dams. By storing the water of such floods, and discharging it during low-water-time, these channels are kept open and a more equable volume is preserved.

There is another use to which flood waters are put. Experience has shown that they contain vast stores of fertilizing elements. All other fertilizers that man can utilize sink into insignificance when compared with those furnished by flood waters. In highly civilized and densely populated lands this source of fertilization is already used, and it will be used more and more as the years go by. In the United States we are just beginning to appreciate this. The conditions under which agricultural operations have hitherto been carried on have not directed the attention of our farmers to this subject until of late years. It is far within the facts to state that any region of our country may have its agricultural production doubled by the use of its flowing waters for the fertilization of the lands. The time is rapidly coming when the flood waters of the country will be used for this purpose on a grand scale, and reservoirs will be constructed all over the land, as they are now in process of building in England, Germany, France, Italy, and other countries.

About two-fifths of the area of the United States is so arid that agriculture is impossible without artificial irrigation, the rainfall being insufficient for the fertilization of ordinary crops. In this region all agriculture depends upon the use of running streams. In all of this country, wherever agriculture is prosecuted, dams must be constructed, and the waters spread upon the lands through the agency of canals. Again, as the season of growing crops is comparatively short—in most of the country it lasts from two to three months only—the waters of the non-irrigating season will run to waste unless they are stored in reservoirs. Already the storing of these waters is begun; the people are constructing reservoirs, and will continue the process until all of the streams of the arid region are wholly utilized in this manner, so that no waste water runs to the sea. Less than a third of the streams of the arid region run to the sea, even now, as the great majority are "lost rivers." A little further explanation is necessary to understand how these waters are to be utilized.

The arid region is mountainous. Mountain ranges enclose valleys, while plains, mesas, and plateaus carry dead volcanoes on their backs. The precipitation of moisture on these lands is confined to the mountains, where it is excessive. The fertile lands along the plains and mountains are arid. In all the region agriculture is possible only by collecting the mountain waters and using them on the plains and valleys. Wherever a farm, a village, or a city is made, hydraulic works are necessary, and dams must be constructed and reservoirs built. Considering the whole country at large, its hydraulic industries are gigantic. In the region of country where land is more abundant than water, the value inheres in the water, not in the land. Land, like air, is found in greater quantities than can be used; water is the necessary, and value is given to the land by the water-right which it carries; if the water-right is disservered, the land is valueless. These are not unfavorable conditions for agriculture, however. The farmer's industry is more attractive and more profitable in an arid than a humid region. All of the early civilization of the world began in arid lands, and the best agriculture of the world today is carried on by means of artificial irrigation. The seemingly-desert plains of the arid region of the West are, in fact, abundantly rich when watered artificially. The gentle storms of a humid region fructify the land, but its tempests drown vegetation. In such regions the planting season is now too dry and now too wet, and many a prospectively rich harvest has been destroyed by a harvest-time storm. Agriculture in arid lands is not subject to these vicissitudes. The mountains catch the floods, while the valleys are fertilized by the hand of man, who turns the waters upon them at his will. At the day and hour he pleases he spreads the water upon his garden, his vineyard, or his field in quantities governed by his judgment. When harvest time comes, he reaps his field with a mind free from the fear of storms. Ultimately one of the great agricultural regions of this country will be found in the irrigated plains and valleys of the West. Sage-brush plains, sand-dune deserts, and alkaline valleys will be covered by gardens, fields, and groves, all perennially fertilized from thousands of mountain lakes.

Enough has been said to show that the storage of water in reservoirs is not one of the trivial incidents of modern industry, but one of its most important factors, and that in this country we have only reached the beginning of its development. We may expect, in the course of a few generations, that all the highland streams of America will be controlled and utilized, and that the floods will be bridled and become the trained servants of man, as wild beasts have been domesticated for his use.

In view of these facts, it is only the thoughtless man, governed by the impulse of the hour, and dragged from the throne of his reason by the emotions which arise at human suffering, who will believe that the vast industries which have been mentioned must be stopped because hydraulic power, when improperly controlled, may become an agent of destruction. Badly constructed houses may fall and over-whelm families, but no check to the construction of houses will be made thereby. Fires will cause conflagration, yet homes will be warmed. Bridges may give way and trains leap into the abyss, yet bridges will be erected. Cars will leave the track and plunge travellers over embankments, but railroads will be operated. Dams will give way and waters overwhelm the people of the valley below, but dams will still be built.

What lesson, then, is there in the Conemaugh disaster? Nothing new to scientific engineering, but a very old lesson, that must needs be taught to mankind again and again. From the accounts which have appeared in the scientific journals, it seems that the dam was properly constructed. Earth dams are more common than all others. Most of the dams constructed for four thousand years have been, in all essential particulars, like that at Conemaugh. Where, then, was the trouble? In the construction of the dam there was a total neglect to consider the first and fundamental problem—the duty the dam was required to perform. The works were not properly related to the natural conditions, and so a lake was made at Conemaugh which was for a long time a menace to the people below, and at last swept them to destruction.

When the construction of such a dam is proposed, the first thing to be done is to determine the amount of water to be controlled and the rate at which it will be delivered to the reservoir under maximum conditions of rainfall or snow-melting. The proper method of proce-dure is to determine, first, the area of the drainage basin supplying the reservoir; second, the declivities of the supplying basin.

The very first thing, then, is a topographic survey.

The second need is a hydrographic survey.

The precipitation in rain and snow over the basin must be

determined as an average from year to year, and also the maximum precipitation at the times of great flood. This must be supplemented by the gauging of streams to determine their average volume and maximum volumes. All of these factors are necessary and preliminary to the construction of a safe and efficient reservoir system by making mountain lakes. Before a reservoir dam is constructed, it is of prime importance to determine what will be required of it. With these facts ascertained, the engineer can easily plan works adequate to control the forces involved; he can readily determine how much water he can store, and what waste-way will be necessary to discharge the surplus.

The art of dam construction is quite within the grasp of every intelligent engineer. In the case of solid masonry dams, the waste-way is over the whole surface of the dam, as at the Great Falls of the Potomac, where a dam has been constructed to divert the water into the reservoirs that supply Washington. But masonry dams are few; earth dams, and those related to them, are many, and, with these, special waste-ways must be provided, adequate to meet all possible emergencies. The rules for their construction are well known, and have been known for tens of centuries. In American engineering, that which has been most neglected is a precise determination of the duty of the dam—the conditions which it must fulfil or else be destroyed. These can be determined only by a topographic survey, which gives the area of the drainage basin and its grade-curves. To this must be added a hydrographic survey, which may have to extend over some years. It is not necessary that this survey in all its parts should be over each basin where a reservoir is to be constructed. The average and maximum rate of precipitation may be determined for large regions, and the general facts used for the several cases, always allowing a margin for safety. But the topographic survey and the stream-gauging are essential to each individual basin.

There are other factors to be determined that are important to persons engaged in constructing reservoirs for industrial purposes. Two may be mentioned here. The streams feeding the reservoir should be gauged for the purpose of determining the amount of sediment they carry, in order that the life of the reservoirs may be known, or that the proper engineering appliances may be devised to discharge such sediment; and the rate of evaporation should be ascertained, so as to know how much water is lost thereby.

In the construction of reservoirs in the arid region there are important problems not pertaining to humid regions. To a large extent the sources of the water are in high mountains, where the chief precipitation is snow, which, to some extent, stores itself in snow-banks and glacial fields, to be melted by the summer sun at the time when irrigation is required. The upper portions of these mountains are largely treeless—a condition favorable to the storage of snow. In a forest region the snows are evenly distributed over the entire surface, and are quickly melted when the summer rains and suns come; but in a treeless region the snows are accumulated in great drifts in the lee of rocks and cliffs and under the walls of gorges and canyons. Such great drifts are themselves stupendous reservoirs of water, and artificial works are necessary only to control the flow properly and distribute the water at the places and times needed. Wherever the chief precipitation is snow, forests are a disadvantage if the waters are needed in the valleys below for irrigation, for the forests keep the snow distributed over broad areas of ground and expose it to the winds of their trunks, branches, and leaves, so that altogether the mountain evaporation is enormously increased as compared with the evaporation from snow-drifts and ice-fields. On the other hand, in low mountain and hilly regions of humid lands, forests about the sources of the streams are of advantage in two ways: the water being in excess, increased evaporation is advantageous; and the forests serve to hold back the water and thus equalize the flow through the year and greatly mitigate the floods.

Whether forests increase the amount of rainfall has long been discussed, and lately it has been the subject of careful scientific investigation. The outcome of all this research is that, if forests do, in fact, increase rainfall, it is to such a slight extent that our present means of investigation are not sufficiently refined to prove it.

Such are the facts to be collected as preliminary to the construction of a reservoir system. To neglect the essential facts is to be guilty of criminal neglect. The history of mountain-lake construction, throughout all the countries of engineering enterprise, is full of lessons like that taught at Conemaugh, and the lessons have always been enforced by the destruction of property and life; they have always been emphasized by dire disaster. Modern industries are handling the forces of nature on a stupendous scale. The coal-fields of the world are now on fire to work for man; chemical forces, as giant explosives, are used as his servants; the lightnings are harnessed and floods are tamed. Woe to the people who trust these powers to the hands of fools! Then wealth is destroyed, homes are overwhelmed, and loved ones killed.

3

THE FOUNDATIONS OF
INDUSTRIAL EMPIRE IN THE WEST

John Wesley Powell
INSTITUTIONS FOR THE ARID LANDS

Powell's environmental classic Report on the Arid Lands of the West *(1879) ranks with Marsh's book in shaping a more realistic and better-informed attitude toward the land. It provided the first thorough documentation for the argument that much of the continent was too dry to be farmed in the traditional, independent, humid-land fashion—a revelation strongly resisted by those convinced of the unbounded benevolence of nature and captured by the moral ideal of the small yeoman farmer. The* Report *did not win instant acclaim from Congress, but eventually out of necessity a few of Powell's recommendations became public policy. In this later essay Powell restates in more concise form his main proposals, especially the idea that irrigated farming and resource conservation should be carried out as self-governing community enterprises. The prospect of turning public forests over to western cooperatives was not especially appealing to most conservationists; consequently they generally ignored Powell's fears of excessive central power and corruption. But in his determination to see the western wilderness "redeemed" by rational and socially benevolent planning, Powell was the accepted prophet of the first conservation movement.*

Industrial civilization in America began with the building of log cabins. Where Piedmont plain merges into coastal plain, there rivers are transformed—dashing waters are changed to tidal waters and navigation heads, and there "powers" are found. Beside these transformed waters, in a narrow zone from north to south across the United States, the first real settlement of the country began by the building of log-cabin homes. This first cabin zone ultimately became the site of the great cities of the east—Boston, New York, Philadelphia, Baltimore, Washington, Richmond, Charleston, and Augusta;

SOURCE. John Wesley Powell, "Institutions for the Arid Lands," *The Century,* May 1890.

and steadily, while the cities were growing, the log-cabin zone moved westward until it reached the border of the Great Plains, which it never crossed.

The arid region of the west was settled by gold and silver hunters aggregated in comparatively large bodies. Their shanties of logs, slabs, boards, and adobes were speedily replaced by the more costly structures of towns and cities, which suddenly sprang into existence where gold or silver was found. These towns and cities were thus scattered promiscuously through the mountain land. In them avenues of trees were planted and parks were laid out and about them gardens, vineyards, and orchards were cultivated. From this horticulture sprang the agriculture of the region.

In the east the log cabin was the beginning of civilization; in the west, the miner's camp. In the east agriculture began with the settler's clearing; in the west, with the exploitation of wealthy men. In the log-cabin years a poor man in Ohio might clear an acre at a time and extend his potato-patch, his cornfield, and his meadow from year to year, and do all with his own hands and energy, and thus hew his way from poverty to plenty. At the same time his wife could plant hollyhocks, sweet-williams, marigolds, and roses in boxed beds of earth around the cabin door. So field and garden were all within the compass of a poor man's means, his own love of industry, and his wife's love of beauty. In western Europe, where our civilization was born, a farmer might carry on his work in his own way, on his own soil or on the land of his feudal lord, and in the higher phases of this industry he could himself enjoy the products of his labor, subject only to taxes and rents. Out of this grew the modern agriculture with which we are so familiar in America, where the farmer owns his land, cultivates the soil with his own hands, and reaps the reward of his own toil, subject only to the conditions necessary to the welfare of the body politic.

The farming of the arid region cannot be carried on in this manner. Individual farmers with small holdings cannot sustain themselves as individual men; for the little farm is, perchance, dependent upon the waters of some great river that can be turned out and controlled from year to year only by the combined labor of many men. And in modern times great machinery is used, and dams, reservoirs, canals, and many minor hydraulic appliances are necessary. These cost large sums of money, and in their construction and maintenance many men are employed. In the practice of agriculture by irrigation in high antiquity, men were organized as communal bodies or as slaves to carry on such operations by united labor. Thus the means of obtaining subsistence were of such a character as to give excuse and cogent argument for the establishment of despotism. The soil could be cultivated, great nations could be sustained, only by the organization of large bodies of men working together on the great enterprises of irrigation under despotic rulers. But such a system cannot obtain in the United States, where the love of liberty is universal.

What, then, shall be the organization of this new industry of agriculture by irrigation? Shall the farmers labor for themselves and own the agricultural properties severally? or shall the farmers be a few capitalists, employing labor on a large scale, as is done in the great mines and manufactories of the United States? The history of two decades of this industry exhibits this fact: that in part the irrigated lands are owned and cultivated by men having small holdings, but in larger part they are held in great tracts by capitalists, and the tendency to this is on the increase. When the springs and creeks are utilized small holdings are developed, but when the rivers are taken out upon the lands great holdings are acquired ; and thus the farming industries of the West are falling into the hands of a wealthy few.

Various conditions have led to this. In some portions of the arid region, especially in California, the Spanish land grants were utilized for the purpose of aggregating large tracts for wholesale farming. Sometimes the lands granted to railroads were utilized for the same purpose. Then, to promote the irrigation of this desert land, an act was passed by Congress giving a section of land for a small price to any man who would irrigate it. Still other lands were acquired under the Homestead Act, the Preemption Act, and the Timber-Culture Act. Through these privileges title could be secured to two square miles of land by one individual. Companies wishing to engage in irrigation followed, in the main, one of two plans: they either bought the lands and irrigated their own tracts, or they constructed irrigating works and supplied water to the farmers. Through the one system land monopoly is developed; through the other, water monopoly.

Such has been the general course of the development of irrigation. But there are three notable exceptions. The people of the southwest came originally, by the way of Mexico, from Spain, where irrigation and the institutions necessary for its control had been developing from high antiquity, and these people well understood that their institutions must be adapted to their industries, and so they organized their settlements as pueblos, or "irrigating municipalities," by which the lands were held in severalty while the tenure of waters and works was communal or municipal. The Mormons, settling in Utah, borrowed the Mexican system. The lands in small tracts were held in severalty by the people, but the waters were controlled by bishops of the church, who among the "Latter-Day Saints" are priests of the "Order of Aaron" and have secular functions. In southern California, also, many colonies were planted in which the lands were held in severalty and in small parcels. Gradually in these communities the waters are passing from the control of irrigating corporations into the control of the municipalities which the colonies have formed. Besides these three great exceptions there are some minor ones, which need not here be recounted. In general, farming by irrigation has been developed as wholesale irrigating by large companies. Some of these water companies are foreign, others are capitalists of the eastern cities, while a few are composed of capitalists of the west.

Where agriculture is dependent upon an artificial supply of water, and where there is more land than can be served by the water, values inhere in water, not in land; the land without the water is without value. A stream may be competent to irrigate 100,000 acres of land, and there may be 500,000 acres of land to which it is possible to carry the water. If one man holds that water he practically owns that land; whatever value is given to any portion of it is derived from the water owned by the one person. In the far west a man may turn a spring or a brook upon a little valley stretch and make him a home with his own resources, or a few neighbors may unite to turn a small creek from its natural channel and gradually make a cluster of farms. This has been done, and the available springs and brooks are almost exhausted. But the chief resource of irrigation is from the use of the rivers and from the storage of waters which run to waste during a greater part of the year; for the season of irrigation is short, and during most of the months the waters are lost unless held in reservoirs. In the development of these water companies there has been much conflict. In the main improvident franchises have been granted, and when found onerous the people have impaired or more or less destroyed them by unfriendly legislation and administration. The whole subject, however, is in its infancy, and the laws of the western territory are inadequate to give security to capital invested in irrigating works on the one hand and protection to the farmer from extortion on the other. For this reason the tendency is to organize land companies. At present there is a large class of promoters who obtain options on lands and make contracts to supply water, and then enlist capital in the east and in Europe and organize and control construction companies, which, sometimes at least, make large profits. There seems to be little difficulty in interesting capitalists in these enterprises. The great increase in value given to land through its redemption by irrigation makes such investments exceedingly attractive. But at present investors and farmers are alike badly protected, and the lands and waters are falling into the hands of "middlemen." If the last few years' experience throws any light upon the future the people of the west are entering upon an era of unparalleled speculation, which will result in the aggregation of the lands and waters in the hands of a comparatively few persons. Let us hope that there is wisdom enough in the statesmen of America to avert the impending evil.

Whence, then, shall the capital come? and how shall the labor be organized by which these 100,000,000 acres of land are to be redeemed? This is the problem that to-day confronts our statesmen and financiers. Capital must come, for the work is demanded and will pay. Let us look at the statistics of this subject in round numbers, and always quite within probable limits. Let us speak of 100,000,000 acres of land to be redeemed by the use of rivers and reservoirs. This will cost about ten dollars per acre, or $1,000,000,000. In the near future a demand for this amount will be made, and it will be forthcoming beyond a peradventure. The experience obtained by the redemption of 6,000,000 acres of land, already under cultivation, abundantly warrents the statement that an average of fity dollars per acre is a small estimate to be placed upon the value of the lands yet to be redeemed as they come to be used. Thus there is a prize to be secured of $5,000,000,000 by the investment of $1,000,000,000. Such vast undertakings will not be overlooked by the enterprising men of America.

In a former article on "The Irrigable Lands of the Arid Region," in The Century Magazine for March 1890, it was explained that the waters of the arid lands flowing in the great rivers must somehow be divided among the States, and that in two cases important international problems are involved. It was also shown that contests are arising between different districts of the same State. But the waters must be still further subdivided in order that they may be distributed to individual owners. How can this be done? Lands can be staked out, corner-posts can be established, dividing lines can be run, and titles to tracts in terms of metes and bounds can be recorded. But who can establish the corner-posts of flowing waters? When the waters are gathered into streams they rush on to the desert sands or to the sea; and how shall we describe the metes and bounds of a wave? The farmer may brand his horses, but who can brand the clouds or put a mark of ownership on the current of a river? The waters of today have values and must be divided; the waters of the morrow have values, and the waters of all coming time, and these values must be distributed among the people. How shall it be done?

It is proposed to present a plan for the solution of these problems, and others connected therewith, in an outline of institutions necessary for the arid lands. Some of these problems have been discussed in former articles, and it may be well to summarize them all once more, as follows:

First. The capital to redeem by irrigation 100,000,000 acres of land is to be obtained, and $1,000,000,000 is necessary.

Second. The lands are to be distributed to the people, and as yet we have no proper system of land laws by which it can be done.

Third. The waters must be divided among the States, and as yet there is no law for it, and the States are now in conflict.

Fourth. The waters are to be divided among the people, so that each man may have the amount necessary to fertilize his farm, each hamlet, town, and city the amount necessary for domestic purposes, and that every thirsty garden may quaff from the crystal waters that come from the mountains.

Fifth. The great forests that clothe the hills, plateaus, and mountains with verdure must be saved from devastation by fire and preserved for the use of man, that the sources of water may be protected, that farms may be fenced and homes built, and that all this wealth of forest may be distributed among the people.

Sixth. The grasses that are to feed the flocks and herds must be protected and utilized.

Seventh. The great mineral deposits—the fuel of the future, the iron for the railroads, and the gold and silver for our money—must be kept ready to the hand of industry and the brain of enterprise.

Eighth. The powers of the factories of that great land are to be created and utilized, that the hum of busy machinery may echo among the mountains—the symphonic music of industry.

A thousand millions of money must be used; who shall furnish it? Great and many industries are to be established; who shall control them? Millions of men are to labor; who shall employ them? This is a great nation, the government is powerful; shall it engage in this work? So dreamers may dream, and so ambition may dictate, but in the name of the men who labor I demand that the laborers shall employ themselves; that the enterprise shall be controlled by the men who have the genius to organize, and whose homes are in the lands developed, and that the money shall be furnished by the people; and I say to the government: Hands off! Furnish the people with institutions of justice, and let them do the work for themselves. The solution to be propounded, then, is one of institutions to be organized for the establishment of justice, not of appropriations to be made and offices created by the government.

In a group of mountains a small river has its source. A dozen or a score of creeks unite to form the trunk. The creeks higher up divide into brooks. All these streams combined form the drainage system of a hydrographic basin, a unit of country well defined in nature, for it is bounded above and on each side by heights of land that rise as crests to part the waters. Thus hydraulic basin is segregated from hydraulic basin by nature herself, and the landmarks are practically perpetual. In such a basin of the arid region the irrigable lands lie below; not chiefly by the river's side, but on the mesas and low plains that stretch back on each side. Above these lands the pasturage hills and mountains stand, and there the forests and sources of water supply are found. Such a district of country is a commonwealth by itself. The people who live therein are interdependent in all their industries. Every man is interested in the conservation and management of the water supply, for all the waters are needed within the district. The men who control the farming below must also control the upper regions where the waters are gathered from the heavens and stored in the reservoirs. Every farm and garden in the valley below is dependent upon each fountain above.

All of the lands that lie within the basin above the farming districts are the catchment areas for all the waters poured upon the fields below. The waters that control these works all constitute one system, are dependent one upon another, and are independent of all other systems. Not a spring or a creek can be touched without affecting the interests of every man who cultivates the soil in the region. All the waters are common property until they reach the main canal, where they are to be distributed among the people. How these waters are to be caught and the common source of wealth utilized by the individual settlers interested therein is a problem for the men of the district to solve, and for them alone.

But these same people are interested in the forests that crown the heights of the hydrographic basin. If they permit the forests to be destroyed, the source of their water supply is injured and the timber values are wiped out. If the forests are to be guarded, the people directly interested should perform the task. Any army of aliens set to watch the forests would need another army of aliens to watch them, and a forestry organization under the hands of the general government would become a hotbed of corruption; for it would be impossible to fix responsibility and difficult to secure integrity of administration, because ill-defined values in great quantities are involved.

Then the pasturage is to be protected. The men who protect these lands for the water they supply to agriculture can best protect the grasses for the summer pasturage of the cattle and horses and sheep that are to be fed on their farms during the months of winter. Again, the men who create water powers by constructing dams and digging canals should be permitted to utilize these powers for themselves, or to use the income from these powers which they themselves create, for the purpose of constructing and maintaining the works necessary to their agriculture.

Thus it is that there is a body of interdependent and unified interests and values, all collected in one hydrographic basin, and all segregated by well-defined boundary lines from the rest of the world. The people in such a district have common interests, common rights, and common duties, and must necessarily work together for common purposes. Let such a people organize, under national and state laws, a great irrigation district, including an entire hydrographic basin, and let them make their own laws for the division of the waters, for the protection and use of the forests, for the protection of the pasturage on the hills, and for the use of the powers. This, then, is the proposition I make: that the entire arid region be organized into natural hydrographic districts, each one to be a commonwealth within itself for the purpose of controlling and using the great values which have been pointed out. There are some great rivers where the larger trunks would have to be divided into two or more districts, but the majority would be of the character described. Each such community should possess its own irrigation works; it would have to erect diverting dams, dig canals, and construct reservoirs; and such works would have to be maintained from year to year. The plan is to establish local self-government by hydrographic basins.

Let us consider next the part which should be taken by the local governments, the state governments, and the general government in the establishment and maintenance of these institutions. Let there be established in each district a court to adjudicate questions of water rights, timber rights, pasturage rights, and power rights, in compliance with the special laws of the community and the more general laws of the state and the nation. Let there be appeal from these lower courts to the higher courts. Let the people of the district provide their own officers for the management and control of the waters, for the protection and utilization of the forests, for the protection and management of the pasturage, and for the use of the powers; and with district courts, water masters, foresters, and herders they would be equipped with the local officers necessary for the protection of their own property and the maintenance of individual rights. The interests are theirs, the rights are theirs, the duties are theirs; let them control their own actions. To some extent this can be accomplished by cooperative labor; but ultimately and gradually great capital must be employed in each district. Let them obtain this capital by their own enterprise as a community. Constituting a body corporate, they can tax themselves and they can borrow moneys. They have a basis of land titles, water rights, pasturage rights, forest rights, and power rights; all of these will furnish ample security for the necessary investments; and these district communities, having it in their power to obtain a vast increment by the development of the lands, and to distribute it among the people in severalty, will speedily understand how to attract capital by learning that honesty is the best policy.

Each state should provide courts for the adjudication of litigation between people of different districts, and courts of appeal from the irrigation district courts. It should also establish a general inspection system, and provide that the irrigation reservoirs shall not be constructed in such a manner as to menace the people below and place them in peril from floods. And finally, it should provide general statutes regulating water rights.

But the general government must bear its part in the establishment of the institutions for the arid region. It is now the owner of most of the lands, and it must provide for the distribution of these lands to the people in part, and in part it must retain possession of them and hold them in trust for the districts. It must also divide the waters of the great rivers among the states. All this can be accomplished in the following manner. Let the general government make a survey of the lands, segregating and designating the irrigable lands, the timber lands, the pasturage lands, and the mining lands; let the general government retain possession of all except the irrigable lands, but give these to the people in severalty as homesteads. Then let the general government declare and provide by statute that the people of each district may control and use the timber, the pasturage, and the water powers, under specific laws enacted by themselves and by the states to which they belong. Then let the general government further declare and establish by statute how the waters are to be divided among the districts and used on the lands segregated as irrigable lands, and then provide that the waters of each district may be distributed among the people by the authorities of each district under state and national laws. By these means the water would be relegated to the several districts in proper manner, interstate problems would be solved, and the national courts could settle all interstate litigation.

But the mining industries of the country must be considered. Undeveloped mining lands should remain in the possession of the general government, and titles thereto should pass to individuals, under provisions of statutes already existing, only where such lands are obtained by actual occupation and development, and then in quantities sufficient for mining purposes only. Then mining regions must have mining towns. For these the townsite laws already enacted provide ample resource.

It is thus proposed to divide responsibility for these institutions between the general government, the state governments, and the local governments. Having done this, it is proposed to allow the people to regulate their own affairs in their own way—borrow money, levy taxes, issue bonds, as they themselves shall determine; construct reservoirs, dig canals, when and how they please; make their own laws and choose their own officers; protect their own forests, utilize their own pasturage, and do as they please with their own powers; and to say to them that "with wisdom you may prosper, but with folly you must fail."

It should be remembered that the far west is no longer an uninhabited region. Towns and cities are planted on the mountain sides, and stupendous mining enterprises are in operation. On the streams sawmills have been erected, and the woodman's ax echoes through every forest. In many a valley and by many a stream may be found a field, a vineyard, an orchard, and a garden; and the hills are covered with flocks and herds. In almost every hydrographic basin there is already found a population sufficient for the organization of the necessary irrigation districts. The people are intelligent, industrious, enterprising, and wide awake to their interests. Their hearts beat high with hope, and their aspirations are for industrial empire. On this round globe and in all the centuries of human history there has never before been such a people. Their love of liberty is unbounded, their obedience to law unparalleled, and their reverence for justice profound; every man is a freeman king with power to rule himself, and they may be trusted with their own interests.

Many of the great industrial undertakings of mankind require organized labor, and this demand grows with the development of inventions and the use of machinery. The transfer of toil from the muscles of men to the sinews of nature has a double result—social solidarity is increased, and mind is developed. In the past, civilization has combined the labor of men through the agency of despotism; and this was possible when the chief powers were muscular. But when the physical powers of nature are employed and human powers engaged in their control men cannot be enslaved; they assert their liberty and despotism falls. Under free governments the tendency is to transfer power from hereditary and chosen rulers to money kings, as the integration of society in industrial operations is accomplished through the agency of capital. This organization of physical power with human industry for great ends by the employment of capital is accomplished by instituting corporations. Corporations furnish money and machinery, and employ men organized under superintendents, to accomplish the works necessary to our modern civilization. Gradually society is being organized into a congeries of such corporations to control the leading industries of the land.

Hitherto agriculture in this country has not come under the domination of these modern rulers. Throughout all the humid regions the farmer is an independent man, but in the arid regions corporations have sought to take control of agriculture. This is rendered possible by the physical conditions under which the industry is carried on. Sometimes the corporations have attempted to own the lands and the water, and to construct the great works and operate them as part and parcel of wholesale farming. In other cases the corporations have sought to construct the works and sell the water to individual farmers with small holdings. By neither of these methods has more than partial success been achieved. There is a sentiment in the land that the farmer must be free, that the laborer in the field should be the owner of the field. Hence by unfriendly legislation and by judicial decision—which ultimately reflect the sentiment of the people—- these farming corporations and water corporations of the west have often failed to secure brilliant financial results, and many have been almost destroyed. Thus there is a war in the west between capital and labor—a bitter, relentless war, disastrous to both parties. The effort has been made to present a plan by which the agriculture of the arid lands may be held as a vast field of exploitation for individual farmers who cultivate the soil with their own hands; and at the same time and by the same institutions to open to capital a field for safe investment and remunerative return, and yet to secure to the toiling farmers the natural increment of profit which comes from the land with the progress of industrial civilization.

The great enterprises of mining, manufacturing, transporting, exchanging, and financiering in which the business kings of America are engaged challenge admiration, and I rejoice at their prosperity and am glad that blessings thus shower upon the people; but the brilliancy of great industrial operations does not daze my vision. I love the cradle more than the bank counter. The cottage home is more beautiful to me than the palace. I believe that the school-house is primal, the university secondary; and I believe that the justice's court in the hamlet is the only permanent foundation for the Supreme Court at the capital. Such are the interests which I advocate. Without occult powers of prophecy, the man of common sense sees a wonderful future for this land. Hard is the heart, dull is the mind, and weak is the will of the man who does not strive to secure wise institutions for the developing world of America.

The lofty peaks of the arid land are silvered with eternal rime; the slopes of the mountains and the great plateaus are covered with forest groves; the hills billow in beauty, the valleys are parks of delight, and the deep canons thrill with the music of laughing waters. Over them all a clear sky is spread, through which the light of heaven freely shines. Clouds rarely mask the skies, but come at times like hosts of winged beauty floating past, as they change from gray to gold, to crimson, and to gorgeous purple. The soul must worship these glories, yet with the old Scotch poet I can exclaim:

> It's rare to see the morning bleeze,
> Like a bonfire frae the sea;
> It's fair to see the burnie kiss
> The lip o' the flow'ry lea;
> An' fine it is on green hillside,
> Where hums the bonnie bee,
> But rarer, fairer, finer far
> Is the ingleside for me.

4

NATURAL RESOURCES
IN THE WELFARE STATE

Bernard E. Fernow
ECONOMICS OF FORESTRY

Historians of conservation consistently have ignored or underrated the career and ideas of Bernhard Fernow (1851–1923). A Prussian who immigrated to America in 1876, Fernow, within ten years of his arrival, was appointed chief of the forestry division in the Department of Agriculture, where he served until 1898. Unlike his two predecessors he had an excellent technical preparation for his position, first at the University of Konigsberg and then at the Hanover-Munden Forest Academy. With few forests to administer here and meager presidential or popular support, he could do little but keep his desk tidy. But for all his forced inaction he held an ideal, as this selection shows, of energetic, positive government that outran even that of most of his fellow conservationists. In the 1890s he laid these ideas before the classes of Wisconsin economist Richard T. Ely, who recognized in Fernow a mind sympathetic to his own German-trained theories of political economy—especially the view of the State as the highest expression of the social organism and the promotion of academics and professionals in government service. The conservation thought of Fernow satisfied both these principles, resting as it did, in Ely's words, on "the philosophy of social solidarity" and disciplined, public intelligence. In the theory of "providential government" sketched here by Fernow the conservation movement merged with the evolving doctrine of the welfare state.

The natural resources of the earth have in all ages and in all countries, for a time at least, been squandered by man with a wanton disregard of the future, and are still being squandered wherever absolute necessity has not yet forced a more careful utilization.

This is natural, as long as the exploitation of these resources is left

SOURCE. Bernhard E. Fernow, *Economics of Forestry* (New York, 1902), pp. 1–20.

unrestricted in private hands; for private enterprise, private interest, knows only the immediate future—has only one aim in the use of these resources, namely, to obtain from them the greatest possible personal and present gain.

Occasionally there may enter into its consideration a desire to prolong the source of profit, so that it may not only hold out during the lifetime of the individual, but continue flowing for his heirs; or else other than business considerations may, for a while at least, preserve possible sources of profit from mismanagement, usually by mere non-use, much more rarely by conscious management for continuity. In most cases it will be found that the busy competition of the present has a destructive tendency and leads to wasteful methods, especially if the resources are large in comparison with the population and its needs. Density of population is the index of the intensity with which resources will be husbanded. Plenty breeds extravagance; dearth breeds care.

Thus in the United States, with its enormous resources in fields and forests and mines, which are open to the unrestricted, licentious use of a comparatively small population, the destruction of valuable material in the exploitation of these natural riches, the careless and extravagant use of them, the neglect to which they are abandoned as soon as the cream is taken, are simply characteristic of all pioneering populations. With us, moreover, the pioneering stage fell into a period when the invention and development of railroad transportation intensified the disproportion of population and resources, opening up new territory and making virgin supplies available more rapidly than the needs of a resident population required, thus creating destructive competition in the attempts to profit from a non-intensive, rapacious exploitation and exportation. For, in the absence of a resident population to use the less valuable portions of the products, these had to go to waste, since only the best portions could bear the cost of transportation to distant centres of consumption.

The amount of waste in materials, natural resources, and in energy, which this uneven settlement and development of the country has produced, has been enormous in all directions, and more especially in fields and forests. The desire for a tangible share in the wealth that can be derived by the exploitation of these resources, the greed of the individual, together with the unfavorable distribution of population, have led to their careless and wasteful use.

From the standpoint of the individual, that use of his opportunities which gives him greatest satisfaction in the present appears justifiable; while society may incidentally benefit from his efforts in producing and distributing wealth, the individual, as a rule, cares little about that result of his activity, nor does he care if the results of his endeavors are the opposite from beneficial to society, unless society itself step in and protect its interests.

From the fact that within any aggregation of people inimical interests arise, that the interests of one set of individuals may clash with those of another set, or that the welfare of the whole may be jeopardized by the unrestricted exercise of the rights of the few, the necessity for the limitation of the rights of the members arises, which, as far as the exercise of property rights goes, finds expression in the old Roman law, *"Utere tuo ne alterum noceas,"* namely, such use of the property as shall not entail damage to another party.

This ancient restrictive principle, which is recognized in all civilized states, was at first probably applied only to interferences between private interests; but finally the protection of the interests of the aggregation against those of the individual must have necessitated its application, whenever a communal interest would suffer by the unrestricted exercise of individual rights.

This restrictive function of the state, in addition to that of defending the aggregation against outsiders, will probably be admitted by all parties and schools as elementary and essential to the existence of the state. Divergence of opinion arises, however, not only when additional, more positive and directive functions are claimed for the state—as, for instance, when the *laissez-faire* policy is to be supplanted by a *faire-marcher* promotive policy—but also in the interpretation of the meaning of the terms of the mere restrictive function, when the question arises, what is to be considered damage and who the other is that is to be protected.

The very nature of the modern civilized government necessitates the very widest interpretation of these terms. Civilized states of today are intended and built for permanency; they are not held together by mere compacts of the single members of society, which may be broken at any time. While forms of government may change, the organization, the state idea, promises to be permanent. This conception of the permanency of the state, the realization that it is not a thing of today and for a limited time, but forever, widens its functions and extends its sphere of action; for it is no longer to be regarded as merely the arbiter between its present members, but it becomes the guardian of its future members; government becomes the representative, not only of present communal interests, as against individual interests, but also of future interests as against those of the present. Its object is not only for the day, but includes the *perpetuity* of the well-being of society, and the *perpetuity* of such favorable conditions as will conduce to the *continued* welfare and improvement of the same; in short, its activity must be with regard to continuity, it must provide for the future, it must be *providential.* We do not create this special providence for the individual, but for society; the individual will have to work out his own salvation to a large extent, with the opportunities for advancement offered by society, but society itself can only act through the state; and, as the representative of the future as well as the present, the state cannot, like the individual, "let the future take care of itself." In our present state activity and legislation there is as yet but little realization of its providential functions. Even the question of education, which in part provides for future improvement, is only imperfectly considered from this point of view. The question of the franchise, as well as that of immigration, both of which are of the greatest influence upon the future composition and condition of our society, are much more often discussed with reference to the rights of present members than with reference to the future of society.

The one condition of social life in which the action of the present influences the future almost more than in any other direction, namely, the condition of the means of material existence and their economical use (the economy of resources), has received perhaps the least recognition in practice as well as in theoretical discussion; and especially is this absence of attention to this most important branch of economics noticeable in English literature.

The reason probably is that the need of careful analysis of this factor of social life has as yet not been pressing. But as the world has been explored in all corners and the extent of its resources has become more nearly known, and as it is being rapidly peopled everywhere and the causes of depopulation are becoming less, the warnings of [Thomas] Malthus and [John Stuart] Mill come home to us with new force; and the study of the nature of resources, their relation to social life and development, and their economy, becomes a most important branch of social science, which will overshadow some of the other branches, now appearing all-important. When the questions of the extension of suffrage to women, of tariff, of taxation, of coinage and currency, which are all merely incidents, will have sunk into the background, the question of the economy of the resources which constitute and sustain the political, commercial, and social power of the nation—long neglected—will still claim attention; for only those nations who develop their natural resources economically, and avoid the waste of that which they produce, can maintain their power or even secure the continuance of their separate existence. A nation may cease to exist as well by the decay of its resources as by the extinction of its patriotic spirit. While we are debating over the best methods of disposing of our wealth, we gradually lose our very capital without even realizing the fact. As Marsh points out in his classical work, man is constantly modifying the earth and making it more and more uninhabitable; he goes over its rich portions and leaves behind a desert.

Whether we have a high tariff or no tariff, an income tax or a head tax, direct or indirect taxation, bimetallism or a single standard, national banks or state banks, are matters which concern, to be sure, the temporary convenience of the members of society, but their prejudicial adjustment is easily remediable; when ill effects become apparent, the inconveniences may be removed with but little harm to the community, and none to mankind at large or to the future. But whether fertile lands are turned into deserts, forests into waste places, brooks into torrents, rivers changed from means of power and intercourse into means of destruction and desolation—these are questions which concern the material existence itself of society; and since such changes become often irreversible, the damage irremediable, and at the same time the extent of available resources becomes smaller in proportion to population, their consideration is finally much more important than those other questions of the day. Increase of population and increased requirements of civilization call for a continual increase of our total economic forces, and increased "intensity" in the management of our resources; and this requires such continued care and administration, that it is not safe to leave it entirely to the incentive of private competition, which always means wasteful use.

It is true that as individuals the knowledge of the near exhaustion of the anthracite coal-fields does not induce any of us to deny ourselves a single scuttle of coal, so as to make the coal-field last for one more generation, unless this knowledge is reflected in increased price. But we can conceive that, as members of society, we may for that very purpose refuse to allow each other or the miner to waste unnecessarily. That this conception is not absurd, and may be practically realized without any strain in our conceptions of government functions, is proved by the fact that it has been carried out in practice in several cases, in our country as well as in others, without opposition.

Absurdly enough we have begun such action with reference to our resources where it is perhaps of least consequence, as, for instance, when, by the establishment of hunting and fishing seasons and by other restrictions, we seek to prevent the exhaustion of the fish and game resources. This is a good illustration of the fact that emotion rather than reason, sentiment rather than argument, are the prime movers of society. It was only partially fear for the exhaustion of this readily restorable resource or economic reasons which led to this protection of our fisheries and game, but love of sport gave the incentive. And again, it needed the love of sport to set on foot the movement for the improvement of the roads in the United States, which the realization of true economy had not the power to bring about.

While we do not prevent single individuals from ruining themselves financially and hazarding the future of their families, we do prevent associated portions of the community—corporations, towns, and cities—from jeopardizing their future by preventing them from extravagant expenditures and contracting of debts. This, too, is perhaps less designed for the future, than to protect present members against undesirable burdens.

There are, then, enough precedents established to show that, whatever the greed and selfishness of the individual may dictate, society recognizes its right to interfere with the individual in the use of resources, not only for its present objects, but even for considerations of the future.

To recognize how far—to what degree and in what manner—any of the resources must become objects of national concern, it is necessary to understand their relative significance for the present and for the future development of society or of the particular aggregate of society called a nation. From this point of view resources may be classified under four heads, namely:

1. Resources inexhaustible.
2. Resources exhaustible and non-restorable.
3. Resources restorable, but liable to deterioration under private activity.
4. Resources restorable, yielding increased returns under increased activity.

Of the first class, hardly any can be mentioned that are usually denominated as resources; land, water, air, and the forces of nature would fall under this class, but since it is not so much these things themselves as the conditions in which they are found that make them resources, and since these conditions are alterable by human agency, their inexhaustibility with reference to human requirements is not entirely established. With the land it is rather the fertility of the soil that makes it a resource, except so far as it serves for building purposes. With the water, except for the absolute necessity of life, it is

its desirable distribution—terrestrial and atmospheric—which constitutes it a resource in the sense of satisfying human wants.

Of such resources as are in time exhaustible without the possibility
of reproduction, we may mention the mines. The supply of coal, "the
bread of industries," in Europe is calculated to last not more than
three or four centuries, although scarcity is expected long before that
time; and in our own country we are told that anthracite coal mines
do not promise more than seventy-five to one hundred years of supply
under present methods of working. The silver and gold mines, upon
the basis of which Nevada became a state, are said to show signs of
exhaustion. Oil-fields and natural gas wells of very recent discovery
belong to this class of exhaustible resources. With their consumption
in satisfying our wants, they are destroyed forever.

The timber of the virgin forest and its game, the water-power of the
streams, largely dependent on the conditions of the forest, the fisheries, and to some extent the local climatic conditions, are resources of
the third order, capable in most instances of reproduction or restoration under human care, after having been deteriorated by uneconomic
exploitation or by change of contingent conditions, as when brooks
and rivers are lessened in volume or else filled with flood-waters and
debris, in consequence of forest destruction.

The extensive and absolute destruction of forest cover in western
Asia and portions of eastern and southern Europe has desolated vast
regions and transformed them into lifeless deserts. Such rapine has
sterilized almost beyond recovery the once highly productive regions
of Sicily and Algeria; and in our own country we can point to similar
results already apparent, as in Wisconsin, where over 4,000,000 acres
have practically been turned into deserts, in Mississippi, and other
portions of our domain, where erosion carries the fertile soil into
rivers, occasioning, in addition to its loss, disturbance of favorable
water stages and expenditures in river and harbor bills.

Even climatic conditions—a resource which we have hardly yet
appreciated as such—it seems, can be changed by mismanagement
beyond recovery, as exemplified by the experience of France, where, it
is asserted, the cultivation of the olive has become impossible in the
northern departments, due to the removal of forest cover, which
furnishes protection against northern winds.

Lastly, as resources restorable and yielding increased returns to
increased activity, we would find most of those resources which are
the product of human labor, industry, and ingenuity: the accumulated
wealth, the accumulated educational fund, and other conditions of
civilization, the people themselves, capable of performing labor.

It might appear that, of the natural resources, the soil with its fertility, capable under intensive cultivation of increasing its yield, should be placed here; but when this increased activity is unaccompanied by rational method, this resource, too, will deteriorate almost to a degree where its restoration is practically precluded.

Altogether, while possibility of restoration has served in our classification, the practicability of such restoration, *i.e.* the relation of expenditure of energy and money to the result, will have to be taken into consideration when state activity with regard to them is to be discussed.

From yet another point of view we can distinguish between those resources, which yield directly a tangible material, necessaries or conveniences of life, serving the purposes of gain, and which are, therefore, objects of industrial enterprise; while others, though desirable and necessary, serving indirectly for the comforts of society, industry, and progress of civilization, do not call for the exertion of private enterprise and offer no incentive, or only an imperfect one, for private action, or are beyond the limits of control by private individuals.

Thus, if there is the possibility of influencing climatic conditions by human action, which is doubted by some climatologists in defiance of many patent facts, it would be a matter of public concern rather than of private interest to preserve favorable or improve unfavorable conditions. As far as the forest yields useful material for the arts, it is an object of private industry; but when, by its position on a watershed, the forest becomes an influential factor in the water conditions of the plain, it may still serve the purposes of gain and wealth, which are the objects of private industry, but its indirect significance for society at large exceeds the private interest.

Of the proper condition of waterways, of navigation and transportation, it may be said, that while private interest may be concerned with it for private gain, public interest is involved in it to a much greater extent. For private interest lies only in the direction of individual gain, while state interest lies in the direction of social gain, of gain for a larger number. Whenever, therefore, other purposes, which do not contemplate the highest profitableness, are to be subserved, especially purposes which are of interest to the community at large, this class of resources must become an object of public economy by the state or community.

Often it will be a difficult task in practice to assign a particular resource to a proper position with regard to its bearing upon social interests, but conservatism, which is the logical policy of society, will lead us in cases of doubt to lean toward the presumption that the interests of society are more likely to suffer than those of the individual; and a mistake in curtailing private interests will be more easily corrected than a mistake in not having in time guarded social interests. Thus it has been urged against the selection of forest areas as state reserves for the purpose of protecting watersheds, that it would be difficult to decide which areas are necessarily comprised in such selection, without withdrawing those of simply commercial value. That the widest construction of the idea of protective forests will be safer than the opposite, and should be the one adopted by the government, seems quite reasonable.

To properly appreciate the position in any given case, we will have to weigh the present and future significance of the resource, the likelihood of its permanence, and the likelihood of its fate under private treatment, whence the necessity of bringing it under sovereign control of the state and the quality of the control will appear.

That each individual case will require its own consideration and adjudication holds there as well as with legislation in reference to industrial action, and the general classification here attempted offers simply a suggestion as to the general points of view from which each case must be considered.

With the conception of the government before us, as outlined, namely, as the instrument to secure the possibility of not only social life but of social progress, the representative of communal interests as against private interests, of the future as against the present, we can get an idea as to how far the providential functions of the state are to be called into action.

The policy of governmental control over waterways, roads, and lands falling under the operation of eminent domain is well established in most governments. The ownership and management of railways has proved itself to be in the interest of society in several countries. It should be extended with even more reason to all exhaustible, non-restorable resources. That in the interest of society and of production as well the mines should belong to the state in order to prevent waste, we may learn from the actual experience of France, where they are state property, and only the right to work them under supervision is leased to private individuals.

Of the restorable resources it is apparent that, with regard to those which yield increased returns to increased labor, the interests of society and of the individual run on parallel lines. Where interference of the state in their behalf exists it is not from providential reasons. The ameliorative functions only are called into requisition. Whatever tends to stimulate private activity is to be promoted, whatever retards development of intensive methods is to be removed, by government. Industrial education, cultural surveys, bureaus of information, experiment stations, and other aids to private enterprise constitute the chief methods of expressing state interest with regard to these resources.

The three great resources upon which mankind is most dependent, and which, therefore, demand foremost attention of the state, are the soil as food producer, the water, and the climatic conditions. The utilization of these three prime resources by agriculture forms the foundation of all other industries, or, as Sully puts it, "Tillage and pasturage are the two breasts of the state." It is true the manufacturer increases the utility of things, but the farmer multiplies commodities; he is creative, and he therefore above all others can claim a right to first consideration on the part of the state.

The soil is a valuable resource as far as it is fertile and capable of agricultural production; the fertility, while liable to deterioration, can, with few exceptions, be said to be restorable, and it certainly yields increased returns to intelligent increased labor. It ranks, therefore, with those resources which can be left to private enterprise, calling only for the ameliorative functions of the government. But while this condition prevails when the soil is put to agricultural use, it does not exist as long as the soil is not so utilized. By the withdrawal of large sections of land from such use, society is harmed, and deprived of the benefit which it would derive from the use of its property. The proper disposal and the appropriation of the soil to proper use form, therefore, fit functions of government control.

The rational appropriation of soil for either farm use, pasturage, or timber production, one would think, could be left to the regulation of private intelligence; yet the fact is, that the thin, rocky soils of mountain districts are worked for a scanty agricultural crop, when they should be left to timber; while thousands of acres in fertile valleys are still under the shade of virgin forests.

Water and climate are the accessories to agricultural production, and supplement the resources of the soil. Not objects of private enterprise directly, except in a limited manner, it is evident that, as far as they or the conditions which influence them can be at all controlled, they should be under the direct control of the state. A rational management of the water capital of the world in connection with agricultural use of the soil will become the economic problem of the highest importance as the necessity for increased food production calls for intensive methods. And in connection with this problem, it must become a matter of state interest, by a rational management of existing forests and by reforestation at the head waters of rivers and on the plains, to secure the conditions which make a rational utilization of the waters possible. For without forest management, no satisfactory water management is possible for any length of time, no stable basis for continued productive agriculture, industries, and commerce!

It is the object of this volume to elucidate in greater detail the significance and character of the forest resource, to show its relationship to the conditions of social life, to point out the various aspects from which it can be viewed, with the final object of determining the position which the state should take with reference to it, based upon the conception of state functions as outlined in this chapter.

We shall recognize that to the individual it is the timber, the accumulated growth of centuries, which is of interest, and which he exploits for the purpose of making a profit on his labor and outlay without any interest in the future of the exploited area. The relation of the forest to other conditions, direct or indirect, immediate or future, hardly ever enters into his calculations.

On the other hand, the function of the forest, which it exercises as a soil cover by preventing erosion of the soil, by regulating water flow, changing surface drainage into subsoil drainage, and thereby influencing the water stages of rivers, and its possible relation to the local climatic conditions, preeminently renders it an object of government consideration.

Here the general principle of the Roman law, *Utere tuo ne alterum noceas*, prevention of the obnoxious use of private property, readily establishes the propriety of state interference, and by *alterum* we are to understand, not only the other citizen of the present, but of the future as well.

We will see, that the forest resource is one which, under the active competition of private enterprise, is apt to deteriorate, and in its deterioration to affect other conditions of material existence unfavorably; that the maintenance of continued supplies as well as of favorable conditions is possible only under the supervision of permanent institutions with whom present profit is not the only motive. It calls preeminently for the exercise of the providential functions of the state to counteract the destructive tendencies of private exploitation.

5

CONSERVATION AND
THE PROGRESSIVE IDEOLOGY

Gifford Pinchot
THE FIGHT FOR CONSERVATION

In the title of his autobiography, Breaking New Ground (1947), Gifford Pinchot (1865–1946) gave his own succinct evaluation of his importance to American conservation. Despite this self-inflation and easy dismissal of his predecessors' achievements, Pinchot was in fact the popular symbol of resource conservation for perhaps a decade or more. His principal contributions were political and bureaucratic rather than theoretical: he established and directed the Forest Service and dramatized the problem of resource exhaustion to the public during the administration of Theodore Roosevelt and after. For Pinchot as for Roosevelt, conservation was part of a national revival crusade for rectitude, patriotism, efficiency, and strenuous living. In a way seldom made specific or shrill enough to threaten anyone, they also stood for the rights of "the people" to natural resources against the private interests, especially the monopoly powers. But as Pinchot quickly made clear, the people were not to put their hands directly on the national forests—the Forest Service would manage them more expertly for the general welfare. Moreover, if the private interests showed a modicum of social responsibility and businesslike competence, they knew they had nothing to fear from government. Apart from rhetoric the Progressives in fact were deeply worried by signs of widening class hostilities in America; in conservation they perceived a nonpolitical cause that could unite the nation, both the rich and the poor, in a common moral purpose.

The principles which the word conservation has come to embody are not many, and they are exceedingly simple. I have had occasion to say a good many times that no other great movement has ever achieved such progress in so short a time, or made itself felt in so many directions with such vigor and effectiveness, as the movement for the conservation of natural resources.

SOURCE. Gifford Pinchot, *The Fight for Conservation* (Garden City, N.Y., 1910), pp. 40–52, 71–78, 109–119.

Forestry made good its position in the United States before the conservation movement was born. As a forester I am glad to believe that conservation began with forestry, and that the principles which govern the Forest Service in particular and forestry in general are also the ideas that control conservation.

The first idea of real foresight in connection with natural resources arose in connection with the forest. From it sprang the movement which gathered impetus until it culminated in the great convention of governors at Washington in May, 1908. Then came the second official meeting of the National Conservation movement, December 1908, in Washington. Afterward came the various gatherings of citizens in convention, come together to express their judgment on what ought to be done, and to contribute, as only such meetings can, to the formation of effective public opinion.

The movement so begun and so prosecuted has gathered immense swing and impetus. In 1907 few knew what conservation meant. Now it has become a household word. While at first conservation was supposed to apply only to forests, we see now that its sweep extends even beyond the natural resources.

The principles which govern the conservation movement, like all great and effective things, are simple and easily understood. Yet it is often hard to make the simple, easy, and direct facts about a movement of this kind known to the people generally.

The first great fact about conservation is that it stands for development. There has been a fundamental misconception that conservation means nothing but the husbanding of resources for future generations. There could be no more serious mistake. Conservation does mean provision for the future, but it means also and first of all the recognition of the right of the present generation to the fullest necessary use of all the resources with which this country is so abundantly blessed. Conservation demands the welfare of this generation first, and afterward the welfare of the generations to follow.

The first principle of conservation is development, the use of the natural resources now existing on this continent for the benefit of the people who live here now. There may be just as much waste in neglecting the development and use of certain natural resources as there is in their destruction. We have a limited supply of coal, and only a limited supply. Whether it is to last for a hundred or a hundred and fifty or a thousand years, the coal is limited in amount, unless through geological changes which we shall not live to see, there will never be any more of it than there is now. But coal is in a sense the vital essence of our civilization. If it can be preserved, if the life of the mines can be extended, if by preventing waste there can be more coal left in this country after we of this generation have made every needed use of this source of power, then we shall have deserved well of our descendants.

Conservation stands emphatically for the development and use of water-power now, without delay. It stands for the immediate construction of navigable waterways under a broad and comprehensive plan as assistants to the railroads. More coal and more iron are required to move a ton of freight by rail than by water, three to one. In every case and in every direction the conservation movement has development for its first principle, and at the very beginning of its work. The development of our natural resources and the fullest use of them for the present generation is the first duty of this generation. So much for development.

In the second place conservation stands for the prevention of waste. There has come gradually in this country an understanding that waste is not a good thing and that the attack on waste is an industrial necessity. I recall very well indeed how, in the early days of forest fires, they were considered simply and solely as acts of God, against which any opposition was hopeless and any attempt to control them not merely hopeless but childish. It was assumed that they came in the natural order of things, as inevitably as the seasons or the rising and setting of the sun. Today we understand that forest fires are wholly within the control of men. So we are coming in like manner to understand that the prevention of waste in all other directions is a simple matter of good business. The first duty of the human race is to control the earth it lives upon.

We are in a position more and more completely to say how far the waste and destruction of natural resources are to be allowed to go on and where they are to stop. It is curious that the effort to stop waste, like the effort to stop forest fires, has often been considered as a matter controlled wholly by economic law. I think there could be no greater mistake. Forest fires were allowed to burn long after the people had means to stop them. The idea that men were helpless in the face of them held long after the time had passed when the means of control were fully within our reach. It was the old story that "as a man thinketh, so is he"; we came to see that we could stop forest fires, and we found that the means had long been at hand. When at length we came to see that the control of logging in certain directions was profitable, we found it had long been possible. In all these matters of waste of natural resources, the education of the people to understand that they can stop the leakage comes before the actual stopping and after the means of stopping it have long been ready at our hands.

In addition to the principles of development and preservation of our resources there is a third principle. It is this: The natural resources must be developed and preserved for the benefit of the many, and not merely for the profit of a few. We are coming to understand in this country that public action for public benefit has a very much wider field to cover and a much larger part to play than was the case when there were resources enough for every one, and before certain constitutional provisions had given so tremendously strong a position to vested rights and property in general.

A few years ago President Hadley, of Yale, wrote an article which has not attracted the attention it should. The point of it was that by reason of the XIVth amendment to the Constitution, property rights in the United States occupy a stronger position than in any other country in the civilized world. It becomes then a matter of multiplied importance, since property rights once granted are so strongly entrenched, to see that they shall be so granted that the people shall get their fair share of the benefit which comes from the development of the resources which belong to us all. The time to do that is now. By so doing we shall avoid the difficulties and conflicts which will surely arise if we allow vested rights to accrue outside the possibility of governmental and popular control.

The conservation idea covers a wider range than the field of natural resources alone. Conservation means the greatest good to the greatest number for the longest time. One of its great contributions is just this, that it had added to the worn and well-known phrase, "the greatest good to the greatest number," the additional words "for the longest time," thus recognizing that this nation of ours must be made to endure as the best possible home for all its people.

Conservation advocates the use of foresight, prudence, thrift, and intelligence in dealing with public matters, for the same reasons and in the same way that we each use foresight, prudence, thrift, and intelligence in dealing with our own private affairs. It proclaims the right and duty of the people to act for the benefit of the people. Conservation demands the application of common-sense to the common problems for the common good.

The principles of conservation thus described—development, preservation, the common good—have a general application which is growing rapidly wider. The development of resources and the prevention of waste and loss, the protection of the public interests, by foresight, prudence, and the ordinary business and home-making virtues, all these apply to other things as well as to the natural resources. There is, in fact, no interest of the people to which the principles of conservation do not apply.

The conservation point of view is valuable in the education of our people as well as in forestry; it applies to the body politic as well as to the earth and its minerals. A municipal franchise is as properly within its sphere as a franchise for water-power. The same point of view governs in both. It applies as much to the subject of good roads as to waterways, and the training of our people in citizenship is as germane to it as the productiveness of the earth. The application of common-sense to any problem for the nation's good will lead directly to national efficency wherever applied. In other words, and that is the burden of the message, we are coming to see the logical and inevitable outcome that these principles, which arose in forestry and have their bloom in the conservation of natural resources, will have their fruit in the increase and promotion of national efficiency along other lines of national life.

The outgrowth of conservation, the inevitable result, is national efficiency. In the great commercial struggle between nations which is eventually to determine the welfare of all, national efficiency will be the deciding factor. So from every point of view conservation is a good thing for the American people.

The National Forest Service, one of the chief agencies of the conservation movement, is trying to be useful to the people of this nation. The service recognizes, and recognizes it more and more strongly all the time, that whatever it has done or is doing has just one object, and that object is the welfare of the plain American citizen. Unless the Forest Service has served the people, and is able to contribute to their welfare it has failed in its work and should be abolished. But just so far as by cooperation, by intelligence, by attention to the work laid upon it, it contributes to the welfare of our citizens, it is a good thing and should be allowed to go on with its work.

The Natural Forests are in the west. Headquarters of the service have been established throughout the western country, because its work cannot be done effectively and properly without the closest contact and the most hearty cooperation with the western people. It is the duty of the Forest Service to see to it that the timber, water-powers, mines, and every other resource of the forests is used for the benefit of the people who live in the neighborhood or who may have a share in the welfare of each locality. It is equally its duty to cooperate with all our people in every section of our land to conserve a fundamental resource, without which this nation cannot prosper. . . .

The business of the people of the United States, performed by the government of the United States, is a vast and a most important one; it is the house-keeping of the American nation. As a business proposition it does not attract anything like the attention that it ought. Unfortunately we have come into the habit of considering the government of the United States as a political organization rather than as a business organization.

Now this question, which the governors of the states and the representatives of great interests were called to Washington to consider in 1908, is fundamentally a business question, and it is along business lines that it must be considered and solved, if the problem is to be solved at all. Manufacturers are dealing with the necessity for producing a definite output as a result of definite expenditure and definite effort. The government of the United States is doing exactly the same thing. The manufacturer's product can be measured in dollars and cents. The product of the government of the United States can be measured partly in dollars and cents, but far more importantly in the welfare and contentment and happiness of the people over which it is called upon to preside.

The keynote of that conservation conference in Washington was forethought and foresight. The keynote of success in any line of life, or one of the great keynotes, must be forethought and foresight. If we, as a nation, are to continue the wonderful growth we have had, it is forethought and foresight which must give us the capacity to go on as we have been going. I dwell on this because it seems to me to be one of the most curious of all things in the history of the United States today that we should have grasped this principle so tremendously and so vigorously in our daily lives, in the conduct of our own business, and yet have failed so completely to make the obvious application in the things which concern the nation.

It is curiously true that great aggregations of individuals and organized bodies are apt to be less far-sighted, less moral, less intelligent along certain lines than the individual citizen; or at least that their standards are lower; a principle which is illustrated by the fact that we have got over settling disputes between individuals by the strong hand, but not yet between nations.

So we have allowed ourselves as a nation, in the flush of the tremendous progress that we have made, to fail to look at the end from the beginning and to put ourselves in a position where the normal operation of natural laws threatens to bring us to a halt in a way which will make every man, woman, and child in the nation feel the pinch when it comes.

No man may rightly fail to take a great pride in what has been accomplished by means of the destruction of our natural resources so far as it has gone. It is a paradoxical statement, perhaps, but nevertheless true, because out of this attack on what nature has given we have won a kind of prosperity and a kind of civilization and a kind of man that are new in the world. For example, nothing like the rapidity of the destruction of American forests has ever been known in forest history, and nothing like the efficiency and vigor and inventiveness of the American lumberman has ever been developed by any attack on any forests elsewhere. Probably the most effective tool that the human mind and hand have ever made is the American axe. So the American business man has grasped his opportunities and used them and developed them and invented about them, thought them into lines of success, and thus has developed into a new business man, with a vigor and effectiveness and a cutting-edge that has never been equalled anywhere else. We have gained out of the vast destruction of our natural resources a degree of vigor and power and efficiency of which every man of us ought to be proud.

Now that is done. We have accomplished these big things. What is the next step? Shall we go on in the same lines to the certain destruction of the prosperity which we have created, or shall we take the obvious lesson of all human history, turn our backs on the uncivilized point of view, and adopt toward our natural resources the average prudence and average foresight and average care that we long ago adopted as a rule of our daily life?

The conservation movement is calling the attention of the American people to the fact that they are trustees. The fact seems to me so plain as to require only a statement of it, to carry conviction. Can we reasonably fail to recognize the obligation which rests upon us in this matter? And, if we do fail to recognize it, can we reasonably expect even a fairly good reputation at the hands of our descendants?

Business prudence and business common-sense indicate as strongly as anything can the absolute necessity of a change in point of view on the part of the people of the United States regarding their natural resources. The way we have been handling them is not good business. Purely on the side of dollars and cents, it is not good business to kill the goose that lays the golden egg, to burn up half our forests, to waste our coal, and to remove from under the feet of those who are coming after us the opportunity for equal happiness with ourselves. The thing we ought to leave to them is not merely an opportunity for equal happiness and equal prosperity, but for a vastly increased fund of both.

Conservation is not merely a question of business, but a question of a vastly higher duty. In dealing with our natural resources we have come to a place at last where every consideration of patriotism, every consideration of love of country, of gratitude for things that the land

and the institutions of this nation have given us, call upon us for a return. If we owe anything to the United States, if this country has been good to us, if it has given us our prosperity, our education, and our chance of happiness, then there is a duty resting upon us. That duty is to see, so far as in us lies, that those who are coming after us shall have the same opportunity for happiness we have had ourselves. Apart from any business consideration, apart from the question of the immediate dollar, this problem of the future wealth and happiness and prosperity of the people of the United States has a right to our attention. It rises far above all matters of temporary individual business advantage, and becomes a great question of national preservation. We all have the unqestionable right to a reasonable use of natural resources during our lifetime, we all may use, and should use, the good things that were put here for our use, for in the last analysis this question of conservation is the question of national preservation and national efficiency. . .

The American people have evidently made up their minds that our natural resources must be conserved. That is good. But it settles only half the question. For whose benefit shall they be conserved—for the benefit of the many, or for the use and profit of the few? The great conflict now being fought will decide. There is no other question before us that begins to be so important, or that will be so difficult to straddle, as the great question between special interest and equal opportunity, between the privileges of the few and the rights of the many, between government by men for human welfare and government by money for profit, between the men who stand for the Roosevelt policies and the men who stand against them. This is the heart of the conservation problem today.

The conservation issue is a moral issue. When a few men get possession of one of the necessaries of life, either through ownership of a natural resource or through unfair business methods, and use that control to extort undue profits, as in the recent cases of the sugar trust and the beef-packers, they injure the average man without good reason, and they are guilty of a moral wrong. It does not matter whether the undue profit comes through stifling competition by rebates or other crooked devices, through corruption of public officials, or through seizing and monopolizing resources which belong to the people. The result is always the same—a toll levied on the cost of living through special privilege.

The income of the average family in the United States is less than $600 a year. To increase the cost of living to such a family beyond the reasonable profits of legitimate business is wrong. It is not merely a question of a few cents more a day for the necessaries of life, or of a few cents less a day for wages. Far more is at stake—the health or sickness of little babies, the education or ignorance of children, virtue or vice in young daughters, honesty or criminality in young sons, the working power of bread-winners, the integrity of families, the provision for old age—in a word, the welfare and happiness or the misery and degradation of the plain people are involved in the costs of living.

To the special interest an unjust rise in the cost of living means simply higher profit, but to those who pay it, that profit is measured in schooling, warm clothing, a reserve to meet emergencies, a fair chance to make the fight for comfort, decency, and right living.

I believe in our form of government and I believe in the golden rule. But we must face the truth that monopoly of the sources of production makes it impossible for vast numbers of men and women to earn a fair living. Right here the conservation question touches the daily life of the great body of our people, who pay the cost of special privilege. And the price is heavy. That price may be the chance to save the boys from the saloons and the corner gang, and the girls from worse, and to make good citizens of them instead of bad; for an appalling proportion of the tragedies of life spring directly from the lack of a little money. Thousands of daughters of the poor fall into the hands of the white-slave traders because their poverty leaves them without protection. Thousands of families, as the Pittsburg survey has shown us, lead lives of brutalizing overwork in return for the barest living. Is it fair that these thousands of families should have less than they need in order that a few families should have swollen fortunes at their expense? Let him who dares deny that there is wickedness in grinding the faces of the poor, or assert that these are not moral questions which strike the very homes of our people. If these are not moral questions, there are no moral questions.

The people of this country have lost vastly more than they can ever regain by gifts of public property, forever and without charge, to men who gave nothing in return. It is true that we have made superb material progress under this system, but it is not well for us to rejoice too freely in the slices the special interests have given us from the great loaf of the property of all the people.

The people of the United States have been the complacent victims of a system of grab, often perpetrated by men who would have been surprised beyond measure to be accused of wrong-doing, and many of whom in their private lives were model citizens. But they have suffered from a curious moral perversion by which it becomes praiseworthy to do for a corporation things which they would refuse with the loftiest scorn to do for themselves. Fortunately for us all that delusion is passing rapidly away.

President Hadley well said that "the fundamental division of powers in the Constitution of the United States is between voters on the one hand and property-owners on the other." When property gets possession of the voting power also, little is left for the people. That is why the unholy alliance between business and politics is the most dangerous fact in our political life. I believe the American people are tired of that alliance. They are weary of politics for revenue only. It is time to take business out of politics, and keep it out—time for the political activity of this nation to be aimed squarely at the welfare of all of us, and squarely away from the excessive profits of a few of us.

A man is not bad because he is rich, nor good because he is poor. There is no monopoly of virtue. I hold no brief for the poor against the rich nor for the wage-earner against the capitalist. Exceptional capacity in business, as in any other line of life, should meet with exceptional reward. Rich men have served this country greatly. Washington was a rich man. But it is very clear that excessive profits from the control of natural resources, monopolized by a few, are not worth to this nation the tremendous price they cost us.

We have allowed the great corporations to occupy with their own men the strategic points in business, in social, and in political life. It is our fault more than theirs. We have allowed it when we could have stopped it. Too often we have seemed to forget that a man in public life can no more serve both the special interests and the people than he can serve God and mammon. There is no reason why the American people should not take into their hands again the full political power which is theirs by right, and which they exercised before the special interests began to nullify the will of the majority. There are many men who believe, and who will always believe, in the divine right of money to rule. With such men argument, compromise, or conciliation is useless or worse. The only thing to do with them is to fight them and beat them. It has been done, and it can be done again.

It is the honorable distinction of the Forest Service that it has been more constantly, more violently and more bitterly attacked by the representatives of the special interests in recent years than any other government bureau. These attacks have increased in violence and bitterness just in proportion as the service has offered effective opposition to predatory wealth. The more successful the Forest Service has been in preventing land-grabbing and the absorption of water power by the special interests, the more ingenious, the more devious, and the more dangerous these attacks have become. A favorite one is to assert that the Forest Service, in its zeal for the public welfare, has played ducks and drakes with the acts of Congress. The fact is, on the contrary, that the Service has had warrant of law for everything it has done. Not once since it was created has any charge of illegality, despite the most searching investigation and the bitterest attack, ever led to reversal or reproof by either house of Congress or by any congressional committee. Not once has the Forest Service been defeated or reversed as to any vital legal principle underlying its work in any court or administrative tribunal of last resort. It is the first duty of a public officer to obey the law. But it is his second duty, and a close second, to do everything the law will let him do for the public good, and not merely what the law directs or compels him to do. Unless the public service is alive enough to serve the people with enthusiasm, there is very little to be said for it.

Another, and unusually plausible, form of attack, is to demand that all land not now bearing trees shall be thrown out of the National Forests. For centuries forest fires have burned through the western mountains, and much land thus deforested is scattered throughout the National Forests awaiting reforestation. This land is not valuable for agriculture, and will contribute more to the general welfare under forest than in any other way. To exclude it from the National Forests would be no more reasonable than it would be in a city to remove from taxation and municipal control every building lot not now covered by a house. It would be no more reasonable than to condemn and take away from our farmers every acre of land that did not bear a crop last year, or to confiscate a man's winter overcoat because he was not wearing it in July. A generation in the life of a nation is no longer than a season in the life of a man. With a fair chance we can and will reclothe these denuded mountains with forests, and we ask for that chance.

Still another attack, nearly successful two years ago, was an attempt to prevent the Forest Service from telling the people, through the press, what it is accomplishing for them, and how much this nation needs the forests. If the Forest Service can not tell what it is doing the time will come when there will be nothing to tell. It is just as necessary for the people to know what is being done to help them as to know what is being done to hurt them. Publicity is the essential and indispensable condition of clean and effective public service.

Since the Forest Service called public attention to the rapid absorption of the water-power sites and the threatening growth of a great water-power monopoly, the attacks upon it have increased with marked rapidity. I anticipate that they will continue to do so. Still greater opposition is promised in the near future. There is but one protection—an awakened and determined public opinion. That is why I tell the facts.

6

THE END OF MALTHUSIAN SCARCITY

Simon Patten
THE NEW BASIS OF CIVILIZATION

In one sense the conservation philosophy ran directly counter to a deeply engrained, long-standing article of national faith—the unending abundance of wealth in the New World. Only the closing of the frontier in 1890 could shake that optimism and give popular credence to conservation and the depressing ratios of Malthus. At the same time that Pinchot was warning of impending resource "famines," however, an economist at the University of Pennsylvania was announcing that in the continuing perfection of technology lay a promise to end once and for all the threat of scarcity. Simon Patten (1852–1922) did not intend to throw off track the program for careful husbanding of the national resources; perhaps his boyhood on an Illinois farm instilled in him his firm appreciation of the value of conservation economics. But, in the midst of a generation of calamity howlers, he could not refrain from pointing to the swelling surplus that applied science had made possible and to the change which he predicted this surplus would work in the American character—replacing a culture of pain, stinginess, and hard work with more generous, free-spending habits. In effect a new frontier of abundance had been discovered, one limited only by the state of technical knowledge. Although some of the immediate material shortages may have been real, in the long run the threat to prosperity was less severe than the conservationists claimed.

One summer day I took my note-book to a wooden hillside whence I could overlook a rich and beautiful valley. The well-tended farms, the strong stone houses, the busy men and animals moving peacefully over roads and fields, would inspire me, I was sure, with the opening theme of this book. As I seated myself under a chestnut tree a fellow guest at the hotel came by, and glancing at my memoranda asked if I, like himself, was writing a lecture. He too had come to the woods, he

SOURCE. Simon Patten, *The New Basis of Civilization* (New York, 1907), pp. 3–27.

said, to meditate and to be inspired by nature. But his thesis, enthusiastically unfolded, was the opposite to mine. It was a part of his faith as a Second Adventist that the world is becoming more unhappy and more wicked; and it is now so evil that the end of it approaches. On the face of the earth are wars and in the air rumors of war. Disease, famine, and disaster surround us; vice reigns, moral decay spreads, and only the annihilation of mankind can satisfy divine justice and purify the way for the practice of the long-deferred divine plan. To find inspiration for this text my companion had also come to look upon the teeming farm lands owned by clean and well-housed folk. Where I marked the progress of humanity and thrilled with the hope that poverty will soon be banished from the world as it has been from this happy valley, he saw a threatening scene of worldliness where prosperity lulled spiritual alarms to a dangerous moral peace. The general argument that degeneration follows a prolonged period of material success is familiar to the reader, and I need not give the outline colored by the social and religious philosophy of his sect. Yet in spite of the fundamental differences in our training it seemed strange to me that two men looking at the same picture could agree wholly upon the truths it painted and forthwith interpret them as differently as we did. Looking down into this plentiful valley, one fortified his belief that divine wrath must be invoked upon a region carnal and depraved; while the other joyfully exclaimed, "Here is the basis of a new civilization; here is evidence that economic forces can sweep away poverty, banish misery, and by giving men work bring forth right and enduring character within the race."

The eclecticism of the Adventist's views reminded me of a social reformer with whom I had talked not long before. I had recalled to this cultured university man—what he of course knew perfectly well—the series upon series of improvements in the conditions of workingmen's lives which are steadily following economic changes now going on; I reminded him of numerous pleasure-yielding motives to work which have been given to the poor; and I pointed out the familiar truth that their consumption of goods has been enormously increased, widely varied, and remarkably cheapened. He nodded his head affirmatively after these statements: then he quickly shook it in negation, saying, "I have lived in Berlin, Paris, London, New York, and Chicago, and in all of them the misery of the masses is as acute as it ever was." His selective vision settled at once upon large cities where his own life centered about the struggling poor. He waived my evidence as having little bearing on urban poverty, while he seemed to me to be incompletely measuring social progress by symptoms, effects, and local hindrances. Acquaintance with the condition of the poor remains for him a basis broad enough to define the forces beneath our civilization; I believe we approach truth only when we construct our theories from a study of continental resources and a precise knowledge of the effects of inventions and improvements in modes of life upon whole populations.

I mention these conversations because they typify a kind now carried on between men with differing educations. Each disputant comes into the field with an experience gained in one of the many environments which our great world affords, and from its vantage ground, armed with its sympathies and interests, draws local deductions to which he gives a universal application. If men in the same place disagreed upon the main facts within it, or if men in different places refused to accept each other's evidence, then there would be no hope of blending, explaining, and reconstructing these particular experiences into a general and comprehensive viewpoint. But in reality there is surprisingly little difference of opinion concerning the facts within the environments that may be discussed. Few men deny that the working people of industrial centers are ill paid, that employment is uncertain, housing is bad, sickness frequent, and that the abnormally short working life ends in an old age of poverty and fear. There are few, on the other hand, who deny the evidence of growing prosperity. Prosperity is a fact: and so is poverty. Both are too evident to be contested.

The differences of opinion develop from the interpretation of facts. We cannot survey today's occurrences as isolated phenomena uninfluenced by yesterday's conditions from which they issued. Neither can we prophesy what will be the effects tomorrow of today's events by looking backward to see what followed similar circumstances in remote times. Nevertheless, when men do undertake to interpret today and tomorrow they turn their gaze to the past, search there for resembling situations, and having found one or more, use them as premises to the conclusion that what followed in the first case will also follow in the present instance. They confuse the law that like effects follow like causes into the loose axiom that history repeats itself. If two men differ radically about the lessons to be drawn from an historical epoch, they will differ as radically about the future consequences of a present situation at the very moment when they are in entire accord upon the actual data under their eyes. They may visit a country together and note a score of evidences of its prosperity; yet one will conclude that good times are temporary and must inevitably be followed by the accustomed misery and exploitation, while the other stoutly affirms that here is the beginning of a new epoch which is without historical precedent, and which may therefore endure indefinitely longer than the Greek or Roman city cited by his friend. If they walk the squalid streets of a factory town and mark the sodden suffering, one will exclaim that this is the predicted outcome of the exploitation of the workers under present methods of production; the other replies that it is the lingering consequences of social injustice and nature's early violences which modern science and industry are relieving, but which they have not had time to eradicate. The issue in neither case is drawn wholly from the local situation; it is determined by the relative importance the men attach to similar circumstances in bygone eras.

To arrive at a man's opinions one ought to know what he has read and heard rather than what he has seen. The glasses through which we scan the present have been ground, polished, and focussed by the experience of the race in distant ages, and we behold most distinctly the objects at a distance. It is difficult, therefore, to interpret the present according to its own significance, and more difficult still to understand the past through our knowledge of the present. But a careful reversal of the popular method of reasoning would give a clearer view of contemporary life and a corrected impression of the past. It would begin with a scrutiny of today, retrace history, and predict the future from a knowledge tested by joint studies of the two. The other mode of thinking threads an involved path starting in historical episodes, makes a detour around the present, and leads to a goal in the future where its followers expect to find new episodes like those they began with. The one is an economic, the other an historical interpretation. Are we nearer the truth when we hold that like economic antecedents produce like social effects or that like historical antecedents will produce like future results? Shall we search for our postulates among the economic and geographic conditions in which we live or shall we return to the history of our crudest ancestral type?

The choice is fundamentally important and divides social thinkers into opposing camps. Those who would predict tomorrow's economic states from a study of the economic states of Rome or Venice overlook the difference between a society struggling to meet a deficit and one so well situated that thought can be centred on the equitable distribution of a surplus. In the one case the civilization must develop its traditions to keep the deficit as small as possible and eventually to overcome it, and in the other to utilize the surplus for common good, not to undermine energy and productive ability or to create parasitic classes, but to distribute the surplus in ways that will promote general welfare and secure better preparation for the future. The one type of society may be called a pain or deficit economy, the other a pleasure or surplus economy. All civilizations before the nineteenth century, like the primitive societies of the western world today and the backward despotisms of the east, were realms of pain and deficit, in which the traditions and experiences of men were moulded out of the general menaces to life and happiness. When adjustment to nature was defective at many points and lacking altogether at others, forecasts of evil were proved true by the event, and men learned to expect calamity and disorder. If nations established themselves in rich localities where they might have built stable institutions upon natural resources, other nations warred upon them without let or hindrance, and the contests exhausted the land. In short, the story of the rise and fall of nations, repeated again and again, seems to justify the familiar conclusion that the decline of a society after an epoch of prosperity is a natural, incontrovertible law. But are these sad endings the fit sequels of man's ill-doing in a one-time perfect world, as certain moralists have affirmed, or are suffering and defeat the outcome of the purely physical conditions of existence? If the latter, improvements in the environment will construct a new basis for civilization by lessening deficit and destroying the old status between men and nature.

We must admit that such a process of amelioration in world affairs is going on. But the changes wrought by that process are so recent that the effects of old conditions have not disappeared. They persist in a revolutionized order of things which has not yet definitely reconstructed the traditions and orthodox modes of thought. Mental habits continue long after the economic conditions which fashioned them have disappeared, and popular beliefs reflect the passing age of nature's deficit, while the actions of men who hold those beliefs are chiefly governed by the new age of surplus in which they live. The economic revolution is here, but the intellectual revolution that will rouse men to its stupendous meaning has not done its work.

The static condition of men's minds is revealed by the contradictions of current thought, and by premises drawn from data that have ceased to be true. John Stuart Mill is still warmly upheld when he says that the science of economics rests upon the niggardliness of nature. Teachers lay down the Law of Diminishing Returns as emphatically as ever, and expound afresh the sweeping Malthusian doctrine of population. We still tremble at the growth of numbers, and advocate measures to restrict the movement of races from poorer to better surroundings. How many there are who fear a lower wage and greater poverty as the bitter fruit of the throngs of eager workers who press into our ports!

It was the social philosophy of deficit that brought forth the theory of exploitation, and its derivative the Iron Law of Wages, which working men and socialists uphold as ardently as the upper classes do the principles of Mill and Ricardo. In another form it becomes the Single Tax doctrine advanced by Henry George. His followers teach us that good lands and advantageous sites are scarce, and that multitudes are degraded by the pressure forcing them downward to poor locations.

In history this ancient outlook is described in terms of the decadence of places and the degeneration of peoples. In politics the masses are pronounced unworthy of trust, hero-worship is practised, imperialism and government by the few are advocated, and the continuance of military and police power is correspondingly assured.

Shift the viewpoint once more, and race hatreds are explained as the result of the necessary strife for possession of the limited riches of the earth. . . . But have nature's negations remained absolute and are subsistence wars still the principle of social evolution? Do resources diminish with use? Indications of a stupendous change have been accumulating for many years, but their profound significance has been slurred by writers whose eyes have been fixed upon the spectacular history of society. An agriculture that added to nature's endowment was feebly practised here and there while the Law of Diminishing Returns was being written; mother countries were becoming reluctant to denude their colonies of pelts, timber, ivories, and human beings; and England in India was learning to sow scientifically with one hand in order that she might longer reap with the other. But this faint stirring was unnoticed behind the body of facts with which thinkers were dealing. It is as if they were engaged in writing the epilogue of one drama while the curtain was rising upon the prologue of another presenting a new cast of characters. Much of the scenery today is that with which time has made us familiar, and the action seems to follow the ancient tragic model. There is the old motive of exploitation; the stronger men use the weaker, and having destroyed them in their machinery of production, discard them while they are still in their middle life; they capture children and torture the little prisoners of industry; and they prey on the women inside factory walls. Bands of men in great cities undergo disease, hunger, exposure, and contend savagely with shifting masses of immigrants who are a steady overtax upon the local labor market. The lives of the weakest in crowded towns seem still ordered by the Law of Diminishing

Returns. But here the new players intervene and promise that millions of the weak shall be added to industrial civilization without the tragic climax of starvation, disease, and despair. Many of the obstacles that were insuperable a century ago are falling before the young genius of the mechanical age. Militarism, bad sanitation, inadequate protection from heat and cold, a high birth-rate offsetting a high death-rate—all these obstructions to the broadened consuming power of the poor have been reduced. Ground that lay barren because of ignorance and scarcity of capital and of tools is fertile now because there are tools and money for every feat of agriculture.

Immobile masses of men used to die of famine while a few hundred miles away crops rotted on the ground for lack of transportation. Famine no longer threatens a country where railroads carry freight. United States laboratories and food stations are evolving cereals and condensing nutriment in their tissues. Government experts are studying food for men and cattle on the Russian steppes and in half-forgotten oases of the Sahara. Mr. Luther Burbank hopes to overcome nature in the deserts of the West with the science-born thornless cactus; he doubles the size of fruits and brings new ones into being, in a few years outdistancing the pace of thousands of generations of his "master,"—nature. The Secretary of Agriculture recently declared that serious crop failures will occur no more. Agriculture has become a science, our common foods grow in conquered habitats, the desert is sown, and waste land is made fertile. Unseasonable frosts, prolonged droughts and rains, torrid heat, insect pests, plant disease—all these familiar menaces he believes will soon cease to threaten the farmer. Never again will widespread famine, plagues, scarcity prices, or commercial panics be the result of defective husbandry. Stable, progressive farming controls the terror, disorder, and devastation of earlier times. A new agriculture means a new civilization. Physicians and sanitarians tell us that the recent yellow fever epidemic was the last which shall find foothold in the United States. Their knowledge of its causes gives them power to subdue it. To recall the horror that has accompanied the plague since history began is to foresee what a change in social traditions and industrial development this revolution alone will make. The food, housing, and general hygiene of the workers at Panama, for instance, can be cared for so scientifically that the canal will be dug under conditions possible fifty years ago only north of the frost line.

Each gain upon nature adds to the quantity of goods to be consumed by society, and lessens the labor necessary to produce them. Improved conditions make better men, and better men improve conditions.

Professor Shaler says men can double the food supply of the world by expansion of population and double that by engineering devices; if it be true, American possibilities exceed even his amazing estimate, for we occupy one of the most fertile regions of the globe. The fall in the rate of business, the eagerness to invest daringly, the alertness of capital to enter new business, the widespread security of investments, the "saving instinct" which has become a constant, half-automatic pressure toward the growth of funds—these economic truths have been so minutely illustrated by special observers that it is scarcely necessary to assume a general doubt of the nation's present ability to give work to hordes of men equipped with an average physique and some intelligence. Prince Kropotkin epitomizes the change when he writes: "For the first time in the history of civilization, mankind has reached a point where the means of satisfying its needs are in excess of the needs themselves. To impose, therefore, as has hitherto been done, the curse of misery and degradation upon vast divisions of mankind, in order to secure well-being for the few, is needed no more; well-being can be secured for all, without overwork for any. We are thus placed in a position entirely to remodel the very bases and contents of our civilization—provided the civilized nations find in their midst the constructive capacities and the powers of creation required for utilizing the conquests of the human intellect in the interest of all."

The well-being of which the Russian reformer thought doubtless differs greatly from that which men pronounced fair a few years ago. At the beginning of the factory system the standards of comfort for laborers were so low that prosperity was defined as nothing more than free and steady access to the two or three staple foods produced in the workers' localities. Cheapness signified control over the few good foods of each community rather than access to the supplies of a continent. Adam Smith, not dreaming of a transportation system which would shortly organize the resources of a world, named the essentials of civilization "cheapness and plenty"; he probably meant by that the ability to buy bread and potatoes, or whatever the laborer's environment produced in largest quantities. At that time the food area was measured by a narrow belt through the North Temperate Zone, and estimated by the accessible amount of wheat. Now, although wheat in our markets grows close to the polar circle, it has not kept its ancient position as chief resource of the workingman, because the multiplication of other cheap edibles places options upon the laborer's table. The grocery window stacked with "breakfast foods," unimagined ten years ago, witnesses at the same time that the use of non-wheat products has increased the demand for cereals in astonishing multiples. Less monotonous, more palatable, and very easily prepared, these "ready to eat" goods are perhaps the cheapest, in proportion to nutrition and to labor-power saved, that have yet been found. They economize fuel, and they set free a fraction of the housewife's time—it is asserted that they were devised to simplify the servant problem in the houses of the well-to-do. If it is true that certain varieties selling at seven or eight cents are properly accused of lacking the ingredients included in the chemical formula on the box, and are nothing more than simple cereal flakes, they "go further" than a loaf of bread and have two valuable qualities beside: they increase the demand for sugar and milk, and they vary the diet.

No manipulation of a corner can permanently raise the price of bread, for the "natural monopoly" was broken when wheat first came to market from the edge of the tropics and the polar latitudes. In western America extensive cultivation of it has just begun to tap possibilities which in relation to eighty million of people are almost boundless. Sugar, which years ago was too expensive to be lavishly consumed by the well-to-do, now freely gives its heat to the workingman. It is more and more advantageously used as a strength builder among the underfed. The demand that will follow the developing taste for it can be met by the vast quantities latent in Porto Rico and Cuba, and beyond them by the teeming lands of South America, and beyond them by the virgin tropics of another hemisphere. Tomatoes, the hot-house delicacy of the Civil War time, are doing now what many a bloody revolution failed to accomplish: they have relieved the monotony of salt pork and boiled potatoes upon the poor man's table. The clear acid flavor of the canned vegetable lightens ugly heaviness, and adds tonic gratifications for the lack of which men have let each other's blood. The tomato will grow on ground inhospitable to other cultivation, it needs little care either on the vine or in the cannery, and the ease of marketing it, together with the enormous demand, have worn the price rapidly down to eights cents a can for the poorer brands. The "specials" offered by cash groceries at seven, six, and five cents extend the circle of purchasers, and the poor man's wife finds their ragged contents very satisfactory when served with her dull meat stew.

Within the last decade the concentrated food value and the delicate flavor of green peas have been added to the dietary of the workingman. The former high prices have been reduced to nine or ten cents, and the primeval barrenness of Colorado, reclaimed by irrigation, has scarcely begun to yield a quota of its crops. Irrigation permanently fertilizes land, and by quickening growth gives richer flavor to vegetables. If these advantages keep the prices of desert-grown vegetables above those the poor man can pay, the varieties now ranking best will descend to his uses. The preservation of food by canning is to time what transportation is to space. One opens an indefinite territory and the other secures an indefinite time in which to consume what has been quickly perishable. The easy and almost unnoticed fall in the demand for meats during the recent beef-trust scandal shows that meat is not the standard of life in the sense that bread was in the eighteenth century, and that a plundering tax can never again involve the poor in hardships comparable with those formerly laid upon the English by salt and wheat imposts. In America, meat three times a day permits monopoly, twice a day high prices, once a day it means cheapness and plenty; for if we are convinced that meat is the staff of life men use this belief to build an artificial monopoly upon. If meat is relegated to a coordinate place in a well-ordered diet, it must become as cheap as bread and potatoes.

In the specific instance of rumored scarcity and famine prices during a late strike, the workers were by no means seriously affected. The Russian Jews turned without much ado to the fish they had depended upon in Russia but had discarded here because it was less fresh than it had been in their river towns; and the northern meat-eating stocks, like the Germans and Irish Americans, increased the consumption of coarse vegetables by putting less of the cheap tough cuts of beef into their stews. Salaried people and the higher class of laborers felt the embargo more than the vast majority of immigrants who have not yet learned to measure their well-being by the pounds of flesh they consume. A vegetable diet is normal to the Italians and semi-tropical people, and the result of a protracted strike or a packer's monopoly will probably be the loss of a potential market without detriment to the health of South Europeans in America. The development of meat tastes, it is not perhaps too much to say, will depend upon the ascendency of Anglo-Saxon tradition rather than upon the needs of modern men, who are adequately warmed in their homes and protected from extremes of weather while outside them.

Rapid distribution of food carries civilization with it, and the prosperity that gives us a Panama Canal with which to reach untouched tropic riches is a distinctive laborer's resource, ranking with refrigerated express and quick freight carriage. The produce which the railroads bring to cities have made ice a commonplace of the larder. Without it milk would cease to flow into New York from Adirondack farms four hundred miles away; it opens a market for fresh fish to people who have hitherto eaten it only in oil or in a dried form; it gives options upon the winter's market as well as upon the summer's, and adds many perishable fruits and shortlived vegetables to the laborer's menu. In the Philadelphia ghetto one may watch a huckster's wagon, filled with strawberries costing three and four cents a box, move down the block and go away empty on a day when a box uptown is not to be found at less than ten cents. Other wagons offer lettuce, celery, corn, and spinach banked crisply against the blocks of ice in the wagon bed. Banana carts make their rounds during the whole year with excellent fruit for ten and eight—and late on market nights for six—cents a dozen. The consumption of bananas among the poor is very large; it may be said to have become a staple without regard to previous food customs because of its small waste, its solid nutriment, and its low price. Like sugar, the banana can never again be a luxury; its simplicity and economy of preparation and its compact food values have added it permanently to the laborer's fund of goods.

It is the worker who reaps the advantage of food bargains not to be found in stationary shops. The huckster whose expenses are low offers his wares late at night and calls to the windows many purchasers who have waited for him and are ready to take advantage of the exigencies of ten o'clock. The daytime commissary of the streets, spread on stands and hawked from baskets, also feeds the children more delicately than they were fed in their fathers' countries. Much is unwholesome, much is adulterated, but the food is unstintedly there, and plenty does not fail. It is but natural that a badly ordered menu should be one of the first results of the bedecked and festival appeals to the palate that are made to growing young people and the newly arrived immigrant. Periods of excess in unaccustomed "fancy things," like two-cent glasses of soda water, cheap candy and cake, alternate with periods of undereating. The disorganized dietary, in fact, frequently persists for several years in families which are on the bare subsistence level. The reason of it is illustrated by the judgments two factory girls exercised on the way home from work one afternoon. They found themselves hungry and decided to dine as they walked rather than wait for the home fare or the coffee, cake, and ice cream of a settlement club dance in the evening. They bought rye bread sandwiches of strong mustard and two frankfurter sausages, and quenched their thirst with chocolate soda at the next street fountain. They then ate strawberry and coffee ice-cream, and being still unsatisfied, n completed their supper with a chocolate eclair. They spent twenty cents each and were so satiated with sweets that they refused the refreshments at the dance.

The confusion that has followed the breakdown of old dietary customs is now being corrected, in a measure, by a number of social agencies which attempt to bring order by systematic instruction in dietetics. Settlements and training schools give cooking lessons to mothers, children, and young women, in which substitutes for meat are carefully demonstrated and the cost of each dish computed. Many of these courses are simple and practicable and will accomplish their ends. Palatable lunches served in the public schools by semi-philanthropic societies, food and health exhibitions, restaurants and dining-rooms opened by social capital, and the steady advice of kindergarten teachers upon the food sent from home for the children—all these methods are adapting the rude bulk of our prosperity to individual instances.

Beneath this admirable superstructure, however, lies the potent basic fact of a civilization whose bounds are indefinitely widened because the unskilled laborer need be no longer held to the plane of sheer animal terror by uncertainty of food and employment. Artificial culture and experimental science have already fundamentally altered the elemental relations existing two hundred years ago between population and environment. Yet to say that the methods which have made men physically independent of the local food supply are artificial, is to underrate the powers of the new forces by implying that they are constantly opposed by fundamental natural forces which in the end must again triumph. The final victory of man's machinery over nature's materials is the next logical process in evolution, as nature's control of human society was the transition from anarchic and puny individualism to the group acting as a powerful, intelligent organism. Machinery, science, and intelligence moving on the face of the earth may well affect it as the elements do, upbuilding, obliterating, and creating; but they are man's forces and will be used to hasten his dominion over nature.

Each gain upon nature adds to the quantity of goods to be consumed by society and lessens the labor necessary to produce them. In one form the surplus is stored in individuals as surplus energy; in another it is in the goods produced by this energy. Goods become utilities in consumption, utilities are transformed into energy, and energy as work creates new goods. The surplus is not conserved as a permanent fund, but exists and grows only as it is perpetually transformed from goods to energy and from energy back to goods. Life, work, and happiness are thus bound together and their measure is the surplus that vitalizes them. It relieves the present from the menace of a deficit which our forefathers constantly faced and feared. As a concept of our social thinking it differentiates the new from the old and helps to drive away the mists that blur clear thinking. But states of mind are hard to change, and in truth those we so long ago adopted seem to find ever fresh justification in the evils which remain to afflict men long after their inciting causes have disappeared; and in the old wounds of humanity it is easy to see new proofs of accustomed beliefs. The strongest arguments can be presented just as their foundations are crumbling to decay. We know that the military state is gradually being displaced by the industrial state, and yet there never was a time when the power and efficiency of armies were as great as now. They hold the nations in their power just when the disintegration of the forces beneath them is most apparent. And so it is with the evils more directly associated with the industrial world. The poverty, misery, exploitation, oppression of the poor; the greed, indifference, and power of the rich, are glaring truths even while the basis of a new economic order becomes more and more plain. In the age of transition the old thought and the new world abide side by side. But if the foundations of our civilization have been changed, the altering status of men will take clearer aspects in each new age, and the old thought, while apparently verifying the old premises anew, will gradually disappear—not because it is argued away, but because men's sentiments are changed by new activity and an accumulating store of fresh experiences.

Part Three

GARDEN CITY AND SUBURB

1

THE URBAN PLANNER
AS A CIVILIZING FORCE

Frederick Law Olmsted
PUBLIC PARKS AND
THE ENLARGEMENT OF TOWNS

The development of city planning in America generally has been treated as a matter of town plats and geometric designs imposed on the land and the people. From this view the formalism of the World's Columbian Exposition or of the City Beautiful movement are the significant episodes in this period. But there is another, more organic tradition in city planning. The key figure here was Frederick Law Olmsted (1822–1903), who adapted the principles of the English landscape gardening school—which to some degree were "naturalistic"—to urban planning. As the following selection demonstrates, Olmsted's approach was as a social scientist as well as an artist; he begins not with an abstract ideal but with observations on the movements and social needs of urban people. Just as his park designs required ecological knowledge as well as aesthetic purpose, so his larger city schemes evolved from an understanding of human ecology toward a higher pattern of civilized order. For Olmsted the city was the proper home for civilized man and the planner eminently a civilizing influence. But civilization did not require, was on the contrary violated by, the total exclusion of nature from the city's precincts and the exercise of arbitrary authority over the social organism.

The last *Overland Monthly* tells us that in California "only an inferior class of people can be induced to live out of towns. There is something in the country which repels men. In the city alone can they nourish the juices of life."

This of newly built and but half-equipped cities, where the people are never quite free from dread of earthquakes, and of a country in which the productions of agriculture and horticulture are more varied, and the rewards of rural enterprise larger, than in any other under civilized government! With a hundred million acres of arable and

SOURCE Frederick Law Olmsted, "Public Parks and the Enlargement of Towns," *Journal of Social Science,* 1871.

grazing land, with thousands of outcropping gold veins, with the finest forests in the world, fully half the white people live in towns, a quarter of all in one town, and this quarter pays more than half the taxes of all. "Over the mountains the miners," says Mr. [Samuel] Bowles, "talk of going to San Francisco as to Paradise," and the rural members of the Legislature declare that "San Francisco sucks the life out of the country."

At the same time all our great interior towns are reputed to be growing rapidly; their newspapers complain that wheat and gold fall much faster than house-rents, and especially that builders fail to meet the demand for such dwellings as are mostly sought by new-comers, who are mainly men of small means and young families, anxious to make a lodgment in the city on any terms which will give them a chance of earning a right to remain. In Chicago alone, it is said, that there are twenty thousand people seeking employment.

To this I can add, from personal observation, that if we stand, any day before noon, at the railway stations of these cities, we may notice women and girls arriving by the score, who, it will be apparent, have just run in to do a little shopping, intending to return by supper time to farms perhaps a hundred miles away.

It used to be a matter of pride with the better sort of our country people that they could raise on their own land or manufacture within their own households almost everything needed for domestic consumption. But if now you leave the rail, at whatever remote station, the very advertisements on its walls will manifest how greatly this is changed. Push out over the prairie and make your way to the house of any long-settled and prosperous farmer, and the intimacy of his family with the town will constantly appear, in dress, furniture, viands, in all the conversation. If there is a piano, they will be expecting a man from town to tune it. If the baby has outgrown its shoes, the measure is to be sent to town. If a tooth is troublesome, an appointment is to be arranged by telegraph with the dentist. The railway timetable hangs with the almanac. The housewife complains of her servants. There is no difficulty in getting them from the intelligence offices in town, such as they are; but only the poorest, who cannot find employment in the city, will come to the country, and these as soon as they have got a few dollars ahead, are crazy to get back to town. It is much the same with the men, the farmer will add; he has to run up in the morning and get some one to take "Wolf's" place. You will find, too, that one of his sons is in a lawyer's office, another at a commercial college, and his oldest daughter at an "institute," all in town. I know several girls who travel eighty miles a day to attend school in Chicago.

If under these circumstances the occupation of the country schoolmaster, shoemaker, and doctor, the country storekeeper, dressmaker and lawyer, is not actually gone, it must be that the business they have to do is much less relatively to the population about them than it used to be; not less in amount only, but less in importance. An inferior class of men will meet the requirements.

And how are things going here in Massachusetts? A correspondent of the *Springfield Republican* gave the other day an account of a visit lately made to two or three old agricultural neighborhoods, such as fifty years ago were the glory of New England. When he last knew them, their society was spoken of with pride, and the influence of not a few of their citizens was felt throughout the state, and indeed far beyond it. But as he found them now, they might almost be sung by Goldsmith. The meeting-house closed, the church dilapidated; the famous old taverns, stores, shops, mills, and offices dropping to pieces and vacant, or perhaps with a mere corner occupied by day laborers; but a third as many children as formerly to be seen in the school-houses, and of these less than half of American-born parents.

Walking through such a district last summer, my eyes were gladdened by a single house with exceptional signs of thrift in fresh paint, roofs, and fences, and newly planted door-yard trees; but happening as I passed to speak to the owner, in the second sentence of our conversation he told me that he had been slicking his place up in hopes that some city gentleman would take a fancy to it for a country seat. He was getting old, had worked hard, and felt as if the time had fully come when he was entitled to take some enjoyment of what remained to him of life by retiring to the town. Nearly all his old neighbors were gone; his children had left years ago. His town-bred granddaughters were playing croquet in the front yard.

You know how it is here in Boston. Let us go on to the Old World. We read in our youth that among no other people were rural tastes so strong, and rural habits so fixed, as with those of Old England, and there is surely no other country where the rural life of the more fortunate classes compares so attractively with their town life. Yet in the "Transactions of the British Social Science Association," we find one debater asserting that there are now very few more persons living in the rural districts of England and Wales than there were fifty years ago; another referring to "the still increasing growth of our overgrown towns and the stationary or rather retrograding numbers of our rural population;" while a third remarks that the social and educational advantages of the towns are drawing to them a large proportion of "the wealthy and independent," as well as all of the working classes not required for field labor.

When I was last in England, the change that had occurred even in ten years could be perceived by a rapid traveller. Not only had the country gentleman and especially the country gentlewoman of [Washington] Irving departed wholly with all their following, but the very embers had been swept away of that manner of life upon which, so little while ago, everything in England seemed to be dependent. In all the country I found a smack of the suburbs—hampers and packages from metropolitan tradesmen, and purveyors arriving by every train, and a constant communication kept up with town by penny-post and telegraph.

In the early part of the century, the continued growth of London was talked of as something marvelous and fearful; but where ten houses were then required to accommodate new residents, there are now a hundred. The average rate at which population increases in the six principal towns is twice as great as in the country at large, including the hundreds of other flourishing towns. So also Glasgow has been growing six times faster than all Scotland; and Dublin has held its own, while Ireland as a whole has been losing ground.

Crossing to the Continent, we find Paris absorbing half of all the increase of France in population; Berlin growing twice as fast as all Prussia; Hamburg, Stettin, Stuttgart, Brussels, and a score or two of other towns, all building out into the country at a rate never before known, while many agricultural districts are actually losing population. In Russia special provision is made in the laws to regulate the gradual compensation of the nobles for their losses by the emancipation of the serfs, to prevent the depopulation of certain parts of the country, which was in danger of occurring from the eagerness of the peasantry to move into the large towns.

Going still further to the eastward, we may find a people to whom the movement has not thus far been communicated; but it is only where obscurity affords the best hope of safety from oppression, where men number their women with their horses, and where labor-saving inventions are as inventions of the enemy.

There can be no doubt then, that, in all our modern civilization, as in that of the ancients, there is a strong drift townward. But some seem to regard the class of symptoms I have referred to as those of a sort of moral epidemic, the crisis and reaction of which they constantly expect to see. They even detect already a growing disgust with the town and signs of a back-set towards rural simplicity. To avoid prolonged discussion of the question thus suggested I will refer but briefly to the intimate connection which is evident between the growth of towns and the dying out of slavery and feudal customs, of priestcraft and government by divine right, the multiplication of books, newspapers, schools, and other means of popular education and the adoption of improved methods of communication, transportation, and of various labor-saving inventions. No nation has yet begun to give up schools or news papers, railroads or telegraphs, to restore feudal rights or advance rates of postage. King-craft and priestcraft are nowhere gaining any solid ground. On the contrary, considered as elements of human progress, the more apparent forces under which men have thus far been led to gather together in towns are yet growing; never more rapidly than at this moment. It would seem then more rational to prepare for a continued rising of the townward flood than to count upon its subsidence. Examining our own country more particularly, it is to be considered that we have been giving away our public lands under a square form of division, as if for the purpose of preventing the closer agricultural settlement which long and narrow farms would have favored, and that we have used our mineral deposits as premiums for the encouragement of wandering and of forms of enterprise, individual, desultory and sequestered in character, in distinction from those which are organized, systematized and public. This policy has had its day; the choicest lands have been taken up; the most prominent and easiest worked metallic veins have been seized, the richest placers are abandoned to Chinamen, and the only reaction that we can reasonably anticipate is one from, not toward, dispersion.

The same policy, indeed, has had the effect of giving us, for a time, great command of ready money and easy credit, and we have thus been induced to spend an immense sum—say two thousand millions —in providing ourselves with the fixtures and machinery of our railroad system. This system, while encouraging the greater dispersion of our food producers, has tended most of all to render them, as we have seen, independent of all the old neighborhood agencies of demand and supply, manufacture and exchange, and to educate them and their children in familiarity with and dependence on the conveniences and habits of townspeople.

To touch upon another line of argument, we all recognize that the tastes and dispositions of women are more and more potent in shaping the course of civilized progress, and we may see that women are even more susceptible to this townward drift than men. Oft-times the husband and father gives up his country occupations, taking others less attractive to him in town, out of consideration for his wife and daughters. Not long since I conveyed to a very sensible and provident man what I thought to be an offer of great preferment. I was surprised that he hesitated to accept it, until the question was referred to his wife, a bright, tidy American-born woman, who promptly said: "If I were offered a deed of the best farm that I ever saw, on condition of going back to the country to live, I would not take it. I would rather face starvation in town." She had been brought up and lived the greater part of her life in one of the most convenient and agreeable farming countries in the United States.

Is it astonishing? Compare advantages in respect simply to schools, libraries, music, and the fine arts. People of the greatest wealth can hardly command as much of these in the country as the poorest work-girl is offered here in Boston at the mere cost of a walk for a short distance over a good, firm, clean pathway, lighted at night and made interesting to her by shop fronts and the variety of people passing.

It is true the poorer work-girls make little use of these special advantages, but this simply because they are not yet educated up to them. When, however, they come from the country to town, are they not moving in the way of this education? In all probability, as is indicated by the report (in the *New York Tribune*) of a recent skillful examination of the condition and habits of the poor sewing women of that city, a frantic desire to escape from the dull lives which they have seen before them in the country, a craving for recreation, especially for more companionship in yielding to playful girlish impulses, innocent in themselves, drives more young women to the town than anything else. Dr. [Oliver Wendell] Holmes may exaggerate the clumsiness and dreariness of New England village social parties; but go further back into the country among the outlying farms, and if you have ever had part in the working up of some of the rare occasions in which what stands for festivity is attempted, you will hardly think that the ardent desire of a young woman to escape to the town is wholly unreasonable.

The civilized woman is above all things a tidy woman. She enjoys being surrounded by bright and gay things perhaps not less than the savage, but she shrinks from draggling, smirching, fouling things and "things out of keeping" more. By the keenness with which she avoids subjecting herself to annoyances of this class, indeed, we may judge the degree in which a woman has advanced in civilization. Think what a country road and roadside, and what the back yard of a farmhouse, commonly is, in winter and springtime; and what far-away farmers' gardens are in haying time, or most of them at any time. Think, again, how hard it is when you city people go into the country for a few weeks in summer, to keep your things in order, to get a thousand little things done which you regard as trifles when at home, how far you have to go, and with how much uncertainty, how much unaccustomed management you have to exercise. For the perfection and delicacy—the cleanness—with which any human want is provided for depends on the concentration of human ingenuity and skill upon that particular want. The greater the division of labor at any point, the greater the perfection with which all wants may be satisfied. Everywhere in the country the number and variety of workmen, not agricultural laborers, proportionately to the population, is lessening as the facility for reaching workmen in town is increasing. In one year we find fifty-four new divisions of trade added to the "London Directory."

Think of all these things, and you will possibly find yourself growing a little impatient of the common cant which assumes that the strong tendency of women to town life, even though it involves great privations and dangers, is a purely senseless, giddy, vain, frivolous, and degrading one.

The consideration which most influences this tendency of women in families, however, seems to be the amount of time and labor, and wear and tear of nerves and mind, which is saved to them by the organization of labor in those forms, more especially, by which the menial service of households is simplified and reduced. Consider, for instance, what is done (that in the country is not done at all or is done by each household for itself, and, if efficiently, with a wearing, constant effort of superintendence) by the butcher, baker, fishmonger, grocer, by the provision venders of all sorts, by the ice-man, dust-man, scavenger, by the postman, carrier, expressmen, and messengers, all serving you at your house when required; by the sewers, gutters, pavements, crossings, sidewalks, public conveyances, and gas and water works.

But here again there is every reason to suppose that what we see is but a foretaste of what is yet to come. Take the difference of demand upon invention in respect to cheap conveyance for example. We began experimentally with street railways twenty years ago. At present, in New York, one pair of horses serves to convey one hundred people, on an average, every day at a rate of fare about one fiftieth of the old hackney-coach rates, and the total number of fares collected annually is equal to that of the population of the United States. And yet thousands walk a number of miles every day because they cannot be seated in the cars. It is impossible to fix a limit to the amount of travel which really ample, convenient, and still cheap means of transportation for short distances would develop. Certain improvements have caused the whole number of people seeking conveyances in London to be doubled in the last five years, and yet the supply keeps nowhere near the demand.

See how rapidly we are really gaining, and what we have to expect. Two recent inventions give us the means of reducing by a third, under favorable circumstances, the cost of good McAdam roads. There have been sixteen patents issued from one office for other new forms of perfectly smooth and nearly noiseless street pavement, some of which, after two or three years' trial, promise so well as to render it certain that some improvement will soon come by which more than one of the present special annoyances of town life will be abated. An improvement in our sewer system seems near at hand also, which will add considerably to the comparative advantages of a residence in towns, and especially the more open town suburbs.

Experiments indicate that it is feasible to send heated air through a town in pipes like water, and that it may be drawn upon, and the heat which is taken measured and paid for according to quantity required. Thus may come a great saving of fuel and trouble in a very difficult department of domestic economy. No one will think of applying such a system to farmhouses.

Again, it is plain that we have scarcely begun to turn to account the advantages offered to townspeople in the electric telegraph; we really have not made a beginning with those offered in the pneumatic tube, though their substantial character has been demonstrated. By the use of these two instruments, a tradesman ten miles away on the other side of a town may be communicated with, and goods obtained from him by a housekeeper, as quickly and with as little personal inconvenience as now if he were in the next block. A single tube station for five hundred families, acoustic pipes for the transmission of orders to it from each house, with a carriers' service for local distribution of packages, is all that is needed for this purpose.

As to the economy which comes by systematizing and concentrating, by the application of a large apparatus, of processes which are otherwise conducted in a desultory way, wasteful of human strength, as by public laundries, bakeries, and kitchens, we are yet, in America, even in our larger cities, far behind many of the smaller towns of the Old World.

While in all these directions enterprise and the progress of invention are quite sure to add rapidly to the economy and convenience of town life, and thus increase its comparative attractions, in other directions every step tends to reduce the manpower required on the farms for the production of a given amount of the raw material of food. Such is the effect, for instance, of every improvement of apparatus or process in ploughing, mowing, reaping, curing, thrashing, and marketing.

Another tendency arising from the improvement of agricultural apparatus, which will be much accelerated when steam shall have been as successfully applied to tillage as already to harvesting and marketing operations, is that to the enlargement of fields and of farms. From this will follow the greater isolation of rural homesteads; for with our long-fronted farms, it will be long before we can hope to have country roads on which rapid engine-transit will be practicable, though we may be close upon it wherever firm and smooth roads can be afforded.

It should be observed that possession of all the various advantages of the town to which we have referred, while it very certainly cannot be acquired by people living in houses a quarter or a half a mile apart, does not, on the other hand, by any means involve an unhealthy density of population. Probably the advantages of civilization can be found illustrated and demonstrated under no other circumstances so completely as in some suburban neighborhoods where each family abode stands fifty or a hundred feet or more apart from all others, and at some distance from the public road. And it must be remembered, also, that man's enjoyment of rural beauty has clearly increased rather than diminished with his advance in civilization. There is no reason, except in the loss of time, the inconvenience, discomfort, and expense of our present arrangements for short travel, why suburban advantages should not be almost indefinitely extended. Let us have a cheap and enjoyable method of conveyance, and a building law like that of old Rome, and they surely will be.

As railroads are improved, all the important stations will become centers or sub-centers of towns, and all the minor stations suburbs. For most ordinary everyday purposes, especially housekeepers' purposes, these will need no very large population before they can obtain urban advantages. I have seen a settlement, the resident population of which was under three hundred, in which there was a public laundry, bathhouse, barber's shop, billiard room, beer garden, and bakery. Fresh rolls and fresh milk were supplied to families before breakfast time every morning; fair fruit and succulent vegetables were delivered at house doors not half an hour after picking; and newspapers and magazines were distributed by a carrier. I have seen a town of not more than twelve hundred inhabitants, the streets and the yards, alleys, and places of which were swept every day as regularly as the house floors, and all dust removed by a public dust-man.

The construction of good roads and walks, the laying of sewer water, and gas pipes, and the supplying of sufficiently cheap, rapid, and comfortable conveyances to town centers, is all that is necessary to give any farming land in a healthy and attractive situation the value of town lots. And whoever has observed in the French agricultural colonies how much more readily and cheaply railroads, telegraph, gas, water, sewer, and nearly all other advantages of towns may be made available to the whole population than under our present helter-skelter methods of settlement, will not believe that even the occupation of a farm laborer must necessarily and finally exclude his family from a very large share of urban conveniences.

But this opens a subject of speculation, which I am not now free to pursue. It is hardly a matter of speculation, I am disposed to think, but almost of demonstration, that the larger a town becomes because simply of its advantages for commercial purposes, the greater will be the convenience available to those who live in and near it for cooperation, as well with reference to the accumulation of wealth in the higher forms—as in seats of learning, of science, and of art—as with reference to merely domestic economy and the emancipation of both men and women from petty, confining, and narrowing cares.

It also appears to be nearly certain that the recent rapid enlargement of towns and withdrawal of people from rural conditions of living is the result mainly of circumstances of a permanent character.

We have reason to believe, then, that towns which of late have been increasing rapidly on account of their commercial advantages, are likely to be still more attractive to population in the future; that there will in consequence soon be larger towns than any the world has yet known, and that the further progress of civilization is to depend mainly upon the influences by which men's minds and characters will be affected while living in large towns.

Now, knowing that the average length of the life of mankind in towns has been much less than in the country, and that the average amount of disease and misery and of vice and crime has been much greater in towns, this would be a very dark prospect for civilization, if it were not that modern science has beyond all question determined many of the causes of the special evils by which men are afflicted in towns, and placed means in our hands for guarding against them. It has shown, for example, that under ordinary circumstances, in the interior parts of large and closely built towns, a given quantity of air contains considerably less of the elements which we require to receive through the lungs than the air of the country or even of the outer and more open parts of a town, and that instead of them it carries into the lungs highly corrupt and irritating matters, the action of which tends strongly to vitiate all our sources of vigor—how strongly may perhaps be indicated in the shortest way by the statement that even metallic plates and statues corrode and wear away under the atmospheric influences which prevail in the midst of large towns, more rapidly than in the country.

The irritation and waste of the physical powers which result from the same cause, doubtless indirectly affect and very seriously affect the mind and the moral strength; but there is a general impression that a class of men are bred in towns whose peculiarities are not perhaps adequately accounted for in this way. We may understand these better if we consider that whenever we walk through the denser part of a town, to merely avoid collision with those we meet and pass upon the sidewalks, we have constantly to watch, to foresee, and to guard against their movements. This involves a consideration of their intentions, a calculation of their strength and weakness, which is not so much for their benefit as our own. Our minds are thus brought into close dealings with other minds without any friendly flowing toward them, but rather. a drawing from them. Much of the intercourse between men when engaged in the pursuits of commerce has the same tendency—a tendency to regard others in a hard if not always hardening way. Each detail of observation and of the process of thought required in this kind of intercourse or contact of minds is so slight and so common in the experience of townspeople that they are seldom conscious of it. It certainly involves some expenditure nevertheless. People from the country are even conscious of the effect on their nerves and minds of the street contact—often complaining that they feel confused by it; and if we had no relief from it at all during our waking hours, we should all be conscious of suffering from it. It is upon our opportunities of relief from it, therefore, that not only our comfort in town life, but our ability to maintain a temperate, good-natured, and healthy state of mind, depends. This is one of many ways in which it happens that men who have been brought up, as the saying is, in the streets, who have been most directly and completely affected by town influences, so generally show, along with a remarkable quickness of apprehension, a peculiarly hard sort of selfishness. Every day of their lives they have seen thousands of their fellow men, have met them face to face, have brushed against them, and yet have had no experience of anything in common with them.

It has happened several times within the last century, when old artificial obstructions to the spreading out of a city have been removed, and especially when there has been a demolition of and rebuilding on a new ground plan of some part which had previously been noted for the frequency of certain crimes, the prevalence of certain diseases, and the shortness of life among its inhabitants, that a marked improvement in all these respects has immediately followed, and has been maintained not alone in the dark parts, but in the city as a whole.

But although it has been demonstrated by such experiments that we have it in our power to greatly lessen and counteract the two classes of evils we have had under consideration, it must be remembered that these means are made use of only with great difficulty—how great, one or two illustrations from experience will enable us perhaps better to understand.

When the business quarter of New York was burnt over, thirty years ago, there was a rare opportunity for laying out a district expressly with a view to facilitate commerce. The old plan had been arrived at in a desultory way; and so far as it had been the result of design, it had been with reference more especially to the residence of a semi-rural population. This had long since passed away; its inconvenience for commercial purposes had been experienced for many years; no one supposed from the relation of the ground to the adjacent navigable waters that it would ever be required for other than commercial purposes. Yet the difficulties of equalizing benefits and damages among the various owners of the land prevented any considerable change of the old street lines. Every working day thousands of dollars are subtracted from the profits of business, by the disadvantages thus reestablished. The annual loss amounts to millions.

Men of barbarous habits laid out a part of London in a way which a thousand years later was found to be a cause of an immeasurable waste of life, strength, and property. There had been much talk, but no effective action, looking toward improvement, when the great fire came, and left every building a heap of ashes. Immediately upon this, while the fire was still burning, a great man, Sir Christopher Wren, prepared a plan for avoiding the old evils. This plan, a simple, excellent, and economical one, he took to the king, who at once approved it, took a strong interest in it, and used all his royal power to have it carried out. It was hailed with satisfaction by all wise and good men, and yet so difficult was it to overcome the difficulties entailed by the original rural laying out of the ground, that the attempt was finally abandoned, and the new city was built with immaterial modifications under the old barbarous plan; and so it remains with only slight improvement, and that purchased at enormous cost, to this day.

Remedy for a bad plan, once built upon, being thus impracticable, now that we understand the matter we are surely bound, wherever it is by any means in our power, to prevent mistakes in the construction of towns. Strange to say, however, here in the New World, where great towns by the hundred are springing into existence, no care at all is taken to avoid bad plans. The most brutal Pagans to whom we have sent our missionaries have never shown greater indifference to the sufferings of others than is exhibited in the plans of some of our most promising cities, for which men now living in them are responsible.

Not long since I was asked by the mayor of one of these to go before its common council and explain the advantages of certain suggested changes, including especially the widening of two roads leading out of town and as yet but partially opened and not at all built upon. After I had done so, two of the aldermen in succession came to me, and each privately said in effect: "It is quite plain that the proposition is a good one, and it ought to be adopted; the city would undoubtedly gain by it; but the people of the ward I represent have less interest in it than some others: they do not look far ahead, and they are jealous of those who would be more directly benefited than themselves; consequently I don't think that they would like it if I voted for it, and I shall not, but I hope it will be carried."

They were unwilling that even a stranger should have so poor an opinion of their own intelligence as to suppose that they did not see the advantage of the change proposed; but it was not even suggested to their minds that there might be something shameful in repudiating their obligations to serve, according to the best of their judgment, the general and permanent interests committed to them as legislators of the city.

It is evident that if we go on in this way, the progress of civilized mankind in health, virtue, and happiness will be seriously endangered.

It is practically certain that the Boston of today is the mere nucleus of the Boston that is to be. It is practically certain that it is to extend over many miles of country now thoroughly rural in character, in parts of which farmers are now laying out roads with a view to shortening the teaming distance between their wood-lots and a railway station, being governed in their courses by old property lines, which were first run simply with reference to the equitable division of heritages, and in other parts of which, perhaps, some wild speculators are having streets staked off from plans which they have formed with a rule and pencil in a broker's office, with a view chiefly to the impressions they would make when seen by other speculators on a lithographed map. And by this manner of planning, unless views of duty or of interest prevail that are not yet common, if Boston continued to grow at its present rate even for but a few generations longer, and then simply holds its own until it shall be as old as the Boston in Lincolnshire now is, more men, women, and children are to be seriously affected in health and morals than are now living on this Continent.

Is this a small matter—a mere matter of taste; a sentimental speculation?

It must be within the observation of most of us that where, in the city, wheel-ways originally twenty feet wide were with great difficulty and cost enlarged to thirty, the present width is already less nearly adequate to the present business than the former was to the former business; obstructions are more frequent, movements are slower and oftener arrested, and the liability to collision is greater. The same is true of sidewalks. Trees thus have been cut down, porches, bow-windows, and other encroachments removed, but every year the walk is less sufficient for the comfortable passing of those who wish to use it. It is certain that as the distance from the interior to the circumference of towns shall increase with the enlargement of their population, the less sufficient relatively to the service to be performed will be any given space between buildings.

In like manner every evil to which men are specially liable when living in towns, is likely to be aggravated in the future, unless means are devised and adapted in advance to prevent it.

Let us proceed, then, to the question of means, and with a seriousness in some degree befitting a question, upon our dealing with which we know the misery or happiness of many millions of our fellow beings will depend.

We will for the present set before our minds the two sources of wear and corruption which we have seen to be remediable and therefore preventible. We may admit that commerce requires that in some parts of a town there shall be an arrangement of buildings, and a character of streets and of traffic in them which will establish conditions of corruption and of irritation, physical and mental. But commerce does not require the same conditions to be maintained in all parts of a town.

Air is disinfected by sunlight and foliage. Foliage also acts mechanically to purify the air by screening it. Opportunity and inducement to escape at frequent intervals from the confined and vitiated air of the commercial quarter, and to supply the lungs with air screened and purified by trees, and recently acted upon by sunlight, together with opportunity and inducement to escape from conditions requiring vigilance, wariness, and activity toward other men—if these could be supplied economically, our problem would be solved.

In the old days of walled towns all tradesmen lived under the roof of their shops, and their children and apprentices and servants sat together with them in the evening about the kitchen fire. But now that the dwelling is built by itself and there is greater room, the inmates have a parlor to spend their evenings in; they spread carpets on the floor to gain in quiet, and hang drapery in their windows and papers on their walls to gain in seclusion and beauty. Now that our towns are built without walls, and we can have all the room that we like, is there any good reason why we should not make some similar difference between parts which are likely to be dwelt in, and those which will be required exclusively for commerce?

Would trees, for seclusion and shade and beauty, be out of place, for instance, by the side of certain of our streets? It will, perhaps, appear to you that it is hardly necessary to ask such a question, as throughout the United States trees are commonly planted at the sides of streets. Unfortunately they are seldom so planted as to have fairly settled the question of the desirableness of systematically maintaining trees under these circumstances. In the first place, the streets are planned, wherever they are, essentially alike. Trees are planted in the space assigned for sidewalks, where at first, while they are saplings, and the vicinity is rural or suburban, they are not much in the way, but where, as they grow larger, and the vicinity becomes urban, they take up more and more space, while space is more and more required for passage. That is not all. Thousands and tens of thousands are planted every year in a manner and under conditions as nearly certain as possible either to kill them outright, or to so lessen their vitality as to prevent their natural and beautiful development, and to cause premature decrepitude. Often, too, as their lower limbs are found inconvenient, no space having been provided for trees in laying out the street, they are deformed by butcherly amputations. If by rare good fortune they are suffered to become beautiful, they still stand subject to be condemned to death at any time, as obstructions in the highway.

What I would ask is, whether we might not with economy make special provision in some of our streets—in a twentieth or a fiftieth part, if your please, of all—for trees to remain as a permanent furniture of the city? I mean, to make a place for them in which they would have room to grow naturally and gracefully. Even if the distance between the houses should have to be made half as much again as it is required to be in our commercial streets, could not the space be afforded? Out of town space is not costly when measures to secure it are taken early. The assessments for benefit where such streets were provided for, would, in nearly all cases, defray the cost of the land required. The strips of ground reserved for the trees, six, twelve, twenty feet wide, would cost nothing for paving or flagging.

The change both of scene and of air which would be obtained by people engaged for the most part in the necessarily confined interior commercial parts of the town, on passing into a street of this character after the trees had become stately and graceful, would be worth a good deal. If such streets were made still broader in some parts, with spacious malls, the advantage would be increased. If each of them were given the proper capacity, and laid out with laterals and connections in suitable directions to serve as a convenient trunk line of communication between two large districts of the town or the business center and the suburbs, a very great number of people might thus be placed ever day under influences counteracting those with which we desire to contend.

These, however, would be merely very simple improvements upon arrangements which are in common use in every considerable town. Their advantages would be incidental to the general uses of streets as they are. But people are willing very often to seek recreation, as well as receive it by the way. Provisions may indeed be made expressly for public recreations, with certainty that if convenient they will be resorted to.

We come then to the question: what accommodations for recreation can we provide which shall be so agreeable and so accessible as to be efficiently attractive to the great body of citizens, and which, while giving decided gratification, shall also cause those who resort to them for pleasure to subject themselves, for the time being, to conditions strongly counteractive to the special enervating conditions of the town?

In the study of this question all forms of recreation may, in the first place, be conveniently arranged under two general heads. One will include all of which the predominating influence is to stimulate exertion of any part or parts needing it; the other, all which cause us to receive pleasure without conscious exertion. Games chiefly of mental skill, as chess, or athletic sports, as baseball, are examples of means of recreation of the first class, which may be termed that of *exertive* recreation; music and the fine arts generally of the second or *receptive* division.

Considering the first by itself, much consideration will be needed in determining what classes of exercises may be advantageously provided for. In the Bois de Boulogne there is a race-course; in the Bois de Vincennes a ground for artillery target-practice. Military parades are held in Hyde Park. A few cricket clubs are accommodated in most of the London parks, and swimming is permitted in the lakes at certain hours. In the New York Park, on the other hand, none of these exercises are provided for or permitted, except that the boys of the public schools are given the use on holidays of certain large spaces for ball playing. It is considered that the advantage to individuals which would be gained in providing for them would not compensate for the general inconvenience and expense they would cause.

I do not propose to discuss this part of the subject at present, as it is only necessary to my immediate purpose to point out that if recreations requiring large spaces to be given up to the use of a comparatively small number, are not considered essential, numerous small grounds so distributed through a large town that some one of them could be easily reached by a short walk from every house, would be more desirable than a single area of great extent, however rich in landscape attractions it might be. Especially would this be the case if the numerous local grounds were connected and supplemented by a series of trunk-roads or boulevards such as has already been suggested. Proceeding to the consideration of receptive recreations, it is necessary to ask you to adopt and bear in mind a further subdivision, under two heads, according to the degree in which the average enjoyment is greater when a large congregation assembles for a purpose of receptive recreation, or when the number coming together is small and the circumstances are favorable to the exercise of personal friendliness.

The first I shall term *gregarious;* the second, *neighborly.* Remembering that the immediate matter in hand is a study of fitting accommodations, you will, I trust, see the practical necessity of this classification.

Purely gregarious recreation seems to be generally looked upon in New England society as childish and savage, because, I suppose, there is so little of what we call intellectual gratification in it. We are inclined to engage in it indirectly, furtively, and with complication. Yet there are certain forms of recreation, a large share of the attraction of which must, I think, lie in the gratification of the gregarious inclination, and which, with those who can afford to indulge in them, are so popular as to establish the importance of the requirement.

If I ask myself where I have experienced the most complete gratification of this instinct in public and out of doors, among trees, I find that it has been in the promenade of the Champs Elysees. As closely following it I should name other promenades of Europe, and our own upon the New York parks. I have studiously watched the latter for several years. I have several times seen fifty thousand people participating in them; and the more I have seen of them, the more highly have I been led to estimate their value as means of counteracting the evils of town life.

Consider that the New York Park and the Brooklyn Park are the only places in those associated cities where, in this eighteen hundred and seventieth year after Christ, you will find a body of Christians coming together, and with an evident glee in the prospect of coming together, all classes largely represented, with a common purpose, not at all intellectual, competitive with none, disposing to jealousy and spiritual or intellectual pride toward none, each individual adding by his mere presence to the pleasure of all others, all helping to the greater happiness of each. You may thus often see vast numbers of persons brought closely together, poor and rich, young and old, Jew and Gentile. I have seen a hundred thousand thus congregated, and I assure you that though there have been not a few that seemed a little dazed, as if they did not quite understand it, and were, perhaps, a little ashamed of it, I have looked studiously but vainly among them for a single face completely unsympathetic with the prevailing expression of good nature and light-heartedness.

Is it doubtful that it does men good to come together in this way in pure air and under the light of heaven, or that it must have an influence directly counteractive to that of the ordinary hard, hustling working hours of town life?

You will agree with me, I am sure, that it is not, and that opportunity, convenient, attractive opportunity, for such congregation, is a very good thing to provide for, in planning the extension of a town.

I referred especially to the Champs Elysees, because the promenade there is a very old custom, not a fashion of the day, and because I must needs admit that this most striking example is one in which no large area of ground—nothing like a park—has been appropriated for the purpose. I must acknowledge, also, that the alamedas of Spain and Portugal supply another and very interesting instance of the same fact. You will observe, however, that small local grounds, such as we have said might be the best for most exertive recreations, are not at all adapted to receptive recreations of the type described.

One thing more under this head. I have but little personal familiarity with Boston customs; but I have lived or sojourned in several other towns of New England, as well as of other parts of the country, and I have never been long in any locality, south or north, east or west, without observing a *custom* of gregarious out-of-door recreation in some miserably imperfect form, usually covered by a wretched pretext of a wholly different purpose, as perhaps, for instance, visiting a grave-yard. I am sure that it would be much better, less expensive, less harmful in all ways, more health-giving to body, mind, and soul, if it were admitted to be a distinct requirement of all human beings, and appropriately provided for.

I have next to see what opportunities are wanted to induce people to engage in what I have termed *neighborly* receptive recreations, under conditions which shall be highly counteractive to the prevailing bias to degeneration and demoralization in large towns. To make clearer what I mean, I need an illustration which I find in a familiar domestic gathering, where the prattle of the children mingles with the easy conversation of the more sedate, the bodily requirements satisfied with good cheer, fresh air, agreeable light, moderate temperature, snug shelter, and furniture and decorations adapted to please the eye, without calling for profound admiration on the one hand, or tending to fatigue or disgust on the other. The circumstances are all favorable to a pleasurable wakefulness of the mind without stimulating exertion; and the close relation of family life, the association of children, of mothers, of lovers, or those who may be lovers, stimulate and keep alive the more tender sympathies, and give play to faculties such as may be dormant in business or on the promenade; while at the same time the cares of providing in detail for all the wants of the family, guidance, instruction, reproof, and the dutiful reception of guidance, instruction, and reproof, are, as matters of conscious exertion, as far as possible laid aside.

There is an instinctive inclination to this social, neighborly, unexertive form of recreation among all of us. In one way or another it is sure to be constantly operating upon those millions on millions of men and women who are to pass their lives within a few miles of where we now stand. To what extent it shall operate so as to develop health and virtue, will, on many occasions, be simply a question of opportunity and inducement. And this question is one for the determination of which for a thousand years we here today are largely responsible.

Think what the ordinary state of things to many is at this beginning of the town. The public is reading just now a little book in which some of your streets of which you are not proud are described. Go into one of those red cross streets any fine evening next summer, and ask how it is with ther residents? Oftentimes you will see half a dozen sitting together on the door-steps, or, all in a row, on the curb-stones, with their feet in the gutter, driven out of doors by the closeness within; mothers among them anxiously regarding their children who are dodging about at their play, among the noisy wheels on the pavement.

Again, consider how often you see young men in knots of perhaps half a dozen in lounging attitudes rudely obstructing the sidewalks, chiefly led in their little conversation by the suggestions given to their minds by what or whom they may see passing in the street, men, women, or children, whom they do not know, and for whom they have no respect or sympathy. There is nothing among them or about them which is adapted to bring into play a spark of admiration, of delicacy, manliness, or tenderness. You see them presently descend in search of physical comfort to a brilliantly lighted basement, where they find others of their sort, see, hear, smell, drink, and eat all manner of vile things.

Whether on the curb-stones or in the dram-shops, these young men are all under the influence of the same impulse which some satisfy about the tea-table with neighbors and wives and mothers and children, and all things clean and wholesome, softening and refining.

If the great city to arise here is to be laid out little by little, and chiefly to suit the views of land-owners, acting only individually, and thinking only of how what they do is to affect the value in the next week or the next year of the few lots that each may hold at the time, the opportunities of so obeying this inclination as at the same time to give the lungs a bath of pure sunny air, to give the mind a suggestion of rest from the devouring eagerness and intellectual strife of town life, will always be few to any, to many will amount to nothing.

But is it possible to make public provision for recreation of this class, essentially domestic and secluded as it is?

It is a question which can, of course, be conclusively answered only from experience. And from experience in some slight degree I shall answer it. There is one large American town in which it may happen that a man of any class shall say to his wife when he is going out in the morning: "my dear, when the children come home from school, put some bread and butter and salad in a basket, and go to the spring under the chestnut-tree where we found the Johnsons last week. I will join you there as soon as I can get away from the office. We will walk to the dairy-man's cottage and get some tea, and some fresh milk for the children, and take our supper by the brook-side"; and this shall be no joke, but the most refreshing earnest.

There will be room enough in the Brooklyn Park, when it is finished, for several thousand little family and neighborly parties to bivouac at frequent intervals through the summer, without discommoding one another, or interfering with any other purpose, to say nothing of those who can be drawn out to make a day of it, as many thousand were last year. And although the arrangements for the purpose were yet very incomplete, and but little ground was *at all* prepared for such use, besides these small parties, consisting of one or two families, there came also, in companies of from thirty to a hundred and fifty, somewhere near twenty thousand children with their parents, Sunday-school teachers, or other guides and friends, who spent the best part of a day under the trees and on the turf, in recreations of which the predominating element was of this neighborly receptive class. Often they would bring a fiddle, flute, and harp, or other music. Tables, seats, shade, turf, swings, cool spring-water, and a pleasing rural prospect, stretching off half a mile or more each way, unbroken by a carriage road or the slightest evidence of the vicinity of the town, were supplied them without charge, and bread and milk and ice-cream at moderate fixed charges. In all my life I have never seen such joyous collections of people. I have, in fact, more than once observed tears of gratitude in the eyes of poor women, as they watched their children thus enjoying themselves.

The whole cost of such neighborly festivals, even when they

include excursions by rail from the distant parts of the town, does not exceed for each person, on an average, a quarter of a dollar; and when the arrangements are complete, I see no reason why thousands should not come every day where hundreds come now to use them; and if so, who can measure the value, generation after generation, of such provisions for recreation to the overwrought, much-confined people of the great town that is to be?

For this purpose neither of the forms of ground we have heretofore considered are at all suitable. We want a ground to which people may easily go after their day's work is done, and where they may stroll for an hour, seeing, hearing, and feeling nothing of the bustle and jar of the streets, where they shall, in effect, find the city put far away from them. We want the greatest possible contrast with the streets and the shops and the rooms of the town which will be consistent with convenience and the preservation of good order and neatness. We want, especially, the greatest possible contrast with the restraining and confining conditions of the town, those conditions which compel us to walk circumspectly, watchfully, jealously, which compel us to look closely upon others without sympathy. Practically, what we most want is a simple, broad, open space of clean greensward, with sufficient play of surface and a sufficient number of trees about it to supply a variety of light and shade. This we want as a central feature. We want depth of wood enough about it not only for comfort in hot weather, but to completely shut out the city from our landscapes.

The word *park*, in town nomenclature, should, I think, be reserved for grounds of the character and purpose thus described.

Not only as being the most valuable of all possible forms of public places, but regarded simply as a large space which will seriously interrupt cross-town communication wherever it occurs, the question of the site and bounds of the park requires to be determined with much more deliberation and art than is often secured for any problem of distant and extended municipal interests.

A Promenade may, with great advantage, be carried along the outer part of the surrounding groves of a park; and it will do no harm if here and there a broad opening among the trees discloses its open landscapes to those upon the promenade. But recollect that the object of the latter for the time being should be to see *congregated human life* under glorious and necessarily artificial conditions, and the natural landscape is not essential to them; though there is no more beautiful picture, and none can be more pleasing incidentally to the gregarious purpose, than that of beautiful meadows, over which clusters of level-armed sheltering trees cast broad shadows, and upon which are scattered dainty cows and flocks of black-faced sheep, while men, women, and children are seen sitting here and there, forming groups in the shade, or moving in and out among the woody points and bays.

It may be inferred from what I have said, that very rugged ground, abrupt eminences, and what is technically called picturesque in distinction from merely beautiful or simply pleasing scenery, is not the most desirable for a town park. Decidedly not in my opinion. The park should, as far as possible, complement the town. Openness is the one thing you cannot get in buildings. Picturesqueness you can get. Let your buildings be as picturesque as your artists can make them. This is the beauty of a town. Consequently, the beauty of the park should be the other. It should be the beauty of the fields, the meadow, the prairie, of the green pastures, and the still waters. What we want to gain is tranquillity and rest to the mind. Mountains suggest effort. But besides this objection there are others of what I may indicate as the housekeeping class. It is impossible to give the public range over a large extent of ground of a highly picturesque character, unless under very exceptional circumstances, and sufficiently guard against the occurrence of opportunities and temptations to shabbiness, disorder, indecorum, and indecency, that will be subversive of every good purpose the park should be designed to fulfill.

Nor can I think that *in the park proper*, what is called gardenesque beauty is to be courted; still less that highly artificial and exotic form of it, which, under the name of subtropical planting, the French have lately introduced, and in suitable positions with interesting and charming results, but in following which indiscreetly, the English are sacrificing the peculiar beauty of their simple and useful parks of the old time. Both these may have places, and very important places, but they do not belong within a park, unless as side scenes and incidents. Twenty years ago Hyde Park had a most pleasing, open, free, and inviting expression, though certainly it was too rude, too much wanting in art; but now art is vexed with long black lines of repellant iron-work, and here and there behind it bouquets of hot house plants, between which the public pass like hospital convalescents, who have been turned into the yard to walk about while their beds are making. We should undertake nothing in a park which involves the treating of the public as prisoners or wild beasts. A great object of all that is done in a park, of *all* the art of a park, is to influence the mind of men through their imagination, and the influence of iron hurdles can never be good.

2
COMBATING DISEASE
AND POLLUTION IN THE CITY

Edward Dalton
THE METROPOLITAN BOARD OF HEALTH

A full quarter of a century before Jacob Riis and the early Progressives discovered the slums, environmental health officials had initiated programs to make the living conditions of the poor less wretched and dangerous. The turning point in early American public health was the founding of New York's Metropolitan Board of Health in 1866. The following selection is a review of the first annual report of the board. The board's work included not only ameliorating the tenement environment but also controlling epidemics and improving the quality of air for the city as a whole. Edward Dalton (1834–1872), the author of both the report and this review, was a graduate of Harvard and the College of Physicians and Surgeons in New York. After a distinguished and valuable medical career in the field hospitals of the Civil War, he became sanitary superintendent for the Board of Health, where he served from 1866 to 1869.

By the 1880s medical theory had been altered drastically by the discovery of the microbial causes of disease; henceforth American public health departments virtually abandoned their efforts to improve the general physical environment and instead concentrated on controlling the communicable diseases through immunization. The result was a series of dramatic triumphs over specific diseases and almost complete neglect of the quality of the larger urban environment.

It has been said that "the saddest pages in the history of all nations are those which treat of the wholesale sacrifice of human life, through ignorance or neglect of the simplest means of preserving health or averting disease." It is now known that the fearful epidemics, or plagues, so called, that swept with such deadly malignity through the cities of the Middle Ages, had their origin and derived their strength

SOURCE. Edward Dalton, "The Metropolitan Board of Health of New York," *North American Review*, April 1868.

133

from gross neglect of the simplest sanitary laws. Narrow and filthy streets, crowded, ill-ventilated, and dark dwellings, lack of provision for drainage, and of facilities for personal and general cleanliness —these were the causes of pestilence no less in medieval Europe than at the present day. It needs but a glance to see how the frequency and virulence of epidemics have decreased with the application of improved sewerage, the introduction of plentiful supplies of water, the destruction or remodelling of crowded and filthy quarters, and the removal from populous districts of such processes and manufactures as contaminate the atmosphere, and so reduce the vigor and degrade the morale of the inhabitants.

It was a consideration of these facts, together with the daily increasing evidence that the city of New York, or at least a large portion of it, was already in a condition, not only to foster such ordinary forms of disease as depend upon foul air and general uncleanliness, but to invite and rapidly develop contagion and pestilence, that some six years since stimulated the legislative action which resulted in the establishment of the Metropolitan Board of Health.

Many portions of New York and Brooklyn, but especially of New York, had become densely populated, not only, in fact not chiefly, with native citizens, but with immigrants from abroad. Every week added largely to this population. The older portions of the city, where the laboring classes congregated, were becoming overcrowded to a degree that rendered cleanliness and decency almost impossible.

Diseases of every kind, but especially such as have their origin directly or indirectly in the lack of pure air, personal cleanliness, and nutritious food, prevailed constantly and to an alarming extent among the inhabitants of these districts. The mortality was very great, particularly among children; and it was from time to time startlingly evident that the almost utter neglect of sanitary regulation was leaving the city a victim to the poisonous influence of these sources of sickness, which were daily extending their limits, and every year more imminently threatening to destroy the salubrity of a city to which nature had afforded special facilities for the preservation of life and health.

The engrossing interests of commerce and politics seemed to have blinded the public generally to the shadow that was gradually, but steadily, growing wider and deeper.

Some years since, however, several prominent members of the Academy of Medicine, and subsequently the "Citizens' Association," an organization composed of the more intelligent and public-spirited men in the community, inaugurated a systematic and persistent effort at sanitary reform, and the legislature of the state was urgently appealed to for aid.

Each year, however, the effort proved unsuccessful, until at last, in the winter of 1865–1866, when already from the Old World had come the silent, but fearful, warning of the approach of cholera, the importance of a reform was appreciated.

On the 26th of February, 1866, a health law was passed by the legislature. This law was entitled "An Act to create a Metropolitan Sanitary District, and Board of Health therein, for the Preservation of Life and Health, and to prevent the Spread of Disease."

This law created a Metropolitan Sanitary District, comprising the cities of New York and Brooklyn and several adjoining counties, which was to be under the control, in all matters bearing upon the public health, of a Board of Health, to be composed of four health commissioners, three of whom should be medical men, the fourth a layman, the commissioners of police, four in number, *ex officio*, and the health officer of the port, *ex officio*—also the officer, a medical man, who had charge of the quarantine. It provided likewise for the appointment of a sanitary superintendent, an assistant superintendent, sanitary inspectors, clerks, employees, etc. . . .

The field of jurisdiction of the board was very extensive, and presented subjects of reform exceedingly diversified in character and apparently unlimited in number, a large proportion of which demanded, with almost equal urgency, immediate and decisive action. Naturally the cities of New York and Brooklyn exhibited the most pressing demands. Not only were large tracts covered with densely crowded, ill-ventilated, and filthy tenement-houses, but, scattered everywhere, were individual nuisances of the most aggravated character, contributing their noxious exhalations to the deteriorated atmosphere.

In New York alone there are eighteen thousand five hundred and eighty-two tenement-houses, that is, houses occupied by several families, living independently of each other, but having a common right in the halls, stairways, yards, cellars, and sinks. Of this number, when first examined by the inspectors, fifty-two percent were found in bad sanitary condition, that is, in a condition detrimental to the health and dangerous to the lives of the occupants, sources of infection to the neighborhood, and of insalubrity to the city at large. Thirty-two percent were in this condition purely from overcrowding, accumulations of filth, want of water supply, and other results of neglect. The danger to the public health from this state of things, especially in the event of an epidemic, is not, however, adequately expressed by these figures; for while in the upper and newer parts of the city the tenement-houses are comparatively well built and properly looked after, there are many localities where almost entire blocks are composed of such houses, all of which were found to be in bad condition, and where the danger was greatly increased by this grouping.

The causes of the improper sanitary condition of tenement-houses may be classed under two heads, namely: first, those due to faults in the original construction of the buildings; and second, those due to overcrowding and neglect.

Prominent under the first head is—First, *the custom of erecting a front and rear tenement-house on a single lot.* By this plan the rear end of each rear house is within a short distance, varying in different instances from six inches to two feet, of the rear end of the rear house situated upon the reverse lot fronting on the next street, above or below as the case may be. The result of this is, that the back rooms of the rear houses are entirely cut off from direct sunlight, and the ventilation is necessarily very imperfect. The spaces, too, between houses thus contiguous are always damp, and very frequently, from being made receptacles for garbage and other offensive matters, give off the foulest exhalations, which are either diffused through the houses, or compel the tenants to keep the rear windows constantly closed, and thus preclude the slender means of ventilation which they might otherwise afford. Even the front rooms of such houses suffer in a similar manner, though not to so great a degree, the presence of the high front house, separated only by a narrow court, allowing but a meagre share of direct light and fresh air.

Second, *deficient ventilation* is a very common evil in tenement-houses. The halls are close, rarely, except on the lower floor, extending to either front or rear wall, so as to admit of a window. Therefore, as the tenants keep their room-doors closed, the hall is entirely cut off from the external air, save by the chance opening of the street entrance. The dwelling-rooms have no provision for ventilation, except such as may be afforded by the windows, which are usually on but one side of the room. The sleeping-apartments open from these dwelling-rooms, and are simple closets, with absolutely no ventilation.

Third, *absence of light.* For the same reasons that the halls are unventilated, they are also dark and damp. No sunlight can enter them. The space allowed for the hall is so narrow that a proper well is impossible, and no adequate skylight is provided. A large proportion of these halls are so dark that at midday it is difficult to discern objects in them without opening some adjacent room-door. In many instances the floors are damp and rotten, and the walls and banisters sticky with a constant moisture.

Fourth, *basements, or cellars.* The basements, or cellars, are often entirely under ground, the ceiling being a foot or two below the level of the street, and are necessarily far more damp, dark, and ill-ventilated than the rest of the house. Many of these are constantly occupied, and not infrequently used as lodging-rooms, having no communication with the external air save by the entrance, and the occupants being entirely dependent upon artificial light by day as well as by night. In the lower streets of the city they are often subject to regular periodical flooding by tide-water, to the depth of from six to twelve inches, frequently so as to keep the children in bed until ebb-tide.

Fifth, *deficient drainage.* A large number of tenements have no connection with the common sewer, and no provision for drainage but surface gutters, by which all the house slops are conducted across or immediately beneath the sidewalk into the street gutter, where, from lack of the proper grade, they remain stagnant and putrefying during the summer, and during the winter freeze and turn the flow into the cellars. Indeed, at all seasons, much of the fluid matter deposited by the tenants in the yards makes its way into the cellars, and it is by no means exceptional to find entire blocks of houses where cellars are constantly flooded to a greater or lesser extent from this cause. In other instances, the flow from the different sinks and wash-basins on the successive floors is conducted by pipes, devoid of traps, to a common wooden drain of inadequate dimensions, running immediately beneath the basement floors of contiguous houses, and thence passing into the street sewer. The current through these drains is generally sluggish, frequently obstructed by accumulations of solid matter or by the decay and consequent breaking down of the drain itself. In the event of such accidents, collections of stagnant and offensive fluids take place beneath the basement floor, or in the cellar, if there be one; the whole house becomes permeated with a disagreeable stench, the cause of which is not discovered until sickness or intolerance of the odor leads to complaint and investigation. These drains are not infrequently furnished with ventilators, consisting of flues immediately connected with the interior of the drain, and thence passing up through the house, with openings in the various apartments, through which the gases resulting from the decomposition below are diffused. The lack of proper traps gives rise to the same difficulty, the exhalations from the stagnant contents of the drain finding their way up through the waste-pipes into the halls and rooms.

Such, with the occasional absence of Croton water, and the frequent lack of fire-escapes, are the most prominent faults of construction in New York tenement-houses.

Evils of the second class, arising from overcrowding and neglect, are, accumulations of garbage and filth of every description in the yards and cellars; filthy halls, stairways, and rooms, leaky roofs, and broken windows. All these aggravate the results of faults of construction, and render these dwellings unfit for habitation.

To the filthy habits of the occupants, and especially to the indifference of the owners, are due in great measure the origin and continuance of these terrible sources of disease. Some of these tenements are owned by persons of the highest social position, but who fail to appreciate the responsibility which rests upon them. They are frequently entirely ignorant of the condition of their property; and either trust its care to an agent, who of course feels still less responsibility, and whose duty it is in the main so to manage the property as to make it productive of the greatest pecuniary advantage to his employer, or they lease it to "middle men," as they are called, who have no interest in it except its immediate profits, and who destroy even its original ventilation, and aggravate its defects, by dividing the rooms into smaller ones, and crowding three or four families into space hardly sufficient for one.

The latter is not unfrequently the case with houses not originally intended for tenement-houses, but which are abandoned private residences, arranged for the accommodation simply of one family. The "middle men" hire these old houses for a term of years from the owner, who is glad to get rid of them until he is ready to tear them down and improve the property, while meantime it is not for his interest nor that of the lessee to make improvements or repairs.

Disease, especially in the form of fevers of a typhoid character, was constantly present in these dwellings, and every now and then became epidemic in one or more of them. In one it was found that twenty cases of typhus had occurred during the preceding year. In the summer of 1866, tenement-houses were the first resting-place and the permanent abode of cholera.

The effort to ameliorate or remedy these evils has been by far the most difficult labor of the board; the more so because of their strong tendency to recur, and, unless watched with unceasing vigilance, to become as rife and malignant as ever. But the landlords and owners of tenement-houses have been roused to co-operation with the board, and already a great change has been effected in the condition of such dwellings.

The custom of erecting a front and rear tenement-house on a single lot should be discontinued. The front houses might then be made deeper, and yet leave sufficient space between them and abutting houses from the next street to allow of proper provision for ventilation and light.

To improve the ventilation and light of existing tenement-houses, several plans are feasible which involve comparatively moderate expense. To ventilate and light the halls, the hall bedrooms at one end on each floor may be dispensed with, thus giving the halls the benefit of the windows. Into the halls thus improved a moderate-sized window, three feet square, should be cut from the dark bedrooms which have no opening save the door from the dwelling-rooms. In most of the New York tenement-houses these windows have now been introduced, and are of great value. . . .

A proper system of construction, however, will of itself be of no avail in tenement-houses, unless accompanied by constant watchfulness. Rooms will be overcrowded; windows and doors will be persistently closed; apertures for ventilation will be stuffed with rags; refuse matters will be thrown into the sinks, clogging the waste-pipes, and destroying the efficiency of the plumbing, however perfect; drains will be broken and obstructed; filth will accumulate in the cellars and halls; periodical scrubbing and whitewashing, a most essential measure, will be neglected; the walls will become foul and saturated with the various exhalations of crowded rooms; and the model tenement-house will soon become as unwholesome as the worst.

Reform in this matter can, in our opinion, be made permanent only by forcing upon the owners of such property the responsibility of its management. Weekly, or, if desirable, more frequent inspections of every tenement-house, from garret to cellar, should be made by the owner or other competent authority, who should exact from each tenant strict compliance with such rules as are necessary to the salubrity of a dwelling; and any tenant who persists in living in a manner detrimental to the health of his neighbors should no longer be allowed to remain. Such a system would soon improve the habits of the tenants; and the certainty of a weekly inspection would at least secure a vigorous cleansing at those times, which of itself would prevent the terrible accumulations of filth which are now a disgrace to so many landlords. A competent housekeeper should also reside on or near the premises, whose duty it should be to keep the halls, sinks, and other portions of the house used in common by the tenants clean and in repair. It is in a great measure due to the neglect of these reasonable precautions that so much labor and expense are entailed upon the public for sanitary measures.

These remarks on the subject of tenement-houses are not theoretical, but express the results of observation of the reforms which have been actually carried out in New York during the last two years.

In addition to this greatest source of peril to the health of the city, the neglected condition of the dwellings of the laboring classes, there were establishments for slaughtering animals, for the melting of fat, for the various processes for utilizing the different kinds of offal, for the manufacture of fertilizing agents, and the preparation of chemicals, besides numbers of crowded and filthy cow-stables, hog-yards, and other nuisances of minor character, which together presented such an array of evils as made it a matter of considerable difficulty to decide where and how to begin the work of reform.

But far more appalling than the magnitude of the material labor before the board was the apathy which possessed the minds of those who were the more immediate sufferers from these nuisances, and the sullen, but obstinate, opposition of those to whom they had long been a source of profit.

Accustomed for years to the undisturbed possession of what they considered, or pretended to consider, their rights, this latter class stigmatized as tyranny and usurpation every effort to abate the causes of physical disease and moral degradation; while those in whom long-continued submission had engendered a lethargic content were, in many instances, almost equally ready to join in resistance to any measure which would tend to disturb them in their habitual mode of life.

To herd human beings in buildings and rooms almost devoid of ventilation, and without the commonest provision for cleanliness or even decent privacy, to crowd them into dark, damp cellars, to lodge them in subterranean dormitories where not a ray of sunlight nor a breath of fresh air ever penetrated, and to allow these dwellings from year to year to accumulate filth and infection from this dense mass of humanity without an effort at renovation, was, in very many cases, the alleged inalienable right of a property-holder.

To carry on a business or manufacture, in the midst of a dense population, the processes of which resulted in the corruption of the atmosphere, thus undermining the health and destroying the lives of those whom poverty debarred from escape, was also a practice which long-continued indulgence had transformed into a fancied right.

To use the public streets as common receptacles for refuse and filth of every description, and to leave the foul mass there to putrefy and load the air with its poisonous exhalations, was, in some parts of the city, a practice so universal and popular, that to prevent it was to take away one of the first privileges of a citizen.

We mention these matters merely to show how comparatively easy it is to discover and appreciate the causes of deterioration in the public health, and theoretically to devise measures for their removal, and yet how difficult, and at times almost discouraging, it is to effectually apply the remedy.

The aim of the Metropolitan Board of Health from the beginning was to do its work with a gentle, though firm hand. It was at once apparent that to be successful it must be cautious, and that very often, although the object to be gained might be distinctly recognized from the first, its accomplishment must be reached by slow approaches, lest by too impetuous an attack a recoil should be the result, and the popular support, upon which the ultimate usefulness of the board must rest, should be lost.

A people long accustomed to order their lives, each individual in his own way, without reference to those about him, cannot all at once be brought to see the benefit of a measure which shall subordinate personal advantage to the general good.

To any measure of this sort the people must be educated. They must be led by their own observation to believe in it. They must be given time, from step to step, to see in what direction the work is tending, and to discern that each individual will in the end enjoy far greater benefits when all shall so live as to contribute to the public welfare.

Trite as these observations are, the principle which they set forth is not always appreciated. In the early days of the Metropolitan Board of Health, there were many of its friends who grew very impatient at what they regarded its timidity, and called upon it, now that it had the power, to use it vigorously, and sweep away at once the evils which it was created to remove.

Happily the board was guided by wiser counsels. It began by inviting conferences, by appealing to the citizens generally, and especially to such as were principally engaged in avocations which were in some of their results objectionable, to meet with the board and advise as to the best method of obviating the existing difficulties.

These conferences, although by no means always successful in reconciling the parties interested to the proposed changes, and in preventing the necessity for subsequent coercive measures, were still of great advantage, in showing to the public generally that the board had no disposition to use its powers in any unnecessarily arbitrary manner, but, on the contrary, were ready to accord the fullest respect to the rights of every citizen, and so to accomplish the reforms which it was its duty to insist upon as to entail the least possible pecuniary loss or other embarrassment to any individual or class.

A notable instance was the conference with the butchers. Private slaughter-houses of every size and description, some two hundred in number, were scattered through the most populous portions of the city, and especially those chiefly occupied by tenement-houses.

The evil influence of these establishments upon the public health was very decided, not only from the filthy and neglected condition of many of them, but from the defilement of the streets through which the cattle had to be driven, and the constant necessity of carting offal and other offensive accumulations through the city, as well as the corruption of the atmosphere from the crowding together of heated and travel-worn animals in small, confined yards and pens. The constant bellowing of the footsore and homesick cattle, the ceaseless moaning and bleating of the calves and sheep, and the squealing and grunting of the pigs, disturbed and indeed oftentimes entirely destroyed the sleep of the occupants of the surrounding tenements, which were filled with the laboring classes, who could ill afford to be thus robbed of their natural rest. There was no cause for hesitation or delay as to the proper action to be taken regarding these places. The bitter and universal complaints of the throngs of work-people who filled the lofty tenements that overlooked and received the exhalations from these establishments—their stifling rooms, which were frequently found by the sanitary inspectors with every window closed, especially in hot weather, lest the ingress of noisome odors and swarms of flies should render them untenantable—the sickly and vicious children, rendered so by the noxious effluvia and the brutalizing exhibitions of the slaughter-pen—all pointed with a significance which none could reasonably deny to the expulsion of these nuisances from the city. That this should be the ultimate disposal of them was the early determination of the board; but as the change would involve serious modifications, on the part of the butchers, in the method of conducting their business, it was deemed best to lay the matter fairly before them, and, if possible, gain their cooperation.

A call was accordingly issued for a meeting of all persons interested in the slaughtering of animals, to consider with the board the question of the removal of the whole business beyond the city limits. A large concourse of butchers responded to this call.

The views of the board were laid before them, and a free interchange of opinion was invited. An animated discussion ensued. It was declared by the butchers that the two hundred private slaughter-houses scattered through the city, with their daily and nightly contributions of noxious gases above ground, and of putrid blood and offal to the sewers below, were the necessary and only means for supplying the citizens of New York with meat. In the light of the experience of Paris and London this needed no refutation; yet the butchers remained determined to hold to the existing plan, if possible. But the very publicity of their avowal, and the display of selfishness in their arguments, proved of great advantage to the board. Showing as it did to the public that these nuisances, the evil effects of which had long been generally recognized, were by no means necessarily incident to a great city, as the proprietors claimed, there was at once a general endorsement of the proposed action of the board, and throughout the entire year of injunctions, suits, and vexatious contests which followed, to the final banishment of the business of slaughtering from the populous portions of the city, the commission received the cordial sympathy and encouragement of all classes of the community, save that alone which would be temporarily incommoded by the change.

The erection of ample slaughter-houses upon the outskirts of the city, immediately upon the water, provided with every facility for cleanliness and decorum, and efficient means for utilizing hides, hoofs, horns, bones, blood, and offal upon the spot, before the commencement of putrefaction, is fast adding the evidence of this city to that of the cities of the Old World, that public *abattoirs*, under public inspection, insure the best meat-supply, and at the cheapest rates.

The experience of the board was similar with reference to the nuisance arising out of the process by which the illuminating gas was purified at the various manufactories—a process which resulted in periodically deluging the city, especially in the upper portions, with sulphuretted hydrogen gas. This, too, had been bitterly complained of, but had been regarded as necessarily attaching to this mode of lighting the city. Representatives of the different gas companies were therefore assembled at the chambers of the board, when, after considerable discussion, it appeared that the continuance of this offensive method of purification was a measure, not of necessity, but simply of economy to the manufacturer. This once clearly demonstrated, the mere pressure of public opinion so strengthened the hands of the board, that this most grievous nuisance was abated with but little exercise of authority on their part. Here was a business which none could deny was certainly most important to the city, and yet the brilliancy of its results was dimmed, and the enjoyment of its benefits grievously impaired, by the penetrating and disgusting odors which accompanied one of its essential processes. The purification of the crude coal gas was accomplished by passing it through immense chambers filled with lime. This lime absorbed, that is, took up and mechanically held within its substance, the impurities, which consisted chiefly of sulphuretted hydrogen gas, the most offensive of all gases. At certain regular intervals the lime became saturated with the gas, when it was necessary to empty the purifying chambers, and renew the lime. Then came the nuisance. The lime, surcharged with the noxious constituents of the crude gas, as soon as it was removed from the confinement of the close tank, evolved clouds of the noisome sulphuretted hydrogen, which floated over the city, poisoning the atmosphere, and penetrating the houses in spite of the most prompt and careful closing of every window and door.

When the question of abating this nuisance was first agitated, the reply was, that there was no remedy: the city must either be in darkness, or pay this dreadful penalty for light. The alternative, however, was not accepted. The subject was fully investigated, and a satisfactory result soon reached. The process of purification was changed, and the trouble disappeared. It was ascertained, that, by the use of oxide of iron instead of lime, the offensive elements of the crude gas were chemically destroyed, entering into combination with the iron, instead of being merely held mechanically, as with the lime. The requisite substitution was made, and the gas companies still continue to illumine the city, without contributing their former liberal share to the corruption of its atmosphere.

Very many other manufactures are essential to the maintenance of a populous community, which, if conducted in improper situations or without the proper appliances, are most prolific sources of disease. Many such attracted the early notice of the Board—for example, fat-melting, the utilization of various kinds of offal, and the manufacture of fertilizing agents from refuse bones and other material.

The deleterious effect of these processes upon the public health was frequently and strenuously denied, on the ground that the employees in the manufactures were healthy, that no specific disease in the neighborhood could be traced to emanations from the establishments, and sometimes even that chemistry itself failed to detect in the fumes any substance directly injurious to any organ or function of the human body. A little reflection will show the sophistry of these arguments. The fact that men and women may by long and constant habit become inured to the presence of offensive gases is no proof that they are innocuous to those who are unaccustomed to them. Nor is it necessary that any specific disease shall result to prove their deleterious character. That they lower the general tone of the system, disturb digestion, and impair the healthful and pleasurable exercise of all the functions of the body, is, even more than the production of a definite and recognizable form of disease, a reason for condemning and prohibiting their continuance. This radical course, however, is frequently found to be unnecessary. The advance of science, and improvements in apparatus, have rendered it possible to conduct almost any process, however offensive and unwholesome the gases resulting therefrom may be, in such a manner as to cause no pollution of the surrounding atmosphere. Thus it is with the business of fat-melting, which two years since was carried on in New York very extensively in large open kettles, the foul steam from which, loaded with organic matter frequently in a putrid condition, escaped in dense volumes into the streets, and was borne by the wind over wide and populous districts, compelling the inhabitants to close every window and door, and endure the confined and heated air of their own apartments, rather than the intolerable stench from the outside. When the nuisance was attacked by the board, the reply was, that these odors were the unavoidable results of a business essential to the life of the city, and must be submitted to; and it was only after a long and hot contest in the courts that the board was finally sustained in its order that no fat-melting should be permitted at any factory until the apparatus employed should be so modified as to prevent the escape of any offensive odors into the external air. This prohibition at once caused a change in the whole business; and the prompt substitution of the steam tank for the open kettle completely abated one of the foulest nuisances with which the city was afflicted, and that not only without really damaging the interests of the fat-melters, but, on the contrary, permanently benefiting them. This business is carried on today as extensively as it was two years ago; but now the offensive vapor, instead of rising from the large open caldrons, and escaping unhindered into the air, is conducted from the tight tank in which it is generated, through a pipe, into a condenser, whence, in a liquid form, it passes beneath the factory and is discharged into the street sewer.

Such was the course pursued, not only with reference to nuisances of this general character, but also in dealing with those of more limited influence. No individual has ever been compelled to change the mode of conducting his business, or alter the condition of his premises, without an opportunity being first offered him of personally appearing before the board or some responsible officer of it, and showing cause why an order on the subject should be modified or rescinded. In very many instances the execution of an order has been stayed, on the representation by the party upon whom it was served that its delay or modification would enable him to protect himself from undue damage without causing the public to suffer in consequence. . . .

Undoubtedly, during the first year of the existence of this department of the metropolitan government, the presence of cholera, with the vague dread which it inspired, had a powerful influence in recommending the measures adopted by the board. When it became evident that the pestilence had actually reached the country, and was searching out the places where congenial surroundings should add to its power and promote its development, the efforts of the board to anticipate its progress, and destroy everything that could nourish its strength, were warmly seconded, and an occasional summary exercise of authority was applauded; and it was in this emergency only that peremptory orders were issued and promptly executed.

The course of the epidemic corroborated the evidence which the

history of previous ones had invariably afforded, namely, that tenement-houses offered by far the most favorable fields for the development and spread of the disease. The first victim was an occupant of
one in a conspicuously insalubrious condition, and its immediate
evacuation by order of the board, and its prompt cleansing and disinfection, were followed by entire immunity throughout the season,
although the occupants were allowed to return after a few days. This
action, arbitrary and usurping as it might seem, was cheerfully
acquiesced in by the owner of the property, and the expenses attending it were defrayed without complaint. During the prevalence of the
epidemic, each new case was treated in a similar manner, and even all
the houses in the vicinity of the one infected were subjected to
precautionary measures without giving rise in any instance to serious
complaint.

In all cases disinfectants were promptly and freely used, though
necessarily at first in a somewhat experimental manner, owing to a
lack of accurate knowledge as to the peculiar power of disinfectants,
the exact quantity required, the time for which it was necessary to
subject articles to their action, and other practical details. It was
therefore frequently thought best to burn soiled articles, especially
beds, lest the disinfection should be slow or imperfect. . . .

A large quantity of common lime and charcoal-dust was purchased,
and used in the general disinfection of filthy localities, without reference to the occurrence of cholera. A number of horses and carts were
hired, with a sufficient number of men to furnish each cart with one
helper besides the driver, to distribute this material. The plan adopted
was to pass through each street in the filthy parts of the city once a
week, and in some instances twice, and sprinkle the disinfectants
freely along the gutters and through the alleys and yards, and deposit a
certain amount in each garbage-box and foul cellar. Now and then a
few cart-loads of sulphate of iron and chloride of lime were used in the
worst places. At first the inhabitants misunderstood the proceeding,
but it soon became popular and received their hearty cooperation.

Additional instructions were issued to the sanitary inspectors "to
immediately investigate any case of supposed cholera reported to
them at any hour by any officer of the Metropolitan Police, to do what
might be immediately necessary professionally, and give instructions
as to the proper method of obtaining medical attendance from the
dispensaries, or, if the case required it, of gaining admission to hospital, and to furnish the necessary certificate." They were at once to
decide what was requisite in the way of disinfection; and if the parties
were able to procure and employ the necessary articles themselves, to
give them detailed instructions regarding the same, and make a rein-

spection of the premises six hours later to ascertain if their instructions had been carried out. In any case where the parties were unable to procure and employ the necessary articles, the inspector was to apply at the nearest police station, and, through the officer in charge, telegraph to the office of the superintendent that disinfection was required at such premises, giving the street, number, and room accurately. It was his duty then to reinspect after six hours and ascertain whether the proper measures had been taken, and to report his action at the office of the superintendent, in person, by telegraph, or in writing.

The sanitary inspectors kept watch of every case of cholera investigated by them until either recovery or death took place, and then promptly reported the result to the superintendent—in writing, if recovery, by telegraph, if death. The inspectors in the country districts were instructed to "forward to the office of the superintendent a written report upon each case of supposed cholera investigated by them, whether proved to be genuine or not, within twenty-four hours subsequent to said investigation." The inspectors also made thorough examination of premises where any cases of cholera occurred, and visited every family residing on or near such premises, inquiring carefully for any premonitory symptoms resembling those of cholera, and, on finding such, giving advice, and, if necessary, treatment. This investigation extended through the whole block, and as much farther as the situation and circumstances required. These visits were repeated from time to time during the week or two following the occurrence of any case, so as either to make sure that no second case was to appear, or, in the event of such appearance, to meet it promptly.

The practical application of disinfectants was soon reduced to a simple system, which was followed in every case, and with apparently satisfactory results. Whenever a despatch was received at the central office that disinfection was needed at any house, men of the disinfectant corps, with a wagon loaded with the requisite material, were at once sent to the spot. The officers and men of the police force were prompt in their cooperation, and the disinfecting men were usually at their work on the premises within an hour from the time at which the despatch was forwarded from the station-house.

The plan of disinfection thus described gave entire satisfaction as regards clothing and other immediate surroundings of the patient; but frequently the recurrence of successive cases in tenement-houses showed that the power of such measures was too limited, and at an early date general fumigation of such buildings was resorted to, either with chlorine or sulphurous-acid gas. The process was this. All tenants were removed from the house, being allowed to take out nothing more than the clothing then upon them. All the windows and chimneys were closed. The gas was then set free in quantity—if chlorine, by the addition of sulphuric acid to chloride of lime,—if sulphurous acid, by the burning of sulphur in large open pans supported by long iron legs. The men employed commenced the process on the upper floors, and descended, leaving the pans in operation on the different floors, and finally closed the street-door. The house thus filled with the gas was left undisturbed from eight to twelve hours. It was then opened and freely aired, and finally the tenants were allowed to reoccupy.

After the subsidence of cholera, the plan of disinfection and cleansing was continued, though with less magnitude of apparatus, and applied to houses where the existence of fever of an infectious character was discovered, or the condition of which was found to be such as to impair the health of the occupants.

The practice thus instituted and submitted to under the fear of contagion became, by an easy transition, a permanent custom. The tenement-houses, as well as other premises likely to be detrimental to the public health, remained constantly under the strict supervision of the board, and subject to its authority, until, at the assembling of the legislature in 1867, new and more extensive powers were given to the board, and a tenement-house law was passed, which it is hoped will establish on a permanent basis improvements which might otherwise be but temporary.

The control of small-pox by periodical inspections of all public schools and other educational institutions, and the vaccination of the inmates, we need not dwell upon, and will only mention in passing.

There is still great necessity for the regulation of occupations injurious to health, such as those followed by needle-women, tailors, bakers, printers, etc., whose work-rooms are generally crowded and ill-ventilated, and whose modes of life, induced by the conditions under which they earn their livelihood, are in a high degree conducive to disease, especially consumption.

In several of the suits that the board has been engaged in, having reference to the abatement of nuisances consisting of offensive odors, the question has been mooted as to what particular odors are and what are not detrimental to health. We are convinced that the only consistent and philosophical position on this question is, that all odors are detrimental to heath,—that is, that unadulterated atmospheric air is best adapted to preserve all the organs in a perfectly healthful condition, and that anything which impairs the absolute purity of the atmosphere must of necessity be deleterious.

When, however, we consider the conditions under which a great city exists, the multitudinous necessities which attach to its traffic and its growth, we cannot expect that the atmosphere which pervades it shall be absolutely pure; still, we must not lose sight of the principle that the odors which attend on the various life of the city are so many warnings of danger, and that it is incumbent upon us to watch jealously these warnings, and see to it that they do not reach an intensity beyond that demanded by actual necessity.

The vast multitudes that throng the avenues of a metropolis, whose thoroughfares are bounded on either side by lofty warehouses or dwellings, whose streets are tunnelled with sewers, the contents of which, made up of all the various *debris* of the growth and decay of the community, are poured into the rivers that wash its shores, whose buildings are illumined with gas, the manufacture of which must be carried on either within or close upon the city precincts, whose wharves are crowded with vessels from every foreign port, and whose population is made up in great measure of the surplus of every country of the Old World, cannot expect to breathe the bracing air of the mountains or the sea-shore. But they can expect, and should demand, that the impurities be reduced to the minimum that unavoidably attaches to the prosperity and progress of the city. To reach this point is the aim of the Metropolitan Board of Health.

3

AN EARLY EXPERIMENT
IN WASTE RECYCLING

C. A. Leas
ON THE SANITARY CARE AND
UTILIZATION OF REFUSE IN CITIES

The following address was delivered before the American Public Health Association in 1872 by a Baltimore physician and sanitarian. No one has given a more vivid, detailed, and unexpectedly enthusiastic description of the practices of urban waste removal and treatment in the days of the backyard privy. In 1877 Philadelphia counted 82,000 privy vaults and cesspools, and Washington, 56,000. Those cities such as Boston, New York, and Chicago which had built underground conduits leading to nearby rivers or lakes intended them primarily for draining surface water rather than for collecting sewage. But by 1900 even cities as small as Providence had replaced most of their vaults with sewer lines, and these were being used heavily to discharge human wastes. By the same date city garbage was still commonly fed to hogs, or in some cases was carried by barges out to sea; but in about ninety cities it was burned in furnaces. The cultural import of these technological advances was that Americans discovered they could flush their nastier problems away—though, as in the case of New York, they had to pay for their sins by being forced to build expensive aqueducts and reservoirs to bring water from the purer reaches of the Adirondacks. What happened in ensuing years to the ecological awareness and old-fashioned economy displayed in this address by Leas poses an interesting question.

It has been said, and I think with much truth, that the disposition made of the offal from human habitations may with much propriety be received as an evidence or indication, not only of the cleanliness, decency, self-respect, and industry of a people, but of their moral and social condition, and when we see with what unconcern and indifference this grave and important subject of the disposal of refuse has

SOURCE. C. A. Leas, "On the Sanitary Care and Utilization of Refuse in Cities," *The Journal of the Franklin Institute*, March 1874.

been received and approached by legislative and executive bodies, during the past ages, we are filled with unbounded wonder and surprise, especially when we reflect that vigilant and astute sanitarians have, in all civilized countries, again and again, through many decades of the past, sounded the alarm from their watch-towers, and cried aloud from the house-tops, that these besoms of destruction, the epidemic and zymotic diseases, owe their existence in the main to defective sanitary regulations; to those active deteriorators of the public health, the heaps of festering and fermenting refuse matters, left unremoved and unutilized in and around the dwellings in our cities and towns. And not only do they thus speak forth in tones of thunder from the eternal world, but by their noxious effluvia demand removal, and are continually revealing and exclaiming, by this still small voice, that there are rich fertilizing qualities reposing within, which, if yielded up to the exhausted soils, to the demands of husbandry, will aid to promote abundance, cheapen food, and increase the demand for honest toil. Man, however, in sanitary affairs learns slowly the very important lesson that prevention is better than cure. He seems in these to have but little faith in the axiom that time ought to be grasped by the forelock, and hence he frequently slumbers and sleeps over volcanos of deadly miasma and noxious or pestilential effluvium, until, suddenly aroused by the bursting forth of blighting, withering, and devastating epidemics, which cost, besides the fearful loss of human life, sanitary reputation and commercial prestige, the expenditure of much treasure in crushing out that which might have been for a trifling outlay year by year altogether prevented. And therefore we cannot, in our mission as sanitarians, too strongly impress upon all people the important truth that in all matters relating to sanitary police and public hygiene, that what is deemed worthy to be done ought to be promptly undertaken, and speedily and efficiently accomplished. Looking, therefore, at the question from all standpoints, we arrive at the conclusion that it is no economy to neglect or postpone the thorough cleansing of towns and cities until cholera or yellow fever has broken out, and it is no economy to discharge the contents of closets with kitchen offal into drains and sewers which debouch into tidal streams, causing thereby not only the loss of millions of dollars worth of rich manurial materials, but strewing, through the agency of the winds and tides upon the shores and docks, myriads of festering nuclii which in warm seasons exhale noxious gases to poison the atmosphere, and thus scatter disease and death among the people, to say nothing of the foul stenches that are forced back by the winds through the sewers, drains, and traps into dwellings and sleeping-chambers, causing diseases of a low type, aggravating others of a mild character, and lessening the ordinary powers of vital resistance to other morbific and destructive agencies and influences, and, indeed, man's general capability for good. Nor is it compatible with common decency to thus pollute the waters of non-tidal streams from which others must draw a supply of water for drinking, cooking, and cleaning purposes.

But it is not the subject of sanitary police, or public hygiene, in their very direct bearings that I am called upon at this time to contemplate; nor is it the baneful and destructive influence that unremoved excreta and other refuse matters have upon human life and health that I am expected to consider, but it is the utilization of the refuse of towns and cities, or the best and most economical mode of treating and manipulating the refuse materials of large communities, so as to place them to good account, to render them sources of wealth and happiness instead of causes of misery, disease, and death. And yet this very subject has a somewhat intimate collateral connection with sanitary police and public hygiene, because, before we can utilize these refuse matters we must first get possession of them. We are, therefore, at the very threshold of our inquiry compelled to consider the best and most economical mode for their collection and transmission to safe and convenient localities, such as are out of the way and well suited for the process of manipulation.

To discuss the soundness of the wisdom which demands the restoration, as far as possible, to the soil, of such elements as were taken from it, in its efforts to furnish man with an abundant supply of food and raiment, in order that this great storehouse of nature may be replenished with the materials wherewith to bring forth new evidences of its munificence and exhibit the infinite benevolence and loving kindness of God, would, it seems to me, be the height of folly. The economic and agricultural interests demand it, and our own common sense tells us that it is right, because in these offals and excrementitious matters, from the very nature of man's ingesta, that we find contained most valuable manurial and fertilizing qualities. And when we reflect upon the vast consumption of cereals and meats in various forms in the cities and towns of this and other countries, drawn from our fields and gardens, never again to return, then, and only then, do we begin to realize how solemn is the obligation to economize the wastes of our dwellings, stables, slaughter-houses, and streets, lanes, and alleys, and in a convenient and concentrated form, present them again to the soil from whence they came, and not only so, but at the same time to enrich the people's treasury?

With a view to a clearer comprehension of the nature or character of the substances refused by man, that collect about his dwelling-places, and require removal from considerations of health and convenience, we will say that they consist of all refuse and offal from houses, such as ordure and excreta; the vegetable and animal garbage from kitchens, including coal and other ashes; the sweepings of houses and yards; old and worn-out pans, kettles, and boots and shoes; the scrapings and sweepings of streets, lanes, alleys, and courts; dead animals; the unutilized materials from factories and workshops; and last, but not least, the offal and garbage from slaughtering establishments. Happily, however, for our public treasuries, that some of the substances here enumerated do not fall for their removal upon the public authorities, hence I have concluded to embrace within the scope of these remarks the utilization of only such of the refuse matters as come under the immediate and daily observation of public sanitary authorities, and as fall into their possession, either direct or indirect, for removal and disposal. And although the garbage and offal from slaughter houses as a general thing do not come under this head, and are in the main removed soon or late by the owners of such establishments to the country, and their most valuable fertilizing properties in some way or other utilized for agricultural, horticultural, or other purposes, yet I will here remark that nevertheless the efforts of many gentlemen engaged in the butchering and slaughtering of animals to preserve their premises in a cleanly and sweet condition, a greater outrage can hardly be perpetrated upon a people than the toleration within towns and cities of such establishments. They, together with their kindred, melting and boiling houses, soap and glue factories, and bone-grinding and crushing establishments, ought to be banished into suburban places, and the atmosphere of crowded localities saved from the contaminating influences which result from the retained filth and offal for hours, and sometimes days, in closets and dung pens, festering and fermenting out in warm weather pestiferous gases, which act like slow but sure poison upon the human organism; and, besides, in suburban localities or open country the flesh of slaughtered animals can be better prepared for the markets; the atmosphere being purer, the meats are less liable to take on speedy putrefactive action. The animals themselves, from the same cause, are in a more healthy condition, and, besides, the people saved the further danger, annoyance, and damage to health and traffic, resulting from the driving of sheep, oxen, and swine through crowded thoroughfares. But it ought not to be forgotten that these open country localities for abattoirs or slaughtering purposes should be located upon streams, the waters of which are not afterwards to be used for drinking, culinary or cleansing purposes.

Various and dissimilar have been and are the modes of scavenging large towns and cities, and collecting for removal the ordinary offal and garbage from the streets and dwellings, both in this and other countries. In parts of the West Indies the dead animals and some other portions of refuse matter are referred to the buzzards for removal, and it may be said that as scavengers in this relation they are prompt and efficient, doing their work quick and well. In some European localities the owners of property are required to cleanse the public thorough-fares in front of their respective premises, and to remove the house offal, which generally accumulates in the courtyards and other places for days and weeks, until the amount proves equal to one or more wagon-loads. Such, for example, was the case in the imperial city of St. Petersburg, until the inauguration of an American scavenging system; hence it may not be wondered at that cholera had previously prevailed in that city more or less the whole year round. In other places the contiguous farmers and gardeners, with their long covered wagons and the help of their women, collect the garbage and street manure, and apply them to their lands, the removal costing the authorities nothing. Again, in others, the scavenging service is, in whole or in part, confided to contractors, who in the main regard more attending to their own pockets than the public health and conveni-ence. The municipal authorities of some towns and cities employ the scavenging forces, but lack fixed regulations, especially in the remo-val of the garbage from dwellings, the carts visiting at any and all hours of the day, thus causing the exposure of masses of filth and rubbish upon the sidewalks, in the gutters, and in and about dwellings for hours, to the great detriment of health, sight, and smell. Others cause the collection of kitchen offal and house ashes separately by two sets of carts, with the view to the utilization of the ashes for the filling of sunken lots, and the vegetable and animal offal for the feeding of swine, while others collect all together, making the same cart one heterogeneous mass of vegetable, animal, and mineral matter, and either depositing the same upon open and sunken lots, where it acts as a poison to the atmosphere of whole neighborhoods, or, to avoid this, it is covered with a layer of good earth, which makes a fair show outwardly, and smothers up, and renders less rapid the process of putrefaction. Nevertheless, it is true that good earth is a most valuable deodorant; yet it may also be regarded as certain that, if this deposited mass should be disturbed or uncovered in the process of cellar digging short of three or four years, the gases sent through the houses built upon such foundations will be productive of fearful disease and general bad health.

To secure and maintain the confidence of the people in any effort at refuse utilization, the mode and manner of its collection and removal must combine both economy and efficiency. You will, therefore, be pleased to pardon a little digression, with the view that I may, in a succinct form, lay before you my views in this relation. The garbage or kitchen offal, including coal and other ashes, yard and cellar sweepings, ought to be collected daily in the warm seasons, and at least three times per week during the other portions of the year, and with the view to constant cleanliness within doors, and a proper utilization of refuse matters, housekeepers, and all others interested, ought to be required to separate the ashes and earthy substances from the vegetable and animal offal, and in this form to present them with absolute regularity to the garbage collector, when he shall appear before the premises, and further to remove from public view the empty vessels immediately after the departure of the cart, which, together with the horses, ought to be large and substantial, and the former provided with a movable division board, so arranged as to shift little by little, fore and aft, and with an upright bolt, so that by the drawing of which the board will fly open from below upward when the cart is tilted. This partition will furnish two compartments, one for the ashes and the other for the animal and vegetable refuse, and can be shifted as the seasons advance, one upon the other, or in proportion as the ashes predominate over the vegetable and animal materials collected. Housekeepers and others ought to have sufficient warning, through the frequent sounding of a horn, aided by the ringing of team bells upon the hames of the horse, of the near approach of the cart, so that then, and not before, they may bring out their garbage; and they ought to be strictly enjoined not to expose their refuse matters upon the streets and sidewalks in advance of the time for the visit of the cart; but the officer in charge of the service ought to see to it, through the proper districting of the town or city into garbage beats, and the maintenance of proper order and discipline; that the carts appear, as to time, with almost the same degree of regularity as characterizes the arrival and departure of railroad trains. Unfaithfulness, loitering, or drunkenness on the part of employes ought to be promptly punished, as the people's health, lives, and convenience ought not to be compromised or placed in jeopardy through political or other influences. The garbage and refuse thus collected ought to be removed, either by water, rail, or carts into the country, and as much as possible out of the way of habitations and into grounds inclosed and prepared for their reception, the ashes placed under sheds and sifted, and held in stores as an absorbent and deodorant, and the vegetable and animal portions dumped into compost pits.

I had the honor of inaugurating in the city of Baltimore, nearly twenty years ago, a system of collecting garbage, and it has maintained its place and popularity for nearly two decades, amid all the changes of men, measures, and parties, and when honestly, energetically and conscientiously executed, has given uniform pleasure and satisfaction to the people. And not only so, but the present Emperor of Russia, some years ago, ordered one like it to be put in execution in the city of St. Petersburg, after an Imperial Commission had reported that in all the European cities visited for the purpose of investigation, none was found equal to it as a scavenging system. The housewives of Baltimore have been so trained and schooled, through the kindness, gentleness, and firmness of the Sanitary Department, added to their own good practical judgment and dispositions of cleanliness, to regard the garbage-cart, not only as a necessity, but its regularity even to hours as of such grave importance as to call forth complaints when failure occur, and all such complaints ought not only to be encouraged, but carefully and promptly inquired into. The improvements or additions to this system—namely, the separation by families of the garbage from the ashes, the movable division-board in the carts, and the hauling by cart nearly two miles into the country—were adopted at my suggestion, and inaugurated nearly one year ago, with the view to the utilization of all this refuse, together with the nightsoil or contents of privies, which cess-pool matter was at the same time ordered to be removed by the independent nightmen, in their carts, to the city dumping-grounds, which last regulation gave rise to an advance in the cost to property-owners of cleaning privy-vaults, and which, in its turn, together with other wise sanitary reasons, created the necessity of inaugurating the system of cleaning these places by the pneumatic suction plan, which, in case the machinery can be so perfected as to remove by suction the ordinary solid excrementitious matter, I consider to be a decided improvement, and ought by all means to form a part of the sanitary system of all large towns and cities. And again, besides the advantages in a sanitary or hygienic point, it ought to give rise to a reduction in the cost of cleaning closets nearly if not quite one-half, from the fact that the worst can and is done by day, thus giving full opportunity for double the working hours and larger loads. And, furthermore, propertyowners and others interested, can see or determine with exactness the amount of service given by the night-men, and thus be enabled to audit the bills and save unrighteous drafts upon their purses and patience.

The movable division board in the cart saves the expense of duplicated carts in the collection of garbage—an expense the politicians feared very much. Then, again, it was supposed that to require families to provide a second garbage vessel would give rise to such an avalanche of indignation that no political party could stand against it; but, on the contrary, it was found that on the day fixed for the commencement of the garbage-separation system—which was fully made known to every family, by means of advertising and handbills circulated into every house, through the agency of the police—every family in the city of Baltimore—a city of over fifty thousand houses--had their garbage separated, and ready at the appointed hour for the garbage collector, save very few, and the neglect of these few was found, upon investigation, to be the result of ignorance rather than unwillingness; and up to this day I am not aware of a single fine having been imposed, as provided in the law. And indeed the whole thing has become popular with the people, and thus this objection, a mere *ignis fatuus* in the minds of those that scare at shadows, has vanished, and when these fearful ones expected this overwhelming ruin they found only praise and eulogiums. At first was feared that the weight in the cart would be unequal; that either the load would be too heavy in front, and thus crush down the horse, or in the rear, and thus tilt the cart backward and hang the animal; but this difficulty soon also vanished when I showed the garbage men how to load in order to preserve the centre of gravity through the axletree.

Night-soil possesses, next to bullock's blood, the most valuable manurial properties, being well adapted to the growth of all kinds of crops, but especially those requiring a large amount of nitrogen or ammonia. I therefore ask, then, if these things be true, is it wisdom, is it true economy to allow these sources of wealth to flow through our drains and sewers into the bays and rivers, to be forever lost, or if returned in any form, to be in the shape of epidemic, pestilential, and low forms of disease, and the expenditure of millions to dredge out our docks, rivers, and ship channels, saying nothing of the damage done to the fresh water streams through their pollution by this system of drainage? Sewers and drains were originally designed to convey away the surface drainage, and this system of sending through them all refuse matters, is a serious departure from this original intention, and which ought not to be continued. I know there are difficulties surrounding this whole matter of closet vaults; the contamination of the atmosphere which they cause, especially when being cleaned by the miserable cart and bucket man and the partial contamination or damage to contiguous wells and spring. But then we must not forget that there are very few large communities dependent for a supply of water upon the resources here referred to, nor yet upon this old rotten borough system of cleansing by cart and bucket. Therefore, in view of these things, the new mode of disposing of kitchen sewage and human excreta by drains and sewers renders, in my judgment, the last end worse than the first. Until, therefore, the people can be educated up to a well-regulated system of earth or ash closets, which ought to be as soon as possible, let us, at least for the present, stand by the cess-pool plan of accumulation, and a perfected pneumatic suction system of cleansing, and utilize, in compliance with the plain dictates of nature, for the benefit of agriculture and the taxpayers, this large mass of refuse material.

But now the question comes up, how are these waste matters to be utilized? The answer I will endeavor to give. And as was before stated, economy should always travel side by side with efficiency, therefore it is recommended to all towns and cities having navigable rivers running through or convenient to them, and not liable to ice blockade, to use these to convey away, in suitable boats, tanks, and hoppers, these refuse matters to proper dumping grounds. If these, however, do not exist, or if existing, cannot be availed of, then the next best agents for transportation are railroads, and lastly, if these are not convenient or will not afford the required facilities, then there remains nothing but the horse and cart, which is the case in Baltimore, where the garbage and excreta are, by this means, transported about one mile and a half into the country. In any effort, however, to successfully utilize refuse, a market for the large amount of compost must not be overlooked in the selecting of depots for dumping purposes. This whole field must be well canvassed in its agricultural and horticultural bearings and relations, and confidence well founded that the outlet is well secured, and the demand will be quite equal to the supply. To this end and for this purpose let the section of country which may be induced under favorable circumstances to draw a supply of fertilizers from the depots, be as large as possible, and with the further view that these fertilizing boons from the towns and cities may penetrate to and enrich as far as possible those whose toil and labor contribute to the wants and necessities of the urban populations. But even if circumstances should demand the removal by horse and cart, yet the necessity will still exist for locating the dumping places so near to either railroads or navigable streams so that collateral tracks may be constructed without much cost either of construction or after working. The poudrette can be readily removed to the city in sacks or barrels and stored in warehouses for sale, but the composts cannot be so treated—those, from their crude nature, must be shipped or hauled direct to the farmers and gardeners. The ground, in quantity, should be sufficient for all present and future purposes, and having a light backward declivity, it should be inclosed by a high board fence, and containing, besides long sheds for the reception for coal and other ashes, stowage-room for sifted ash, poudrette, old coal, old bones and rags, boots and shoes, and implements; also, two rows of night-soil tanks, capable of holding each at least twenty-three thousand gallons; large drying floors; below the tanks a number of compost pits; a small house for the protection of the superintendent by day and the watchman by night; a pump to furnish water for man and beast, and, if necessary, feeding troughs for horses, and lastly, the required supply of forks, shovels, sieves, wheelbarrows, and scrapers; two or three horses and carts will also be wanted to haul materials from one locality to another.

The above is a faithful description of the mode of constructing and manner of furnishing the Baltimore dumps, and I have given them in detail because I advised their construction and equipment, and are, therefore, whether good or bad, the embodiment of my own ideas in this relation, and I will now further, from the same cause and for the same reason, describe the manner of handling and treating the refuse matter after reception within these depots. The ashes are dumped under the sheds, and then separated by the process of sifting from the coal, bones, rags, and other matters, and the vegetable and animal offal from houses into the compost pits for after treatment. The night-soil is dumped or pumped from the wagon-tanks into the first or upper row of tanks, after passing through a grating fixed in front thereof to separate and detain from the ordure all stones, bricks, sticks, hoop-skirts, and old clothes. As the contents of privy vaults contain, as a general thing, a larger amount of urinous than solid matter, the former rises to the surface, and when the upper tank is full, this supernatant liquor is decanted through long troughs into the compost pits containing the vegetable and animal offal before referred to, and a percentage of sifted coal ash added to act as an absorbent and deodorant. The filling from the carts and the decanting is carried forward until the first tank is full of solid, or rather semi-solid matter. This mass or residuum is then allowed to pass through a flood-gate into the second row of tanks, where sifted coal-ash is added, which acts immediately as an absorbent and deodorant. Indeed, practical experience and observation have fully demonstrated that two thousand pounds of sifted coal-ash will, in fifteen minutes, completely deodorize six hundred gallons of manure. The amount of sifted ash now ordered to be added to the ordure for the making of poudrette is two parts of the latter to one of the former, or one of ash to two of night-soil, though, for the purposes of greater strength and concentration for transportation purposes, one part of sifted coal-ash may be added to three or four parts of night-soil, which makes a beautiful dry poudrette, and will, I doubt not, prove quite equal in its fertilizing qualities to the best guano, and far superior to many of the fertilizing agents now sold in the markets for from $40 to $60 the ton. The mixture thus made in the second row of tanks is, after deodorization, thrown upon the drying floor about three inches deep, which, if the weather be favorable, will dry in a few hours. The mass is then removed and thrown out upon a heap; a process of heating takes place, in which the great and small lumps or clods that were formed upon the drying-floor fall or crumble into powder. The whole is then run through a sieve or screen, and is the fine or double-refined poudrette—according to the capacity of the sieve—which is sold by the Corporation of Baltimore for from $15 to $20 the ton, and its popularity is I am informed, being well established with the farmers and gardeners who have used it upon their lands. This poudrette, thus made from no other materials than the raw contents of privies and coal-ash, is a fine, dry, inodorous powder, which might, with great propriety, be exhibited in a parlor filled with ladies and gentlemen of the most refined character. Composed of three parts of night-manure to one of coal ash, and upon examination it will be seen how perfectly the ammonia is fixed, and how thorough and complete has been to the deodorization. The compost made from the kitchen offal, a portion of sifted ash and the supernatant liquor from the manure tanks, is sold by the cart load of forty cubic feet, or thirty bushels, at seventy-five cents, but it is an exceedingly rich manure, as can well be understood from its miscellaneous or heterogeneous character, being composed of rich vegetable and animal matters. This manure is the most fertile of all the fertilizing agents, and has, doubtless, a far greater monied value, and which will probably be yet realized, when the authorities shall have connected the dumps with the railroads that pass near them, so that the far distant fields and gardens can be allowed, upon reasonable conditions, to partake of or share in this ocean of marrow and fatness. The old rags and bones are separated as before stated, from the ashes and also from the kitchen offal and night-soil and sold, considerable revenue being derived therefrom; and the old boots and shoes can, I understand, be reduced to powder by the process of burning and sold for the case hardening of iron, the old coal either sold for reburning or for the making of roads; so it will be seen that the utilization of everything collected has been provided for, save the old pans and kettles, and I do not despair even of these. It may be, that ere long, some branch of business will require them for some useful purpose.

It has been stated that coal-ashes possess no agricultural or fertilizing value whatever, but such is evidently not the case, for besides the trace of wood-ash that they contain, which yield alkaline salts, they have in themselves properties, chemical and mechanical, which the soil requires, and I have seen, in our Baltimore dumping grounds, splendid tomatoes, pumpkins, citrons and tobacco growing from a bed of pure coal-ash and cinders. A sample of the Baltimore city poudrette was submitted to Professor Leibig for analysis, composed of one part of ash to one of night-soil, and it was declared to have a value of $15 per ton of 2000 pounds, when viewed in the light of the report of the United States Commission of Agriculture at Washington, and as compared with the double-refined poudrette of the Lodi Manufacturing Company of New York, an article which, it is said, finds a ready sale at $25 per ton. If, therefore, this Baltimore poudrette of one to one has such a value, what will be the value of a poudrette made of from say four of human ordure to one of ash? The answer will probably prove it to be quite equal to the best guanos. The analysis of Professor Leibig exhibits the constituents to be ammonia, phosphoric acid, bone-phosphate of lime, alkaline salts, and lime, all of which are important and even necessary in the growth of crops.

I have made no special reference to the utilization of the scrapings and sweepings of streets, because these generally find a ready sale. They, however, can be made of greater value by admixture with the compost matters, as the supernatant liquor from the night-soil tanks is quite sufficient for complete saturation, even after these shall be added.

I have also not referred to the plan of utilization by irrigation as practiced in some parts of England and Scotland, through the instrumentality of ditches, pipes and jets. This plan comprehends the utilization in the form of liquid manure or sewer water, in which the kitchen offal and other matters are held in solution, and suspension. This mode of applying refuse matters to useful purposes admits of the discharge of refuse matters into drains and sewers for collection at the mouths of the latter, but I apprehend it could not be availed of to any extent in this country. I, therefore, even if it were compatible with a well regulated sanitary system, dismiss it as being impracticable, at this time at least.

4

NATURE, ART, AND URBANITY

Garden and Forest
SELECTED ARTICLES AND EDITORIALS, 1888-1896

The first issue of Garden and Forest *appeared in February 1888. As its first page announced, it was a journal of "Horticulture, Landscape Art, and Forestry." Initiated by Charles Sprague Sargent (1841-1927) of Boston and edited by William A. Stiles (1837-1897) of New York, the magazine quickly established itself as the voice of the well-educated urban dweller on environmental matters. It was an exceptionally well-written manual for the home gardener, a vigorous campaigner for the scientific management of forests and the preservation of historic sites, a defender of city and national parks, and an earnest tutor in landscape planning. In its pages appeared the writing of Olmsted, Fernow, Pinchot, and Sargent as well as Charles Eliot, Jr., who initiated Massachusetts' Trustees of Public Reservations and Boston's regional park system, and Mrs. Schuyler van Rensselaer, a popular authority on architecture and garden design. The following editorials and articles represent, in a rough composite, the environmental aesthetic propounded by the magazine as a guide to American taste. Their central theme is the necessary stance of the urbane, discriminating artist toward natural materials—his comfortable adjustment of nature to the requirements of a civilized sensibility. Carried beyond the boundaries of the estate or park, this aesthetic became the directing principle for creating the "garden city," which, especially among the upper middle class in America, was a diffuse but fertile environmental ideal: to extend nature into the city and the city into nature.*

A. LANDSCAPE GARDENING

Mrs. Schuyler van Rensselaer, March 28, 1888

When we speak of "natural scenes" we are apt to mean, illogically, all those which have not been modified by the conscious action of art as art. We recognize a park landscape as non-natural; but those rural landscapes in cultivated countries from which the designer of a park

SOURCE. Articles and editorials from Garden and Forest, 1888–1896.

gets his best inspirations—these, too, are non-natural. "If in the idea of a natural state," says an old English writer, "we include ground and wood and water, no spot in this island can be said to be in a state of nature. . . . Wherever cultivation has set its foot—wherever the plow and spade have laid fallow the soil—nature is become extinct."

Extinct, of course, is too strong a word if we take it in its full significance. But it is not too strong if we understand it as referring to those things which are most important to the landscape gardener: the compositions, the broad general pictures, of nature, have become extinct in all thickly settled countries. The effects we see may not be artistic effects—may not have resulted from a conscious effort after beauty; but they are none the less artificial effects. They do not show us what nature wants to do or can do—only what man and nature have chanced to do together. When English artists became dissatisfied with the formal, architectural gardening of the seventeenth century, they fondly imagined that they were learning from nature how to produce those effects of rural freedom, of idyllic repose, of seemingly unstudied beauty, grace and charm, which were their new desire. But, in reality, they were learning from the face of a country which for centuries had been carefully moulded, tended and put to use by man. In some of its parts, of course, the effects of man's presence were comparatively inconspicuous. But of most parts it could be said that for ages not a stream or tree or blade of grass had existed except in answer to his efforts, or, at least, in consequence of his permission; and it was these parts and not the wilder ones which gave most assistance to the artist. An instinctive love for beauty had doubtless often tried to express itself in the neighborhood of dwellings, absent though the idea of art had been from the mind of their inhabitants; nature herself is so good an artist that even in her bondage she had worked admirably and with more suavity and gentleness than in her free estate; and the mere utilitarian treatment of the land had also accidentally given rise to happily suggestive features. Take, for example, the lawn, which is so essential a feature of almost every artistic design in landscape. It is not true to say, as often has been said, that nature never suggests a lawn. But it is true to say that she did not suggest it to those English gardeners who developed it so beautifully. They must have been inspired by the artificially formed meadowlands and glades of the England of their time.

But all the semi-natural, semi-artificial beauty of England would not have taught them how to make beautiful parks and gardens had they not been taught as well by their own imagination. What they wanted to create were landscapes which should charm from all points of view and should bear close as well as distant examination; and, moreover, landscapes which might fitly surround the habitations of man and accommodate his very various needs and pleasures. Such landscapes we can no more expect to find in nature—even in cultivated, semi-artificial nature—than landscapes painted upon canvas. That is, while we can imagine a natural spot which would be an appropriate setting for a hunter's lodge or a hermit's cell, we can imagine none which would appropriately encircle a palace, a mansion, or even a modest home for a man with civilized habits and tastes. Every step in civilization is a step away from that wild estate which alone is really nature; and the further away we get from it, the more imagination is needed to bring the elements of existence which nature still supplies into harmony with those which man has developed. The simplest house in the most rustic situation needs, at least, that a path shall be cut to its door; and to do so much as cut a path in the most pleasing possible way needs a certain amount of imagination, of art. How much more, then, is imagination needed in such a task as the laying-out of a great estate where subordinate buildings are to be grouped around the chief one, and all are to be accommodated to the main unalterable natural features of the scene, where a hundred minor natural features are to be harmoniously disposed, where convenient courses for feet and wheels are to be provided in every direction, where gardens and orchards are to be supplied, where water is to be made at once useful and ornamental, and where every plant, whether great or small, must be beautiful at least in the sense of helping the beauty of the general effect? The stronger the desire to make so artificial an aggregate of features look as though nature might have designed it, the more intimate must be the artist's sympathy with the aims and processes of nature and the keener his eye for the special opportunities of the site; but also the stronger must be his imaginative power, the firmer his grasp of the principles and processes of his art.

B. THE BEAUTIFUL IN THE SURROUNDINGS OF LIFE

Editorial, November 9, 1892

[Philip] Hamerton has well defined the word "landscape" as meaning "the visible material world, or all that can be seen on the surface of the earth by a man who is himself upon that surface." Wild landscape—the scenery of the natural world—possesses infinite interest and charm for those of us who live caged in towns and cramped in houses, and we greatly enjoy both traveling in search of it and reading the praise of it. No age of the world has ever brought forth so many delightful books about the woods, the mountains and the seashore. The beauty of natural scenery stirs us as does the finest music. As [John Addington] Symonds has noted, "there is a profound sympathy between music and fine scenery; they both affect us in the same way, waking strong but undefined emotions which express themselves in 'idle tears' or evoke thoughts which lie, as Wordsworth said, 'too deep for tears' beyond the reach of any words." It seems as if our extreme delight in the beauty of wild landscape, tending, as it seemingly does, "to destroy habits of clear thinking and to sentimentalize the mind," had caused us to overlook for the time the supreme importance of that part of landscape which is necessarily not wild—the landscape of our daily lives—the humanized scenery of the earth. This prevalent carelessness concerning the landscapes of every-day life is something remarkable. Here are our rich men paying enormous sums for painted landscapes to be hung in their houses while they permit the real landscape about them to become ugly in the extreme. Here are poorer people spending liberally for journeys in search of the picturesque while what might be the picturesqueness of their own neighborhood is unperceived or destroyed.

But there are signs that a better day is coming. Some parts of our great America are even now beginning to stir with eager desire for beauty. It is true, the desire is unformed, and our work is too often based upon mistaken conceptions of that beauty which is our hope, and yet we must be thankful when the desire appears among us, for it is something which distinctly ennobles the life of every man and nation in whose heart it is born. Possessed by it, we are compelled to strive and strive again to find "the secret of the beautiful," the foundation upon which beauty is built, the nature of that growth of which beauty is the flower. We shall make our mistakes like other men. We shall attempt to attain our heart's desire by forbidden and impossible ways. We shall probably fell noble forest-trees to make room for brilliant exotics. Perhaps we shall curve our roads because we think we like curves, or build our houses according to some pattern we admired in a foreign land. But, even so, there is hope for us. We shall learn in the end. And, meanwhile, so rash and willful and so generally unsuccessful are we in all this field of work that it may be worth while to look back for a moment over the long story of the evolution of landscape in the hope that we may find therein that key to the secret of the really beautiful which we seek.

Not to name others, [John] Ruskin, in his early essay on the Poetry of Architecture, has been before us here. He finds man in primitive ages living precariously upon wild nature, and causing little or no change in the appearance of the wilderness around him. When, at last, he is forced to increase his food supply, he takes some wild thing like maize and plants it in the glades of the forest, and stores the crop in granaries set up on stakes. When he desires to shelter himself, he contrives frail tents like the Bedouins or the Red Indians, or he walls the mouths of cañon caves, or he builds earthern pueblos hardly to be distinguished from the arid ground on which they stand. As he comes to cultivate broad stretches of the earth, he works marked changes in scenery. He fells the woods and marks off fields and draws lines of roads across the country. He plants avenues and orchards, he makes gardens and vineyards, he builds farmsteads of as many types as there are differing climates and differing social circumstances, he builds villages and cities, he rears palaces and temples, doing all to meet his needs and to express his life; and so long as he is sincere and straight-forward in his work, mother Nature stands ready to adopt it as her own, and to make of it landscape rich in meaning and pathos such as no primitive wilderness can show.

Look for a moment upon a typical valley of the interior of our own New England. We are standing upon the eastern wall of upland. The village, with a mill or two and a church or two, lies below us at the mouth of a gap in the northern hills. Southward the valley broadens to contain a fresh green intervale. Opposite us the western wall of the valley is an irregular steep slope of rising woods, with numerous upland farms scattered along the more level heights above. The central intervale, the flanking woods, the village gathered at the valley's head—the whole scene before us possesses unity and beauty to a degree which interests us at once. And how was this delightful general effect produced? Simply by intelligent obedience to the requirements of human life in this valley. The village grew what it is for the sake of nearness to the great water-power which rushes from the gap in the hills. The intervale was cleared and smoothed for raising perfect hay. The steep side hills have been maintained in woods because they are too steep for agriculture, and because, if they were cleared of trees, their sands and gravels would wash down upon the fertile land of the intervale. Similarly upon the upland farms, the greenery along even the tiniest brooks has been preserved in order to obviate that wasteful washing away of soil which results from carrying plowing to the edges of the water-courses. Throughout the landscape before us it is most interesting to note how beauty has resulted from the exercise of common sense and intelligence. The every-day forces of convenience, use and true economy have here conspired with nature to produce beauty, and this beauty is of a very different and much more satisfying kind than that which tries to found itself on mere caprice or fashion.

If, now, we search the world over, do we not find the same truth everywhere? Let us call to mind some of the loveliest of earthly scenes. The red farmstead among the Firs of Sweden, the Ilex-trees and the white villas of the steep bank of Como, the English deer-park and its stately mansion, the towered village of the Italian hills, the broad green and the great elms of our own Hadley or Deerfield. The beauty of these memorable humanized landscapes is nothing extraneous; it is not something added to the landscape after the main lines have been laid down; it springs directly from the fact that these fields, trees, ways and buildings have been arranged first with reference to the needs, uses and enjoyments of real life in their respective lands and climates, and it is their perfect conformity to these principles which constitutes the essence of the beauty we admire. Not by display of knowledge of the styles of architecture and gardening; not by gathering in one place all the trees of the earth; not by imitating the beautiful features of the scenery of foreign lands and climates; not by copying wild nature in places which are not wild; not even by attempting to obey the laws of landscape-painting, will beauty ever be won to dwell among us in the surroundings of modern life. "All that would be fair must be fit." There is no other way to win the beauty we desire.

This truth being accepted, what shall we of this too self-conscious age say to our gardener and our builder when we set out to make "a place of our own"? To the first it must be: Lay out no road or path which is not the most convenient possible in the circumstances. Lay out nothing for mere flourish, but all for use or rational enjoyment. Fell and plant and choose the kinds of plants for good reasons only. In all you do, have constant reference to the general scheme of the whole place.

To the builder we say: plan for convenience first and always. Take advantage of every peculiarity of the purpose, the site and the exposure of the building. Let the exterior of the building faithfully represent the interior, and shape it not as a thing apart, but as the central object in a larger design. In placing doors which involve paths; in arranging drying-yards, kitchen-courts, piazzas and terraces; in all you do, have constant reference to the general scheme of the whole place.

And who shall conceive and insist upon this general landscape scheme in the perfecting of which the artist gardener and the artist builder are to play their respective parts? In these days it is seldom that the need of such a broadly inclusive scheme is realized even by the artists who have part in the work, much less by the managing owner; and yet the time is coming when the landscape-architect, whose province is just this arranging of the building and its surroundings to form one landscape, will be welcomed alike by owner, builder and gardener as the man who will cause the work of each to count for beauty much more effectively than it otherwise can. When this day comes, and either the owner, the gardener, the builder or the professional specialist is looked to as the deviser of a general landscape design based on purpose and fitness, and not upon caprice; then, again, there will be hope of finding the really beautiful in the surroundings of daily life.

C. ART AND NATURE

Editorial, July 4, 1894

We spoke last week of the way in which nature's suggestions are often disregarded in the treatment of our private pleasure-grounds, when a respect for these suggestions would furnish an endless diversity of beautiful effects instead of the monotonous repetition of lawns, flower-beds and popular plants, all arranged after one fashion and without any relation to the original features of any given site. One reason for this unfortunate state of things may be found in the fact that most people seem to feel that there is an eternal opposition between the terms nature and art, and between the qualities they typify as appealing to our admiration and love. Of course, these terms are, in a sense, properly used in contrast. The highest work of art lacks certain qualities which delight the eye and kindle the imagination in a work of nature; and, on the other hand, the most impressive natural object lacks that expression of human emotion and intelligence, that evidence of difficulties overcome and ideals conceived and achieved, which contribute so powerfully to the interest and charm of a successful work of art. The artist cannot really imitate nature any more than nature can copy art; and until this fact is recognized we cannot appreciate the peculiar charm of either natural or artistic beauty. But nature and art are constantly conceived of as hostile to each other in a more radical way than this. Many people say, "We are lovers of nature, and, therefore, we find those things most beautiful which the hand of man has not touched, or in which the traces of his hand are least obtrusive." These people think that a painter should copy as closely as possible some bit of nature, changing nothing, omitting nothing, emphasizing nothing, but trying to be as accurately photographic as possible, and they resent as an impertinence to themselves and an insult to nature any suggestion of the artist that he saw more in the scene before him than they might, or saw it differently, or that he wished to press upon their attention some features more strongly than others. They wish him to be a literal translator, while the true artist is an interpreter who transmutes and perhaps glorifies a scene by infusing into it some of the poetry which inspires him. These same lovers of nature insist on a slavishly accurate reproduction of nature by the landscape-gardener and deny his right to use the transforming power of his imagination in constructing his scenery.

On the other hand, many people say, "We are lovers of art, and, therefore, the less an artist shows dependence upon nature, the better he pleases us"; or, if they do not deliberately say this, they unconsciously act upon it. They are willing that a painter shall dispense with good drawing, natural schemes of color, and logical schemes of light and shade, if by some striking result he can convince them that he has "originality"; and they call his products "artistic" just in proportion as they diverge most palpably from the models offered by the natural world. Canons of taste like this in the domain of gardening have controlled the design of our country places more frequently than those of the opposite extreme, for we have reached a stage of mental development when we all wish to be considered artistic; and too many of us like the bold display of expenditure for its own sake, and "artistic" pleasure-grounds give a better chance for this display than pleasure-grounds adapted more closely to the suggestion of nature.

This belief, that to be artistic we must show little regard for nature, is seen in our excessive love for trees, shrubs and flowers which are novel or particularly showy or eccentric in shape or color, and also in the invention of novel forms and color combinations for the almost invariably ugly clipped flower-bed. This radical mistake of thinking that what is artistic must be unnatural, or, at least, non-natural, has not yet led the American people to an overweening love for absolutely formal gardening; for the traditions of our English ancestry are strong, and we think we have a true preference for landscape-gardening. Our belief that we cannot be artistic without being unnatural is not self-confessed, as it was in France in the time of Louis Quatorze. Like many other beliefs in respect to art, it is a sort of groping desire for we know not exactly what. It would probably declare itself to be a desire to blend the beauties of nature and of art, which is precisely what it ought to be; but when analyzed by its results it shows very clearly as a desire to be "artistic" in defiance of nature. And it has become as conventional in its manifestations as it is unintelligent in the crude feeling upon which these are based.

Not even the formal gardens of the seventeenth century were more alike in essence and in treatment than are most of our American pleasure-grounds. This one fact alone should show their owners that they are on a wrong track; for the key-note of landscape-gardening, if the term means anything at all, must be perpetual variety between one work and another. No two natural landscapes are alike, and within a very few miles we always find many which are surprisingly unlike in radical character and general effect as well as in details. Therefore, an art which is based upon the study of nature cannot be going right when its products all bear a close family likeness to each other, and this not only as regards a single stretch of country-side, but as regards regions that lie far apart and are wholly different in climate, geological conformation and native vegetation. Expedients which are right for one place on the island of Mount Desert would most likely not be quite right for a neighboring place; and certainly they would not be right for one on the banks of the Hudson, in the mountains of North Carolina, on a stretch of western prairie or the coasts of the Pacific Ocean. Yet far and wide we find the same ideals, the same expedients; and the greater the natural beauty of the site the more apt are these ideals and expedients to be wrong. For the essence of all natural beauty is distinctness of character; and the more individual this character is, the more charming we are apt to find it, while the more certainly it is ruined by the unintelligent application of conventional and stereotyped methods of "improvement."

The true scheme for an artist in any branch is to follow out nature's ideals and suggestions, showing his own individuality and his own creative imagination by intensifying the character she presents—ennobling, purifying, glorifying her suggestions. The artist on canvas may choose what he wishes to do at any given time and place, provided that, once his theme is selected, he keeps it clearly in mind and transgresses no essential truth in explaining it. But the artist in landscape must consent, at any given place, to do what nature then and there prescribes, or, at least, permits. To try to wipe out her work is futile; to try to conceal its character and supply a new one can result merely in an abortion which is admirable neither to the genuine lover of Nature nor the genuine lover of art. This is true even when we think of a real artist at work; and if we think how much more true it must be when ignorant owners, assisted by men who may grow plants well, but have no knowledge whatever of art, strive to do artists' work, then we can comprehend why so few American country places, large or small, give any pleasure to intelligent observers. When we really understand in what points art stands in contrast to nature, and in how far it must rest upon nature and get its inspiration from her, then we shall realize that lawns and flower-beds are appropriate, and therefore artistic, in some situations, absolutely formal gardens in others, and almost absolute wildness in others; and that between these types, as within each of them, an infinite number of beautiful gardening schemes may be evolved—infinite because the beauty of nature varies perpetually—and if we search over the whole surface of our wide and fruitful land we can find no scene which is not distinct from every other in its essence, its character and its expression.

D. THE PRESERVATION OF NATURAL BEAUTY

Editorial, August 19, 1896

It is now more than five years since the body known as the Trustees of Public Reservation was incorporated under an act of the Legislature of Massachusetts, for the purpose of preserving tracts of land which were distinguished for their natural beauty or for their historic association. This was the first organization of the kind ever established, so far as we know, and it seemed to us then, as it does yet, a proof of more than ordinary enlightenment and public spirit in the society out of which it grew. We expressed the hope then that this might become a settled policy throughout the country, for it certainly is not too much to expect that a community of civilized people would take upon themselves the duty of preserving and transmitting to their children the treasures of beauty which they have inherited, or of protecting from defacement and ruin places made memorable by patriotic sacrifices and noble deeds and preserving them for the inspiration of their descendants. New York has enacted a similar law, and steps have been taken for saving some of our revolutionary battlefields and other noteworthy places from desecration. The movement for saving the Palisades in New Jersey is the outcome of a similar sentiment, and so is the rescue and devotion to public use of that magnificent river gorge known as the Dalles of the St. Croix, between the states of Minnesota and Wisconsin. The acquisition of Niagara by the state of New York and of Valley Forge by Pennsylvania are noteworthy results of the same feeling.

It was the example of Massachusetts which suggested an article in *The Spectator*, of London, in which it was sharply pointed out that it was quite as important for a nation to secure sites of great natural beauty as it was to buy fine pictures. And since Snowdon had already been in the market, and the waterfall of Lodore was advertised for sale, it was urged that a national trust for places of historic interest or natural beauty was a necessity. Such a trust was therefore organized, and the trustees were made up of men eminent in letters and in public life. In a recent number of *The Spectator*, Miss Octavia Hill, who was one of the original incorporators of the trust, writes that the wild heathy promontory known as Barras Head, one of the headlands which enclose King Arthur's Cove at Tintagel, could be secured for a comparatively small sum; and, no doubt, there are enough people interested in the Arthurian legends and the poetry that has gathered about them, to rescue this delightful spot and dedicate it to public use forever. In the same letter it is stated that a lovely bit of old English architecture, a clergy-house built before the Reformation, in a Sussex village, had been acquired as an inheritance from the middle ages. It is encouraging to see good work like that in Massachusetts bearing fruit across the sea, and we are sure that men and women of public spirit, who urge a policy of this sort upon the general government and the government of the separate states, will minister to some of the noblest and purest emotions that animate the human soul, while they will accomplish a work which is eminently practical, even from the sordid dollar-and-cent point of view, and add a distinct pecuniary value to all property which surrounds these places.

The setting apart of the great forest reservations of the west by the general government is, of course, a different matter. But the establishment of Yellowstone Park and the acquisition of the great battle-fields of the Rebellion are justified only by a sentiment that the places which are remarkable for the sublimity and beauty of their natural features, or which have been consecrated by heroic struggles for principle, are, or ought to be, possessions of the people as a whole. But if the people, speaking through their representatives, have asserted their rights in such conspicuous instances, they certainly must feel that their unwritten rights are often invaded by private persons and corporations when they find the scenery which they have enjoyed all their lives needlessly defaced. In some cases laws have been enacted to protect them in this matter. In this city the obtrusive ugliness of signs and advertisements within a certain distance from park territory can be mitigated by the action of the Park Board, but all over the country, landscapes are blotted out by billboards and made hideous by the paint pot of the advertiser, and there is no redress against the outrage. If a private citizen is willing to devote his property to such use he can violate the sensibilities of his neighbors and of all who travel on the highway with impunity. Since there is law against offensive smells and useless noises, there seems to be no injustice in compelling property owners to respect that love for beauty which, to some degree, is implanted in the nature of every one. A loathsome sight is certainly as disagreeable as a foul smell.

What is needed primarily is not, however, law, but a sensitive public conscience which will impel every citizen to respect the feelings of his neighbors. In a truly enlightened community a corporation which was building a railroad would not needlessly gash and scar the landscape. They would no sooner think of destroying the beauties which are the inheritance of all than they would of recklessly destroying property, for which they would be held in pecuniary damages. We can remember a white oak tree which had stood beside an old highway in New Jersey for generations. It was a stately tree before the war of the Revolution. It was an essential feature in a beautiful prospect, and it had been admired and reverenced by thousands who traveled on that road until they felt a personal interest and proprietorship in it. One day the owner of the abutting land cut down this tree for apparently no reason whatever, for it did no injury to the land, and the log was left to rot by the wayside, but every one who has passed the stump since that day feels a sense of bereavement. A noteworthy landmark of the country is obliterated. The whole place is distinctly less interesting, and will be forever.

The sum of the whole matter is that while the established boards of trustees for acquiring public reservations mark an advance in public sentiment, and while these organizations are already doing a noble work and deserve the fullest sympathy and most substantial aid, what we need still more is a wider appreciation of and love for natural beauty. The people who take a genuine delight in natural scenery and are conscious of its soothing influence are not likely to deface or destroy it. Besides this they can realize that others have rights in the general beauty of the land in which they live, and they can be persuaded to respect those rights. Neither you nor I may have a legal property right in Niagara or the field of Gettysburg, but every American would feel that he was robbed of something to which he had a moral right if either of these places were turned over to sordid use. The sublimity, the poetry, the inspiration of places like these are a common heritage. These influences should be guarded as jealously as any other common right.

E. THE NECESSITY OF PLANNING

Charles Eliot, Jr., August 26, 1896

The daily work of the architect and the landscape-architect is popularly supposed to consist in ornamenting lands and buildings so as to make them appear beautiful. Rooms may be inconveniently and awkwardly shaped, but they can be "beautified" by rich furniture and upholstery. Whole buildings may be irrationally planned, but they may still be made "artistic" by means of mouldings, carvings and mosaic. House grounds and college grounds, private gardens and public parks may be senselessly, as well as ineffectively, arranged, but they may still be glorified by yellow and purple leafage. In short, "The world is still deceived with ornament."

On the other hand, although all seekers for the truth concerning beauty have discerned elements which defy analysis, such special students have nevertheless deduced from the visible and historical facts a whole series of fixed principles, which are quite as surely established as any of the other so-called laws of nature. Among these perhaps the most important is this, that "in all the arts which serve the use, convenience or comfort of man, from gardening and building down to the designing of the humblest utensil which it is desired to make beautiful, utility and fitness for intended purpose must be first considered." It is to be remembered that this is not theory but law. As a matter of fact and experience satisfying beauty is not won unless the law of nature is obeyed.

That faithful and well-reasoned planning for the accomplishment of purpose is necessary to the success of the work of architects of buildings is now generally understood. "A plan" is a skillful combination of convenience with effectiveness of arrangement. "A design" is made up of plan, construction and outward appearance, and by no means consists of the latter only. Indeed, the external aspect of a structure depends directly on the mode of construction, the construction depends, in turn, on the plan, and the plan on the purpose in view, with the result that the whole appearance of the building inevitably and naturally expresses this purpose.

If it be true that expression, character, and even beauty are thus most surely won, in the case of buildings, by keeping decoration subsidiary and designing with purpose in view from the start, it is equally true of all the wide field of architecture, using the word in its broadest imaginable sense. "Architecture, a great subject, truly," says William Morris, "for it embraces the consideration of the whole of the external surroundings of the life of man; we cannot escape from it if we would, for it means the moulding and altering to human needs of the very face of the earth itself." A bushy pasture or a smooth green field in forest-clad New England is as truly a product of human handiwork as a green meadow in treeless and dusty Utah, yet each is beautiful, and neither owes a particle of its beauty to decoration. The English deer-park, with its broad-spreading trees, or the church-yard, with its ancient stones and yews, the typical Yankee farm with its low buildings and great elms, or the live oaks and quaint structures of the plantations of Louisiana, these and all similarly interesting landscapes are interesting, not because they have been decorated, but because they are strongly characterized and highly expressive. Their moving beauty is the natural product of straightforward work for the adaptation of land and landscape to human needs and uses.

Believing these things, it will be impossible for us, when a tract of land is newly dedicated to some special purpose, be it that of a suburban lot, a railroad-station yard, a new village, a country-seat or a public park, to stand by and see it thoughtlessly laid out and then, perhaps, turned over to the decorators. We shall insist on premeditation and careful fundamental planning, knowing that therein lies the best, if not the only, hope of happy results. Once possessed of faith in that law of nature in accordance with which beauty springs from fitness, we shall be ready to agree that, when purpose is served, formal gardens, rectilinear avenues and courts of honor are not only permitted, but commanded. On the other hand, we shall be equally strenuous in demanding studied planning and adaptation to environment and purpose in the laying out of whatever work may need to be done to make the wildest place of private or public resort accessible and enjoyable. Positive injury to the landscape of such places can be avoided only by painstaking, while the available resources of scenery can be economized only by careful devising. So with the whole range of problems which lie between these extremes. No work of man is ever successfully accomplished without taking thought beforehand; in other words, without planning.

And, strange as it may appear, opposition to such planning for effective results will not, in practice, be found to come from those who attempt decoration only because they know not how else to attain to the beautiful. Just as the literary class in China ruinously opposes change of any kind, so there is with us a comparatively small, but influential, body of refined persons, far too well educated to be "deceived by ornament," who most unfortunately, though unintentionally, assist in the triumphs of ugliness by blindly opposing all attempts to adapt land and landscape to changed or new requirements. Enjoying the pleasanter scenery of their surroundings as it exists—certain shady roads, or some lingering fields or farm-lands—these estimable people talk of "letting nature alone" or "keeping nature natural," as if such a thing were possible in a world which was made for man. No, the "moulding and altering" of the earth goes forward of necessity, and if those who ought to be leaders will not help to guide the work aright, the work will surely be done badly; as it is, in fact, done badly in the neighborhood of all our great towns. To refuse to exercise foresight and to adapt to purpose in due season, is simply to court disaster. Instead of hanging back, it ought to be the pride and pleasure of these very people to see to it that proper plans are seasonably laid for the widening of roads so that fine trees shall not be sacrificed, to see to it that electric-car tracks shall be placed only in suitably selected and specially arranged streets, that public reservations of one type or another shall be provided in accordance with some consistent general scheme, and that such reservations shall be saved from both decorative and haphazard development by the early adoption of rational and comprehensive plans. There is needed a little less selfish contentment in the doomed landscape of the present, a sharper sense of responsibility to the future and a living faith in that law of God, in obedience to which everything which is well adapted to use and purpose is sure to be interesting and expressive, and if not beautiful, at least on the way to be.

5

THE REFORMATION OF
THE CITY DWELLER AND HIS HABITAT

Charles W. Eliot
THE NEED OF CONSERVING THE BEAUTY
AND FREEDOM OF NATURE IN MODERN LIFE

*The ruling interests of his life restricted the role the elder Charles Eliot
(1834–1926) could take in environmental reforms. From 1869 to 1909 he was
president of Harvard, the first scientist to be elected to the post; during his
tenure so many important changes were effected that he remains the most
important college administrator in the history of American higher education.
Much of the residue of his energies went into the problems of labor and
industrial relations. Still, he served briefly as president of the National Conservation Congress, and through his son Charles Eliot, Jr., he contributed to
landscape architecture and park development. In this short essay he concisely
articulated several dominant themes of the period in urban planning. Here in
essence is the "garden city" idea—decentralized, low-density housing, with
private gardens, parks, and nature reserves near at hand. Here also is made
apparent the urban agitation for national parks—Mount Desert Island
became Acadia National Park in 1916—which were viewed by the city as
more far-flung and less commodious extensions of Olmsted's Central Park
and the younger Eliot's Middlesex Fells Reservation. In addition Eliot reveals
the moral concern generated by a rapidly industrializing society; perhaps the
environmental planner could become an agent for purging the life of the
factory worker of its "degraded" and "poisonous" tendencies.*

The past hundred years have supplied civilized mankind with a complete demonstration that the evils which attend the growth of modern
cities and the factory system are too great for the human body to
endure; yet these evils are the consequences, or results, of nineteenth-
century civilization, and particularly of that form of liberty which the

SOURCE. Charles W. Eliot, "The Need of Conserving the Beauty and Freedom
of Nature in Modern Life," *The National Geographic Magazine*, July 1914.

first half of the century developed—individualism. Within the last 40 years a different form of liberty, the liberty of association and collective action, has begun to check some of the evils fostered by individualism, and so to improve the human environment.

The sources of the evils which afflict the population massed in cities are partly physical and partly mental or moral. The collective energies of society are now actively directed to the amelioration of bad physical conditions, and considerable improvements in this respect have already been made; and more are in sight. The study, even, of remedies for wrong mental and moral conditions has hardly begun; yet these are the fundamental evils which must be eradicated, if improved physical conditions are to produce their desired effects.

It is therefore a very practical and urgent inquiry: What influences in the environment of civilized mankind make for mental health, for wholesome interests, for rational pleasures, and for exalting delight in the beauty, grace and splendor of nature?

By far the most important social study today is the study of the means of improving men's emotion and thought environment from earliest youth to age. These means are both negative and positive—on the one hand they must shut out poisonous excitements and injurious pleasures, on the other they must develop all wholesome mental interests and enjoyable activities of observation, memory, and imagination.

In order to cure the destructive evils of present urban life and the factory system, it will not be enough to restrict the vices, to diminish the pressure of poverty, to prevent destructive diseases, and prolong the average human life. The human environment must be not only negatively but positively improved; so that the whole people may have the opportunity to cultivate healthy tastes and interests, to acquire just ideals of pleasantness and beauty, and to learn the value toward tranquil happiness of that living with nature which city congestion has within a single generation made almost impossible for multitudes.

While the exclusion of bad influences needs to be unremitting, the good influences—fortunately for the crowded urban populations —need not all be incessantly in action. An occasional holiday in a city park or garden, a week-end in the country now and then, or a fortnight's vacation in summer may make deep and lasting mental impressions, and supply both children and adults with wholesome material to fill the mind and direct its energies for months and years.

Hence the importance of better city and suburban planning, of public reservations of all sorts in city and state, and of national parks and monuments. All these modes of public action tell not only on the physical well-being of both urban and rural populations, but on the mental training of children and on the cultivation in the whole population of thoroughly healthy spiritual interests and uplifting enjoyments, both individual and social.

The profession of landscape architecture is going to be—indeed, it already is—the most direct professional contributor to the improvement of the human environment in the twentieth century, because it is devoted not only to the improvement of housing and of town and city designing, but also to the creation, preservation, and enlargement of opportunities for human enjoyment of mountains and valleys, hills and plains, forests and flowers, ponds and water-courses, spring blossoms and autumn tints, and the wild life of birds and other animals in their natural haunts. These are the things that city dwellers need to have opportunities to see and enjoy; these are the things that serve as antidotes to the unwholesome excitements and tensions of modern city life; these are the delights which, by occupying the mind and satisfying the spirit, keep out degrading thoughts and foul desires.

That good environment can modify favorably the effects of heredity is as true of nations as of individuals. The vital question of modern life is how to feed the mental health and spiritual growth of multitudes. In the modern world life is tightly packed against life, and one life is interwoven with many others. Neither freedom of mind nor health of body can be secured in isolation; for both blessings the individual must hereafter be dependent on social or collective action.

The present evils of city life and the factory system—bad conditions which civilization has itself created—have developed their destructive forces in this country in spite of the schools and churches and of free political institutions, and in spite of many happy influences from art, poetry, music, and the drama. Clearly, society needs to develop a new and better environment for the general life—an environment favorable to both bodily and mental health and to the attainment of genuine happiness—not of mere momentary excitements, pleasures, and gratifications, but of solid contentment, and the lasting satisfactions of life enjoyed in quietness and peace. What are the means of compassing this end?

The readiest means is good planning of city, town, and landscape—first applied to areas still open, and then gradually to areas already occupied in undesirable ways. The new planning must take into account the interests of the whole community, as well as the interests of individual owners, the social or collective interest always prevailing.

The immediate objects to be sought are more light and air for dwellings, offices, shops, and factories, and thus a spreading out of cities; the transfer of factories to suburbs and to country sites along the lines of railway; the multiplication of playgrounds and open decorated areas, and above all the attachment of a piece of arable or garden ground to every family dwelling. Many of these results can certainly be attained; and indeed much work of this sort is already started in regulating the height of buildings, transferring factories and setting up new plants in smaller towns, enlarging school yards, and creating public parks and gardens.

The housing problem for mechanics and operatives has already been solved in a business way by the English Garden City. In cities already too compactly built and with too lofty structures the improvement of the human environment must await better understanding of life's needs or change of taste in populations now unwholesomely congested. With the diffusion of knowledge concerning healthy and happy conditions for family life and the industrial life of the laborious masses this reformation of our cities and manufacturing towns will surely come about, but in coming about it must take account of something more than water supplies, sewers, and street lights; it must take account of beauty and of all that brings cheerfulness and social happiness.

The collective force of the community must further supply the means of making rural and landscape pleasures occasionally accessible to city populations by means of parks and gardens which illustrate all forms of open-country beauty and permit the occasional enjoyment by city families or larger urban groups of the outdoor pleasures which woods, shrubberies, gardens, and broad fields can give. All city dwellers greatly need these occasional delights, and Americans more than any other people: for they have become accustomed to an indoor life, and have come to rely on electricity as a substitute for sunlight, and mechanical ventilation as an equivalent for fresh air. Even the richer sort of Americans are often content to live in houses in which at least one-third of the cubical contents cannot be used without artificial light the year round, and to occupy offices in which electricity has to reinforce sunlight during the greater part of the year.

The proper use of the natural materials for creating on public ground fine landscapes, gardens, and scenes of rural beauty involves an extensive study of these materials. The landscape architect must know how to use a near or distant prospect of hills and woods. He must know the trees, shrubs, and herbaceous plants valuable in landscape or in gardens, or along walks and drives where thousands of people daily pass. He must know all the native materials for creating scenes of beauty, and all the imported materials which have proved available in the climate of the reservation he plans. And in order that the landscape architect may have the opportunity to study these materials, society must furnish places where they may be assembled, appropriately used, and thoroughly tested.

In other words, the collective force of society should be used to provide and maintain living collections of these materials of landscape and garden beauty, where climate, soil, and scenery make it possible to assemble, cultivate, and exhibit them advantageously. The botanic gardens and arboretums which universities and governments maintain do not fully answer this purpose, although they contribute to it; because the lay-out of the botanical gardens and arboretums is made for a scientific purpose quite different from that which directs the thoughts of the landscape architect.

There is another source of keen enjoyment for city people which should be provided for when parks, gardens, and playgrounds are constructed for their pleasure, namely, the natural interest in animal life as well as vegetable life. Most men and nearly all women take a keen interest in bird life—in the migration, nesting, family life, and feeding habits of birds, both land birds and sea fowl. It is one of the advantages of suburban over city life that many varieties of birds can be seen and studied in the suburbs. The collective force of society, therefore, should be exerted to preserve all the species of birds which are profitable, not only for food and crop protection, but also for the stirring of human sympathy and delight in their colors, songs, and alert, sprightly ways. The provision of sanctuaries for birds, of closed spaces as well as closed seasons, is a highly expedient use of the collective protective force of society against individual destroyers of bird life.

The government of the United States has begun to use effectively its constitutional powers for improving the environment of the people by conserving broad scenes of extraordinary natural beauty and single beautiful or striking objects which, without the protection afforded them by government, might be lost to future generations. The national parks are reserved by act of Congress: the president, by executive order, may and does order the preservation of smaller areas or single objects under the title of national monuments. State legislatures have begun to provide state reservations, and have authorized municipalities, or special districts, to acquire both large and small parks. Chartered bodies of trustees have been authorized by state legislatures to acquire and hold considerable areas for perpetual public use.

On the beautiful island of Mount Desert, not far from the northeastern extremity of the Atlantic coast of the United States, there is at this moment opportunity for establishing a national monument of unique interest and large serviceableness. The island is the loftiest piece of land on the Atlantic coast of the United States, and has a sharply differentiated surface of hills and valleys, a climate midway between that of the neighboring lands and that of the surrounding sea, abundant water, and in favorable spots a highly productive soil, well suited for growing a wide variety of trees, flowering shrubs, and herbaceous plants belonging to the temperate and subarctic regions of the world.

Private initiative and enterprise have long since demonstrated the peculiar fitness of the Mount Desert climate and soils for horticultural and aboricultural uses, and leading botanists and garden experts have testified to the remarkable thriftiness of plants grown upon the island, as well as to the unusual beauty and rich coloring of their blooms.

A body of trustees, called the "Hancock County Trustees of Public Reservations," has already acquired the wooded slopes and rocky summits of many of the principal hills, and holds them for perpetual public enjoyment. Possession, too, has been secured by public-spirited private persons of considerable areas exceptionally fitted for the growth and exhibition of all varieties of trees, shrubs, and herbaceous plants which the landscape architect might use in developing all across the continent, in northern climates, parks and gardens for the enjoyment of city populations. Here, too, all the bird-food plants could be appropriately cultivated and bird sanctuaries provided. The cultivated tracts would have a noble background of rocky cliffs and lofty hills, and down the valleys and gorges visitors would look out from time to time over the near bays or the distant ocean. Here, in short, could be brought together under highly favorable conditions and in great variety the botanical and zoological materials of the landscape and garden designer.

If the government of the United States should set aside as a national monument a large area in this picturesque and unique island, it would help to consecrate for all time to the improvement of the human environment one of the most beautiful and interesting regions in the whole country; and in so doing it would take appropriate part in resisting and overcoming the destructive influences on modern civilization of urban life and the factory system.

The powers of the national government have thus far been exerted to these conservation ends chiefly in the far west, where population is sparse and the evils of city life and the factory system are little developed. Is it not just and highly expedient that these beneficent powers should now be exerted in the east, where manufacturing industries occupy the major part of the population and the destructive effects of city life have long been manifest?

Part Four

THE BIOCENTRIC REVOLUTION

1

NATURE VERSUS CULTURE

John Muir
WILD WOOL

"Gardening is civil and social," Henry Thoreau had said, "but it wants the vigor and freedom of the forest and the outlaw. There may be an excess of cultivation as well as anything else, until civilization becomes pathetic." As the forests came under a regimen of rational management and the garden city expanded its domain into the wilderness, carving out by law national parks for urban man, Thoreau's anarchic impulse had a diminishing range for free expansion. In the following selection the mountain zealot John Muir (1838–1914) fashioned anew the case for wildness. Unlike Lester Ward, Muir discovered in the scientific method a foundation for arguing the functional superiority of nature's unimproved devices over man's. Behind his argument lay a personal, moral revolution against the antinaturalism of the Christian training he had received in his youth. Coincident with that awakening was his migration in 1868 from his Wisconsin home to the Sierras of California, which became for him and for those who read his books a means of deliverance from an environment circumscribed by a narrow, exclusive humanism. But by the 1880s Muir reached an inevitable compromise with the institutions of civilization, if not with its landscape. In order to save his unspoiled wilderness, he joined those eastern gentlemen who were seeking to protect with civil authority the more spectacular examples of American scenery.

Moral improvers have calls to preach. I have a friend who has a call to plow, and woe to the daisy sod or azalea thicket that falls under the savage redemption of his keen steel shares. Not content with the so-called subjugation of every terrestrial bog, rock, and moorland, he would fain discover some method of reclamation applicable to the ocean and the sky, that in due calendar time they might be brought to

SOURCE. John Muir, "Wild Wool," *The Overland Monthly*, April 1875.

bud and blossom as the rose. Our efforts are of no avail when we seek to turn his attention to wild roses, or to the fact that both ocean and sky are already about as rosy as possible—the one with stars, the other with dulse, and foam, and wild light. The practical developments of his culture are orchards and clover fields that wear a smiling, benevolent aspect, and are truly excellent in their way, though a near view discloses something barbarous in them all. Wildness charms not my friend, charm it never so wisely; and whatsoever may be the character of his heaven, his earth seems only a chaos of agricultural possibilities calling for grubbing hoes and manures.

Sometimes I venture to approach him with a plea for wildness, when he good-naturedly shakes a big mellow apple in my face and reiterates his favorite aphorism, "Culture is an orchard apple; nature is a crab." All culture, however, is not equally destructive and inappreciative. Azure skies and crystal waters find loving recognition, and few there be who would welcome the axe among mountain pines, or would care to apply any correction to the tones and costumes of mountain waterfalls. Nevertheless, the barbarous notion is almost universally entertained by civilized men, that there is in all the manufactures of nature something essentially coarse which can and must be eradicated by human culture. I was, therefore, delighted in finding that the wild wool growing upon mountain sheep in the neighborhood of Mount Shasta was much finer than the average grades of cultivated wool. This *fine* distinction was made some three months ago, while hunting between Shasta and Lower Klamath Lake. Three fleeces were obtained—one that belonged to a large ram about four years old, another to a ewe about the same age, and another to a yearling lamb. After parting their beautiful wool on the side and many places along the back, shoulders, and hips, and examining it closely with my lens, I shouted:

"Well done for wildness! Wild wool is finer than tame!"

My companions stooped down and examined the fleeces for themselves, pulling out tufts and ringlets, spinning them between their fingers, and measuring the length of the staple, each in turn paying tribute to wildness. It *was* finer, and no mistake; finer than Spanish Merino. Wild wool *is* finer than tame.

"Here," said I, "is an argument for fine wildness that needs no explanation. Not that such arguments are by any means rare, for all wildness is finer than tameness, but because fine wool is appreciable by everybody alike—from the most speculative president of national wool-growers' associations all the way down to the gude-wife spinning by her ingleside."

Nature is a good mother, and sees well to the clothing of her many bairns—birds with smoothly imbricated feathers, beetles with shining jackets, and bears with shaggy furs. In the tropical south, where the sun warms like a fire, they are allowed to go thinly clad; but in the snowy northland she takes care to clothe warmly. The squirrel has socks and mittens, and a tail broad enough for a blanket; the grouse is densely feathered down to the ends of his toes; and the wild sheep, besides his undergarment of fine wool, has a thick overcoat of hair that sheds off both the snow and the rain. Other provisions and adaptations in the dresses of animals, relating less to climate than to the more mechanical circumstances of life, are made with the same consummate skill that characterizes all the love-work of nature. Land, water, and air, jagged rocks, muddy ground, sand beds, forests, underbrush, grassy plains, etc., are considered in all their possible combinations while the clothing of her beautiful wildlings is preparing. No matter what the circumstances of their lives may be, she never allows them to go dirty or ragged. The mole, living always in the dark and in the dirt, is yet as clean as the otter or the wave-washed seal; and our wild sheep, wading in the snow, roaming through bushes, and leaping among jagged storm-beaten cliffs, wears a dress so exquisitely adapted to its mountain life that it is always found as unruffled and stainless as a bird.

On leaving the Shasta hunting grounds I selected a few specimen tufts, and brought them away with a view to making more leisurely examinations; but, owing to the imperfectness of the instruments at my command, the results thus far obtained must be regarded only as rough approximations. . . .

When the fleece is parted and looked into with a good lens, the skin appears of a beautiful pale yellow color, and the delicate wool fibers are seen growing up among the strong hairs, like grass among stalks of corn, every individual fiber being protected about as specially and effectively as if enclosed in a separate husk. Wild wool is too fine to stand by itself, the fibers being about as frail and invisible as the floating threads of spiders, while the hairs against which they lean stand erect like hazel wands; but, notwithstanding their great dissimilarity in size and appearance, the wool and hair are forms of the same thing, modified in just that way and to just that degree that renders them most perfectly subservient to the well-being of the sheep. Furthermore, it will be observed that these wild modifications are entirely distinct from those which are brought chancingly into existence through the accidents and caprices of culture; the former being inventions of God for the attainment of definite ends. Like the modifications of limbs—the fin for swimming, the wing for flying, the foot for walking—so the fine wool for warmth, the hair for additional warmth and to protect the wool, and both together for a fabric to wear well in mountain roughness and wash well in mountain storms.

The effects of human culture upon wild wool are analogous to those produced upon wild roses. In the one case there is an abnormal development of petals at the expense of the stamens, in the other an abnormal development of wool at the expense of the hair. Garden roses frequently exhibit stamens in which the transmutation to petals may be observed in various stages of accomplishment, and analogously the fleeces of tame sheep occasionally contain a few wild hairs that are undergoing transmutation to wool. Even wild wool presents here and there a fiber that appears to be in a state of change. In the course of my examinations of the wild fleeces mentioned above, three fibers were found that were wool at one end and hair at the other. This, however, does not necessarily imply imperfection, or any process of change similar to that caused by human culture. Water lilies contain parts variously developed into stamens at one end, petals at the other, as the constant and normal condition. These half wool, half hair fibers may therefore subserve some fixed requirement essential to the perfection of the whole, or they may simply be the fine boundary lines where an exact balance between the wool and the hair is attained.

I have been offering samples of mountain wool to my friends, demanding in return that the fineness of wildness be fairly recognized and confessed, but the returns are deplorably tame. The first question asked is, "Wild sheep, wild sheep, have you any wool?" while they peer curiously down among the hairs through lenses and spectacles. "Yes, wild sheep, you *have* wool; but Mary's lamb had more. In the name of use, how many wild sheep, think you, would be required to furnish wool sufficient for a pair of socks?" I endeavor to point out the irrelevancy of the latter question, arguing that wild wool was not made for man but for sheep, and that, however deficient as clothing for other animals, it is just the thing for the brave mountain dweller that wears it. Plain, however, as all this appears, the quantity question rises again and again in all its commonplace tameness. To obtain a hearing on behalf of nature from any other standpoint than that of human use is almost impossible. Domestic flocks yield more flannel per sheep than the wild, therefore it is claimed that culture has improved upon wildness; and so it has as far as flannel is concerned, but all to the contrary as far as a sheep's dress is concerned. If every wild sheep inhabiting the Sierra were to put on tame wool, probably only a few would survive the dangers of a single season. With their fine limbs muffled and buried beneath a tangle of hairless wool, they would become short-winded and fall an easy prey to the strong mountain wolves. In descending precipices they would be thrown out of balance and killed, by their taggy wool catching upon sharp points of rocks. Disease would also be brought on by the dirt which always finds a lodgment in tame wool, and by the draggled and water-soaked condition into which it falls during stormy weather.

No dogma taught by the present civilization seems to form so insuperable an obstacle in the way of a right understanding of the relations which culture sustains to wildness, as that which declares that the world was made especially for the uses of man. Every animal, plant, and crystal controverts it in the plainest terms. Yet it is taught from century to century as something ever new and precious, and in the resulting darkness the enormous conceit is allowed to go unchallenged.

I have never yet happened upon a trace of evidence that seemed to show that any one animal was ever made for another as much as it was made for itself. Not that nature manifests any such thing as selfish isolation. In the making of every animal the presence of every other animal has been recognized. Indeed, every atom in creation may be said to be acquainted with and married to every other, but with universal union there is a division sufficient in degree for the purposes of the most intense individuality; and no matter what may be the note which any creature forms in the song of existence, it is made first for itself, then more and more remotely for all the world and worlds.

Were it not for the exercise of individualizing cares on the part of nature, the universe would be felted together like a fleece of tame wool. We are governed more than we know, and most when we are wildest. Plants, animals, and stars are all kept in place, bridled along appointed ways, *with* one another, and *through the midst* of one another—killing and being killed, eating and being eaten, in harmonious proportions and quantities. And it is right that we should thus reciprocally make use of one another, rob, cook, and consume, to the utmost of our healthy abilities and desires. Stars attract one another as they are able, and harmony results. Wild lambs eat as many wild flowers as they can find or desire, and men and wolves eat the lambs to just the same extent. This consumption of one another in its various modifications is a kind of culture varying with the degree of directness with which it is carried out, but we should be careful not to ascribe to such culture any improving qualities upon those on whom it is brought to bear. The water ouzel plucks moss from the river bank to build its nest, but it does not improve the moss by plucking it. We pluck feathers from birds, and less directly wool from wild sheep, for the manufacture of clothing and cradle-nests, without improving the wool for the sheep, or the feathers for the bird that wore them. When a hawk pounces upon a linnet and proceeds to pull out its feathers, preparatory to making a meal, the hawk may be said to be cultivating the linnet, and he certainly does effect an improvement as far as hawk food is concerned; but what of the songster? He ceases to be a linnet as soon as he is snatched from the woodland choir; and when, hawklike, we snatch the wild sheep from its native rock, and, instead of eating and wearing it at once, carry it home, and breed the hair out of its wool and the bones out of its body, it ceases to be a sheep. These breeding and plucking processes are similarly improving as regards the secondary uses aimed at; and, although the one requires but a few minutes for its accomplishment, the other many years or centuries, they are essentially alike. We eat wild oysters alive with great directness, waiting for no cultivation, and leaving scarce a second of distance between the shell and the lip; but we take wild sheep home and subject them to the many extended processes of husbandry, and finish by boiling them—a process which completes all sheep improvements as far as man is concerned. It will be seen, therefore, that wild wool and tame wool—wild sheep and tame sheep—are terms not properly comparable nor are they in any correct sense to be considered as bearing any antagonism toward each other; they are different things, planned and accomplished for wholly different purposes.

Illustrative examples bearing upon this interesting subject may be multiplied indefinitely, for they abound everywhere in the plant and animal kingdoms wherever culture has reached. Recurring for a moment to apples. The beauty and completeness of a wild apple tree living its own life in the woods is heartily acknowledged by all those who have been so happy as to form its acquaintance. The fine wild piquancy of its fruit is unrivaled, but in the great question of quantity as human food wild apples are found wanting. Man, therefore, takes the tree from the woods, manures and prunes and grafts, plans and guesses, adds a little of this and that, until apples of every conceivable size and pulpiness are produced, like nut galls in response to the irritating punctures of insects. Orchard apples are to me the most eloquent words that culture has ever spoken, but they reflect no imperfection upon nature's spicy crab. Every cultivated apple is a crab, not improved, but cooked, variously softened and swelled out in the process, mellowed, sweetened, spiced, and rendered good for food, but as utterly unfit for the uses of nature as a meadowlark killed and plucked and roasted. Give to nature every cultured apple—codling, pippin, russet—and every sheep so laboriously compounded—muffled Southdowns, hairy Cotswolds, wrinkled Merinoes—and she would throw the one to her caterpillars, the other to her wolves. . . .

A little pure wildness is the one great present want, both of men and sheep.

2

THE REVOLT AGAINST UTILITARIANISM

John Muir
THE YOSEMITE

The first national park in America was Yellowstone, established by Congress in 1872. Eighteen years later, due in great measure to John Muir's advocacy, Yosemite Valley was given the same security. Then in 1908 Secretary of the Interior James Garfield approved a long-standing application from the city of San Francisco to build a water reservoir right in the middle of Yosemite Park. The approval ignited a fire that for five years burned straight through the ranks of environmentalists. For Pinchot and the regular conservation technocrats the decision was eminently sound; the benefits of clean water, electric power, and fire protection for the city easily outweighed the loss of what Pinchot called the "swampy floor" of the valley. But by this time another band had formed, bent on preserving the wilderness from the resource experts. Muir had organized the Sierra Club in 1892 to keep Yosemite chaste and unimpaired; now around this nucleus the preservationists across the nation coalesced to delay the project as long as they could. Although Woodrow Wilson finally decided against them, Muir and his activists won a larger victory when the National Park Service was created in 1916, providing new official sanction for the picturesque as well as the productive in nature.

Yosemite is so wonderful that we are apt to regard it as an exceptional creation, the only valley of its kind in the world; but nature is not so poor as to have only one of anything. Several other yosemites have been discovered in the Sierra that occupy the same relative positions on the Range and were formed by the same forces in the same kind of granite. One of these, the Hetch Hetchy Valley, is in the Yosemite National Park about twenty miles from Yosemite and is easily accessible to all sorts of travelers by a road and trail that leaves the Big Oak Flat road at Bronson Meadows a few miles below Crane Flat, and to

SOURCE. John Muir, *The Yosemite* (New York, 1912), pp. 249–262.

mountaineers by way of Yosemite Creek basin and the head of the middle fork of the Tuolumne.

It is said to have been discovered by Joseph Screech, a hunter, in 1850, a year before the discovery of the great Yosemite. After my first visit to it in the autumn of 1871, I have always called it the "Tuolumne Yosemite," for it is a wonderfully exact counterpart of the Merced Yosemite, not only in its sublime rocks and waterfalls but in the gardens, groves and meadows of its flowery parklike floor. The floor of Yosemite is about 4000 feet above the sea; the Hetch Hetchy floor about 3700 feet. And as the Merced River flows through Yosemite, so does the Tuolumne through Hetch Hetchy. The walls of both are of gray granite, rise abruptly from the floor, are sculptured in the same style and in both every rock is a glacier monument.

Standing boldly out from the south wall is a strikingly picturesque rock called by the Indians, Kolana, the outermost of a group 2300 feet high, corresponding with the Cathedral Rocks of Yosemite both in relative position and form. On the opposite side of the valley, facing Kolana, there is a counterpart of the El Capitan that rises sheer and plain to a height of 1800 feet, and over its massive brow flows a stream which makes the most graceful fall I have ever seen. From the edge of the cliff to the top of an earthquake talus it is perfectly free in the air for a thousand feet before it is broken into cascades among talus boulders. It is in all its glory in June, when the snow is melting fast, but fades and vanishes toward the end of summer. The only fall I know with which it may fairly be compared is the Yosemite Bridal Veil; but it excels even that favorite fall both in height and airy-fairy beauty and behavior. Lowlanders are apt to suppose that mountain streams in their wild career over cliffs lose control of themselves and tumble in a noisy chaos of mist and spray. On the contrary, on no part of their travels are they more harmonious and self-controlled. Imagine yourself in Hetch Hetchy on a sunny day in June, standing waist-deep in grass and flowers (as I have often stood), while the great pines sway dreamily with scarcely perceptible motion. Looking northward across the valley you see a plain, gray granite cliff rising abruptly out of the gardens and groves to a height of 1800 feet, and in front of it Tueeula-la's silvery scarf burning with irised sun-fire. In the first white outburst at the head there is abundance of visible energy, but it is speedily hushed and concealed in divine repose, and its tranquil progress to the base of the cliff is like that of a downy feather in a still room. Now observe the fineness and marvelous distinctness of the various sun-illumined fabrics into which the water is woven; they sift and float from form to form down the face of that grand gray rock in so leisurely and unconfused a manner that you can examine their texture, and patterns and tones of color as you would a piece of embroidery held in the hand. Toward the top of the fall you see groups of booming, cometlike masses, their solid, white heads separate, their tails like combed silk interlacing among delicate gray and purple shadows, ever forming and dissolving, worn out by friction in their rush through the air. Most of these vanish a few hundred feet below the summit, changing to varied forms of cloudlike drapery. Near the bottom the width of the fall has increased from about twenty-five feet to a hundred feet. Here it is composed of yet finer tissues, and is still without a trace of disorder—air, water and sunlight woven into stuff that spirits might wear.

So fine a fall might well seem sufficient to glorify any valley; but here, as in Yosemite, nature seems in nowise moderate, for a short distance to the eastward of Tueeulala booms and thunders the great Hetch Hetchy Fall, Wapama, so near that you have both of them in full view from the same standpoint. It is the counterpart of the Yosemite Fall, but has a much greater volume of water, is about 1700 feet in height, and appears to be nearly vertical, though considerably inclined, and is dashed into huge outbounding bosses of foam on projecting shelves and knobs. No two falls could be more un-like—Tueeulala out in the open sunshine descending like thistle-down; Wapama in a jagged, shadowy gorge roaring and thundering, pounding its way like an earthquake avalanche.

Besides this glorious pair there is a broad, massive fall on the main river a short distance above the head of the valley. Its position is something like that of the Vernal in Yosemite, and its roar as it plunges into a surging trout-pool may be heard a long way, though it is only about twenty feet high. On Rancheria Creek, a large stream, corresponding in position with the Yosemite Tenaya Creek, there is a chain of cascades joined here and there with swift flashing plumes like the one between the Vernal and Nevada Falls, making magnifi-cent shows as they go their glacier-sculptured way, sliding, leaping, hurrahing, covered with crisp clashing spray made glorious with sift-ing sunshine. And besides all these a few small streams come over the walls at wide intervals, leaping from ledge to ledge with birdlike song and watering many a hidden cliff-garden and fernery, but they are too unshowy to be noticed in so grand a place.

The correspondence between the Hetch Hetchy walls in their trends, sculpture, physical structure, and general arrangement of the main rock masses and those of the Yosemite Valley has excited the wondering admiration of every observer. We have seen that the El Capitan and Cathedral rocks occupy the same relative positions in both valleys; so also do their Yosemite points and North Domes.

Again, that part of the Yosemite north wall immediately to the east of the Yosemite Fall has two horizontal benches, about 500 and 1500 feet above the floor, timbered with golden-cup oak. Two benches similarly situated and timbered occur on the same relative portion of the Hetch Hetchy north wall, to the east of Wapama Fall, and on no other. The Yosemite is bounded at the head by the great Half Dome. Hetch Hetchy is bounded in the same way, though its head rock is incomparably less wonderful and sublime in form.

The floor of the valley is about three and a half miles long, and from a fourth to half a mile wide. The lower portion is mostly a level meadow about a mile long, with the trees restricted to the sides and the river banks, and partially separated from the main, upper, forested portion by a low bar of glacier-polished granite across which the river breaks in rapids.

The principal trees are the yellow and sugar pines, digger pine, incense cedar, Douglas spruce, silver fir, the California and golden-cup oaks, balsam cottonwood, Nuttall's flowering dogwood, alder, maple, laurel, tumion, etc. The most abundant and influential are the great yellow or silver pines like those of Yosemite, the tallest over two hundred feet in height, and the oaks assembled in magnificent groves with massive rugged trunks four to six feet in diameter, and broad, shady, wide-spreading heads. The shrubs forming conspicuous flowery clumps and tangles are manzanita, azalea, spirea, brier-rose, several species of ceanothus, calycanthus, philadelphus, wild cherry, etc.; with abundance of showy and fragrant herbaceous plants growing about them or out in the open in beds by themselves—lilies, Mariposa tulips, brodiaeas, orchids, iris, spraguea, draperia, collomia, collinsia, castilleja, nemophila, larkspur, columbine, goldenrods, sunflowers, mints of many species, honeysuckle, etc. Many fine ferns dwell here also, especially the beautiful and interesting rockferns—pellaea, and cheilanthes of several species—fringing and rosetting dry rock-piles and ledges; woodwardia and asplenium on damp spots with fronds six or seven feet high; the delicate maidenhair in mossy nooks by the falls, and the sturdy, broad-shouldered pteris covering nearly all the dry ground beneath the oaks and pines.

It appears, therefore, that Hetch Hetchy Valley, far from being a plain, common, rock-bound meadow, as many who have not seen it seem to suppose, is a grand landscape garden, one of nature's rarest and most precious mountain temples. As in Yosemite, the sublime rocks of its walls seem to glow with life, whether leaning back in respose or standing erect in thoughtful attitudes, giving welcome to storms and calms alike, their brows in the sky, their feet set in the groves and gay flowery meadows, while birds, bees, and butterflies

help the river and waterfalls to stir all the air into music—things frail
and fleeting and types of permanence meeting here and blending, just
as they do in Yosemite, to draw her lovers into close and confiding
communion with her.

Sad to say, this most precious and sublime feature of the Yosemite
National Park, one of the greatest of all our natural resources for the
uplifting joy and peace and health of the people, is in danger of being
dammed and made into a reservoir to help supply San Francisco with
water and light, thus flooding it from wall to wall and burying its
gardens and groves one or two hundred feet deep. This grossly destructive commercial scheme has long been planned and urged (though
water as pure and abundant can be got from sources outside of the
people's park, in a dozen different places), because of the comparative
cheapness of the dam and of the territory which it is sought to divert
from the great uses to which it was dedicated in the act of 1890
establishing the Yosemite National Park.

The making of gardens and parks goes on with civilization all over
the world, and they increase both in size and number as their value is
recognized. Everybody needs beauty as well as bread, places to play in
and pray in, where nature may heal and cheer and give strength to
body and soul alike. This natural beauty-hunger is made manifest in
the little windowsill gardens of the poor, though perhaps only a
geranium slip in a broken cup, as well as in the carefully tended rose
and lily gardens of the rich, the thousands of spacious city parks and
botanical gardens, and in our magnificent national parks—the Yellowstone, Yosemite, Sequoia, etc.—nature's sublime wonderlands, the
admiration and joy of the world. Nevertheless, like anything else
worth while, from the very beginning, however well guarded, they
have always been subject to attack by despoiling gainseekers and
mischief-makers of every degree from Satan to Senators, eagerly
trying to make everything immediately and selfishly commercial,
with schemes disguised in smug-smiling philanthropy, industriously,
sham-piously crying, "Conservation, conservation, panutilization,"
that man and beast may be fed and the dear nation made great. Thus
long ago a few enterprising merchants utilized the Jerusalem temple
as a place of business instead of a place of prayer, changing money,
buying and selling cattle and sheep and doves; and earlier still, the
first forest reservation, including only one tree, was likewise de-
spoiled. Ever since the establishment of the Yosemite National Park,
strife has been going on around its borders and I suppose this will go
on as part of the universal battle between right and wrong, however
much its boundaries may be shorn, or its wild beauty destroyed. . . .

The most delightful and wonderful camp grounds in the park are its

196 AMERICAN ENVIRONMENTALISM

three great valleys—Yosemite, Hetch Hetchy, and Upper Tuolumne; and they are also the most important places with reference to their positions relative to the other great features—the Merced and Tuolumne Cañons, and the High Sierra peaks and glaciers, etc., at the head of the rivers. The main part of the Tuolumne Valley is a spacious flowery lawn four or five miles long, surrounded by magnificent snowy mountains, slightly separated from other beautiful meadows, which together make a series about twelve miles in length, the highest reaching to the feet of Mount Dana, Mount Gibbs, Mount Lyell and Mount McClure. It is about 8500 feet above the sea, and forms the grand central High Sierra camp ground from which excursions are made to the noble mountains, domes, glaciers, etc.; across the range to the Mono Lake and volcanoes and down the Tuolumne Cañon to Hetch Hetchy. Should Hetch Hetchy be submerged for a reservoir, as proposed, not only would it be utterly destroyed, but the sublime cañon way to the heart of the High Sierra would be hopelessly blocked and the great camping ground, as the watershed of a city drinking system, virtually would be closed to the public. So far as I have learned, few of all the thousands who have seen the park and seek rest and peace in it are in favor of this outrageous scheme.

One of my later visits to the valley was made in the autumn of 1907 with the late William Keith, the artist. The leaf colors were then ripe, and the great godlike rocks in repose seemed to glow with life. The artist, under their spell, wandered day after day along the river and through the groves and gardens, studying the wonderful scenery; and, after making about forty sketches, declared with enthusiasm that although its walls were less sublime in height, in picturesque beauty and charm Hetch Hetchy surpassed even Yosemite.

That any one would try to destroy such a place seems incredible; but sad experience shows that there are people good enough and bad enough for anything. The proponents of the dam scheme bring forward a lot of bad arguments to prove that the only righteous thing to do with the people's parks is to destroy them bit by bit as they are able. Their arguments are curiously like those of the devil, devised for the destruction of the first garden—so much of the very best Eden fruit going to waste; so much of the best Tuolumne water and Tuolumne scenery going to waste. Few of their statements are even partly true, and all are misleading.

Thus, Hetch Hetchy, they say, is a "low-lying meadow." On the contrary, it is a high-lying natural landscape garden. . . .

"It is a common minor feature, like thousands of others." On the contrary it is a very uncommon feature; after Yosemite, the rarest and in many ways the most important in the National Park.

"Damming and submerging it 175 feet deep would enhance its beauty by forming a crystal-clear lake." Landscape gardens, places of recreation and worship, are never made beautiful by destroying and burying them. The beautiful sham lake, forsooth, would be only an eyesore, a dismal blot on the landscape, like many others to be seen in the Sierra. For, instead of keeping it at the same level all the year, allowing nature centuries of time to make new shores, it would, of course, be full only a month or two in the spring, when the snow is melting fast; then it would be gradually drained, exposing the slimy sides of the basin and shallower parts of the bottom, with the gathered drift and waste, death and decay of the upper basins, caught here instead of being swept on to decent natural burial along the banks of the river or in the sea. Thus the Hetch Hetchy dam-lake would be only a rough imitation of a natural lake for a few of the spring months, an open sepulcher for the others.

"Hetch Hetchy water is the purest of all to be found in the Sierra, unpolluted, and forever unpollutable." On the contrary, excepting that of the Merced below Yosemite, it is less pure than that of most of the other Sierra streams, because of the sewerage of camp grounds draining into it, especially of the Big Tuolumne Meadows camp ground, occupied by hundreds of tourists and mountaineers, with their animals, for months every summer, soon to be followed by thousands from all the world.

These temple destroyers, devotees of ravaging commercialism, seem to have a perfect contempt for nature, and, instead of lifting their eyes to the God of the mountains, lift them to the Almighty Dollar.

Dam Hetch Hetchy! As well dam for water-tanks the people's cathedrals and churches, for no holier temple has ever been consecrated by the heart of man.

3

DARWINISM AND MORAL PHILOSOPHY

Edward Evans
ETHICAL RELATIONS BETWEEN MAN AND BEAST

*The first federal wildlife refuge was created at Pelican Island, Florida, in 1903.
It was the beginning, however timid and belated, of a national attempt to
make amends for the indiscriminate slaughter of wild birds and animals
described much earlier by James Fenimore Cooper and John James Audubon.
Undoubtedly the idea of "refuges" owed much of its public appeal to the
same sentiment that gave rise in the latter part of the nineteenth century to
humane societies. Moreover, the extension of benevolence and "philanthropy" to other species can be explained as part of the moral impact of Darwinian evolution—or perhaps one should rather say Darwin's theory was possible
only in a culture that already had begun to accept man's moral obligation to
lower creatures. In either case the following selection places all these developments in the more general context of traditional western ethics. Edward
Evans (1831–1917) taught modern languages at the University of Michigan for
almost a decade after completing his studies at Berlin, Munich, and Göttin-
gen. In 1870, he resigned from the university and returned to Munich where
he remained until World War I. A scholar of both German literature and
Oriental philosophies, his most important book was* Evolutionary Ethics and
Animal Psychology *(1898). Out of such inquiries into the problem of man's
place in nature was emerging a new environmental ethic, contesting the
confidence of Charles Eliot, Jr., that the earth was made for man.*

Ethnocentric geography, which caused each petty tribe to regard itself
as the center of the earth, and geocentric astronomy, which caused
mankind to regard the earth as the center of the universe, are conceptions that have been gradually outgrown and generally discarded—
not, however, without leaving distinct and indelible traces of themselves in human speech and conduct. But this is not the case with
anthropocentric psychology and ethics, which treat man as a being

SOURCE. Edward Evans, "Ethical Relations between Man and Beast," *The
Popular Science Monthly*, September 1894.

essentially different and inseparably set apart from all other sentient creatures, to which he is bound by no ties of mental affinity or moral obligation. Nevertheless, all these notions spring from the same root, having their origin in man's false and overweening conceit of himself as the member of a tribe, the inhabitant of a planet, or the lord of creation.

It was upon this sort of anthropocentric assumption that teleologists used to build their arguments in proof of the existence and goodness of God as shown by the evidences of beneficent design in the world. All their reasonings in support of this doctrine were based upon the theory that the final purpose of every created thing is the promotion of human happiness. Take away this anthropocentric postulate, and the whole logical structure tumbles into a heap of unfounded and irrelevant assertions leading to lame and impotent conclusions.

Thus Bernardin de Saint-Pierre states that garlic, being a specific for maladies caused by marshy exhalations, grows in swampy places, in order that the antidote may be easily accessible to man when he becomes infected with malarious disease. Also the fruits of spring and summer, he adds, are peculiarly juicy, because man needs them for his refreshment in hot weather, on the other hand, autumn fruits, like nuts, are oily, because oil generates heat and keeps men warm in winter. It is for man's sake, too, that in lands where it seldom or never rains there is always a heavy deposition of dew. If we can show that any product or phenomenon of nature is useful to us, we think we have discovered its sufficient raison d'être, and extol the wisdom and kindness of the Creator; but if anything is harmful to us we can not imagine why it should exist. How much intellectual acuteness and learning have been expended to reconcile the fact that the moon is visible only a very small part of the time, with the theory that it was intended to illuminate the earth in the absence of the sun, for the benefit of its inhabitants!

Gennadius, a Greek presbyter, who flourished at Constantinople about the middle of the fifth century, remarks in his commentary on the first chapter of Genesis that God created the beasts of the earth and the cattle after their kind on the same day on which he created man, in order that these creatures might be there ready to serve him.

But it would be superfluous to multiply examples of the influence of this anthropocentric idea as it has worked itself out in the history of mankind. Every science has had to encounter its opposition, and it has been a stumbling block in the way of every effort to enlarge human knowledge and to promote human happiness. . . .

Not only were the fruits of the earth made to grow for human sustenance, but the flowers of the field were supposed to bud and blossom, putting on their gayest attire and emitting their sweetest perfume, solely as a contribution to human happiness; and it was deemed one of the mysteries and mistakes of nature, never too much to be puzzled over and wondered at, that these things should spring up and expend their beauty and fragrance in remote places untrodden by the foot of man. Gray expresses this feeling in the oft-quoted lines:

> *"Full many a flower is born to blush unseen,*
> *And waste its sweetness on the desert air."*

Science has finally and effectually taken this conceit out of man by showing that the flower blooms not for the purpose of giving him agreeable sensations, but for its own sake, and that it presumed to put forth sweet and beautiful blossoms long before he appeared on the earth as a rude cave-haunting and flint-chipping savage.

The color and odor of the plant are designed not so much to please man as to attract insects, which promote the process of fertilization and thus insure the preservation of the species. The gratification of man's aesthetic sense and taste for the beautiful does not enter into nature's intentions; and although the flower may bloom unseen by any human eye, it does not on that account waste its sweetness, but fully accomplishes its mission, provided there is a bee or a bug abroad to be drawn to it. That the fragrance and variegated petals are alluring to a vagrant insect is a condition of far more importance in determining the fate of the plant than that they should be charming to man.

Plants, on the other hand, which depend upon the force of the wind for fructification, are not distinguished for beauty of color or sweetness of odor, since these qualities, however agreeable to man, would be wasted on the wind. This is an illustration of the prudent economy of nature, which never indulges in superfluities or overburdens her products with useless attributes; but the test of utility which "great creating Nature" sets up in such cases is little flattering to man, and has no reference to his tastes and susceptibilities, but is determined solely by the serviceableness of certain qualities of the plant itself in the struggle for existence.

According to Schopenhauer, anthropocentric egoism is a fundamental and fatal defect in the psychological and ethical teachings of both Judaism and Christianity, and has been the source of untold misery to myriads of sentient and highly sensitive organisms. "These religions," he says, "have unnaturally severed man from the animal world, to which he essentially belongs, and placed him on a pinnacle apart, treating all lower creatures as mere things; whereas Brahmanism and Buddhism insist not only upon his kinship with all forms of animal life, but also upon his vital connection with all animated Nature, binding him up into intimate relationship with them by metempsychosis."

In the Hebrew cosmogony there is no continuity in the process of creation, whereby the genesis of man is in any wise connected with the genesis of the lower animals. After the Lord God, by his fiat, had produced beasts, birds, fishes, and creeping things, he ignored all this mass of protoplastic and organic material, and took an entirely new departure in the production of man, whom he formed out of the dust of the ground. Science shows him to have been originally a little higher than the ape, out of which he was gradually and painfully evolved; Scripture takes him out of his environment, severs him from his antecedents, and makes him a little lower than the angels. Upon the being thus arbitrarily created absolute dominion is conferred over every beast of the earth and every fowl of the air, which are to be to him "for meat." They are given over to his supreme and irresponsible control, without the slightest injunction of kindness or the faintest suggestion of any duties or obligations toward them.

Again, when the earth is to be renewed and replenished after the deluge, the same principles are reiterated and the same line of demarcation is drawn and even deepened. God blesses Noah and his sons, bids them "be fruitful and multiply," and then adds, as regards the lower animals: "The fear of you and the dread of you shall be upon every beast of the earth and upon every fowl of the air, upon all that moveth upon the earth, and upon all the fishes of the sea; into your hand are they delivered. Every moving thing that liveth shall be meat for you; even as the green herb have I given you all things."

This tyrannical mandate is not mitigated by any intimation of the merciful manner in which the human autocrat should treat the creatures thus subjected to his capricious will. On the contrary, the only thing that he is positively commanded to do with reference to them is to eat them. They are to be regarded by him simply as food, having no more rights and deserving no more consideration as means of sating his appetite than a grain of corn or a blade of grass. . . .

Neither the synagogue nor the church, neither sanhedrin nor ecclesiastical council, has ever regarded this subject as falling within its scope, and sought to inculcate as a dogma or to enforce by decree a proper consideration for the rights of the lower animals. One of the chief objections urged by Celsus more than seventeen centuries ago against Christianity was that it "considers everything as having been created solely for man." This stricture is indorsed by Dr. Thomas Arnold of Rugby, who also animadverts on the evils growing out of the anthropocentric character of Christianity as a scheme of redemption and a system of theodicy. "It would seem," he says, "as if the primitive Christian, by laying so much stress upon a future life in contradistinction to this life, and placing the lower creatures out of the pale of hope, placed them at the same time out of the pale of sympathy, and thus laid the foundation for this utter disregard of animals in the light of our fellow creatures. The definition of virtue among the early Christians was the same as [William] Paley's—that it was good performed for the sake of insuring eternal happiness—which of course excluded all the so-called brute creatures. Kind, loving, submissive, conscientious, much-enduring, we know them to be; but because we deprive them of all stake in the future, because they have no selfish, calculated aim, these are not virtues; yet if we say 'a vicious horse,' why not say 'a virtuous horse'?"

We are ready enough, adds Dr. Arnold, to endow animals with our bad moral qualities, but grudge them the possession of our good ones. The Germans, whose natural and hereditary sympathy with the brute creation is stronger than that of any other western people, speak of horses as *"fromm,"* pious, not in the religious, but in the primary and proper sense of the word, meaning thereby kind and docile. The English *"gentle"* and the French *"gentil,"* which are used in the same connection, refer to good conduct as the result of fine breeding.

Archdeacon Paley's definition of virtue, to which Dr. Arnold adverts, is essentially anthropocentric and intensely egoistic. "Virtue," he says, "is the doing good to mankind in obedience to the will of God, for the sake of everlasting happiness." In order to be virtuous, according to this extremely narrow and wholly inadequate conception of virtue, we must, in the first place, do good to mankind, our conduct toward the brute creation not being taken into the account; secondly, our action must be in obedience to the will of God, thus ruling out all generous impulses originating in the spontaneous desire to do good; thirdly, we must have an eye single to our own supreme personal advantage—in other words, our conduct must be utterly selfish, spring not merely from momentary pleasure or temporary profit, but from far-seeing calculations of the effect it may have in securing our eternal happiness. Thus the virtuous man becomes the incarnation of the intensest self-love and self-seeking, and virtue the synonym of excessive venality. From a moral point of view, there is no greater merit in "otherworldliness" than in worldliness, and no reason why the endeavor to attain personal happiness in a future life should differ in quality from the effort to make everything minister to our personal happiness in the present life. . . .

Theocritus, the father of Greek idyllic poetry, represents Hercules as exclaiming, after he had slain the Nemean lion, "Hades received a monster soul"; and he saw nothing incongruous in the spirit of the dead beast joining the company of the departed spirits of men in the lower world. Sydney Smith says, in speaking of the soul of the brute, "To this soul some have impiously allowed immortality." Why such a belief should be deemed impious it is difficult to discover. The question which the psychologist has to consider is not whether the doctrine is impious, but whether it is true. No scientific opinion has ever been advanced that has not seemed impious to some minds, and been denounced and persecuted as such by ecclesiastical authorities. . . .

More than fifty years ago Henry Hallam made the following observations, which are remarkable as an anticipation of the ethical corollary to the doctrine of evolution: "Few at present, who believe in the immortality of the human soul, would deny the same to the elephant; but it must be owned that the discoveries of zoology have pushed this to consequences which some might not readily adopt. The spiritual being of a sponge revolts a little our prejudices; yet there is no resting place, and we must admit this or be content to sink ourselves into a mass of medullary fiber. Brutes have been as slowly emancipated in philosophy as some classes of mankind have been in civil polity; their souls, we see, were almost universally disputed to them at the end of the seventeenth century, even by those who did not absolutely bring them down to machinery. Even within the recollection of many, it was common to deny them any kind of reasoning faculty, and to solve their most sagacious actions by the vague word instinct. We have come in late years to think better of our humble companions; and, as usual in similar cases, the preponderant bias seems rather too much of a leveling character." During the half century that has elapsed since these words were written, not only has zoology made still greater progress in the direction indicated, but a new science of zoopsychology has sprung up, in which the mental traits and moral qualities of the lower animals have been, not merely recorded as curious and comical anecdotes, but systematically investigated and philosophically explained. In consequence of this radical change of view, human society in general has become more philozoic, not upon religious or sentimental but upon strictly scientific grounds, and developed a sympathy and solidarity with the animal world, having its sources less in the tender and transitory emotions of the heart than in the profound and permanent convictions of the mind.

In an essay published a few years ago in *The Dublin Review*, the Right Reverend John Cuthbert Hedley, Bishop of Newport and Menevia, asserts that animals have no rights, because they are not rational creatures and do not exist for their own sake. "The brute creation have only one purpose, and that is to minister to man, or to man's temporary abode." This is the doctrine set forth more than six centuries ago by Thomas Aquinas, and recently expounded by Dr. Leopold Schutz, professor in the theological seminary at Treves, in an elaborate work entitled *The So-called Understanding of Animals or Animal Instinct.* This writer treats the theory of the irrationality of brutes as a dogma of the Church, denouncing all who hold that the mental difference between man and beast is one of degree, and not of kind, as "enemies of the Christian faith"; whereas those who cling to the old notion of instinctive or automatic action in explaining the phenomena of animal intelligence are extolled as "champions of pure truth."

If it was the Creator's intention that the lower animals should minister to man, the divine plan has proved to be a failure, since the number of animals which, after centuries of effort, he has succeeded in bringing more or less under his dominion is extremely small. Millions of living creatures fly in the air, crawl on the earth, dwell in the waters, and roam the fields and the forests, over which he has no control whatever. Not one in twenty thousand is fit for food, and of those which are edible he does not actually eat more than one in ten thousand. In explanation of this lack of effectiveness in the enforcement of a divine decree, it has been asserted that man lost his dominion over the lower world to a great extent when he lost dominion over himself; but this view is wholly untenable even from a biblical standpoint, inasmuch as the promise of universal sovereignty was renewed after the deluge and expressed in even stronger terms than before the fall.

Dugald Stewart admits "a certain latitude of action, which enables the brutes to accommodate themselves in some measure to their accidental situations." In this arrangement he sees a design or purpose of "rendering them, in consequence of this power of accommodation, incomparably more serviceable to our race than they would have been if altogether subjected, like mere matter, to the influence of regular and assignable causes." Of the value of this power of adaptation to the animal itself in the struggle for existence the Scotch philosopher had no conception.

In the great majority of treatises on moral science, especially in such as base their teachings on distinctively Christian tenets, there is seldom any allusion to man's duty toward animals. Dr. [Francis] Wayland, who has perhaps the most to say on this point, sums up his remarks in a note apologetically appended to the body of his work. He denies them the possession of "any moral faculty," and declares that in all cases "our right is paramount and must extinguish theirs." We are to treat them kindly, feed and shelter them adequately, and "kill them with the least possible pain." To inflict suffering upon them for our amusement is wrong, since it tends to harden men and render them brutal and ferocious in temper.

Dr. [Laurens] Hickok takes a similar view and broadly asserts that "neither animate nor inanimate Nature has any rights," and that man is not bound to it "by any duties for its own sake. . . . In the light of his own worthiness as end, . . . he is not permitted to mar the face of Nature, nor wantonly and uselessly to injure any of her products." Maliciously breaking a crystal, defacing a gem, girdling a tree, crushing a flower, painting flaming advertisements on rocks, and worrying and torturing animals are thus placed in the same category as acts tending to degrade man ethically and aesthetically, rendering him coarse and rude, and making him not only a very disagreeable associate, but also, in the long run, "an unsafe member of civil society." These things are considered right or wrong solely from the standpoint of their influence upon human elevation or degradation. "Nature possesses no product too sacred for man. All nature is for man, not man for it."

Man is as truly a part and product of nature as any other animal, and this attempt to set him up on an isolated point outside of it is philosophically false and morally pernicious. It makes fundamental to ethics a principle which once prevailed universally in politics and still survives in the legal fiction that the king can do no wrong. Louis XIV of France firmly believed himself to be the rightful and absolute owner of the lives and property of his subjects. He held that his rights as monarch were paramount and extinguished theirs, that they possessed nothing too sacred for him, and the leading moralists and statists of his day confirmed him in this extravagant opinion of his royal prerogatives. All the outrages which the mad czar, Ivan the Terrible, perpetrated on the inhabitants of Novgorod and Moscow, man has felt and for the most part still feels himself justified in inflicting on domestic animals and beasts of venery.

It is only within the last century that legislators have begun to recognize the claims of brutes to just treatment and to enact laws for their protection. Torturing a beast, if punished at all, was treated solely as an offense against property, like breaking a window, barking a tree, or committing any other act known in Scotch law as "malicious mischief." It was regarded, not as a wrong done to the suffering animal, but as an injury done to its owner, which could be made good by the payment of money. Not until a little more than a hundred years ago was such an act changed from a civil into a criminal offense, for which a simple fine was not deemed a sufficient reparation. It was thus placed in the category of crimes which, like arson, burglary, and murder, are wrongs against society, for which no pecuniary restitution or compensation can make adequate atonement.

Even this legislative reform is by no means universal. The criminal code of the German Empire still punishes with a fine of not more than fifty thalers any person "who publicly, or in such wise as to excite scandal, maliciously tortures or barbarously maltreats animals." This sort of cruelty is classified with drawing plans of fortresses, using official stamps and seals, and putting royal or princely coats of arms on signs without permission, making noises, which disturb the public peace, and playing games of hazard on the streets or market places. The man is punished, not because he puts the animal to pain, but because his conduct is offensive to his fellow men and wounds their sensibilities. The law sets no limit to his cruelty, provided he may practice it in private.

Again, in all enactments regulating the transportation of live stock our legislation is still exceedingly defective. The great majority of people have no conception of the unnecessary and almost incredible suffering inflicted by man upon the lower animals in merely conveying them from one place to another in order to meet the demands of the market. It is well known that German shippers of sheep to England often lose one third of their consignment by suffocation, owing to overcrowding and imperfect ventilation. Beasts are still made to endure all the horrors to which slavers were once wont to subject their cargoes of human chattels in stifling holds on the notorious "middle passage."

The late Henry Bergh states that the loss on cattle by "shrinkage" in transporting them from the western to the eastern portion of the United States is from ten to fifteen percent. The average shrinkage of an ox is one hundred and twenty pounds, and that of a sheep or hog from fifteen to twenty pounds; and the annual loss in money arising from this cause is estimated at more than forty million dollars. The amount of animal suffering which these statistics imply is fearful to contemplate. Here and there a solitary voice is heard in our legislative halls protesting against the horrors of this traffic, but so powerful is the lobby influence of wealthy corporations that no law can be passed to prevent them. Not a word ever falls from the pulpit in rebuke of such barbarity; meanwhile the railroad magnates pay liberal pew rents out of the profits, and listen with complacency one day in the week to denunciations of Jeroboam's idolatry and the wicked deeds of Ahab and Ahaziah, as recorded in the chronicles of the kings of Israel.

The horse, one of the noblest and most sensitive of domestic animals, is put to all kinds of torture by docking, pricking, clipping, peppering, and the use of bearing reins solely to gratify human vanity. As a reward for severe and faithful toil he is often fed with unwholesome and insufficient fodder on the economical principle announced by the manager of a New York tramway that "horses are cheaper than oats." It is an actual fact, verified by Henry Bergh, that the horses of this large corporation were fed on a mixture of meal, gypsum, and marble dust, until the Society for the Prevention of Cruelty to Animals interfered and finally succeeded in putting a stop to the practice.

The Americans, as a people, are notorious for the recklessness with which they squander the products of nature, of which their country is so exceedingly prolific. This extravagance extends to all departments of public, social, and domestic life. No land less rich in material resources could have borne for any length of time the wretched mismanagement of its finances to which the United States has been subjected ever since and even before the close of the Civil War. There is not a government in Europe that would not have been broken down and rendered bankrupt by the tremendous and wholly unnecessary strain put upon it by crass ignorance of the most elementary principles of finance and demagogical tampering with the public credit. The same wasteful spirit involves also, as we have seen, immense suffering to animals on the part of soulless and unscrupulous corporations, in which intense greed of gain is not mitigated by the influence of individual kindness, and by which horses are treated as mere machines, to be worked to their utmost capacity at the smallest expense, and neat cattle as so much butcher's meat to be brought to market in the quickest and cheapest manner.

Erasmus Darwin, in his *Phytologia, or the Philosophy of Agriculture and Gardening*, endeavors to vindicate the goodness of God in permitting the destruction of the lower by the higher animals on the ground that "more pleasurable sensation exists in the world, as the organic matter is taken from a state of less irritability and less sensibility and converted into a greater." By this arrangement, he thinks, the supreme sum of possible happiness is secured to sentient beings. Thus it may be disagreeable for the mouse to be caught and converted into the flesh of the cat, for the lamb to be devoured by the wolf, for the toad to be swallowed by the serpent, and for sheep, swine, and kine to be served up as roasts and ragouts for man; but in all such cases, he argues, the pain inflicted is far less than the amount of pleasure ultimately procured. But how is it when a finely organized human being, with infinite capabilities of happiness in its highest forms, is suddenly transmuted into the bodily substance of a boa constrictor or a tiger? No one will seriously assert that the drosera,

Dionaea muscipula, and other insectivorous and carnivorous plants are organisms superior in sensitiveness to those which they devour, or that this transformation of animal into vegetable structure increases the sum of pleasurable sensation in the world. The doctrine of evolution, which regards these antagonisms as mere episodes in the universal struggle for existence, has forever set aside this sort of theodicy and put an end to all teleological attempts to infer from the nature and operations of creation the moral character of the Creator.

4

THE EMERGENCE OF
AN ECOLOGICAL CONSCIOUSNESS

Nathaniel Shaler
MAN AND THE EARTH

Nathaniel Shaler (1844–1906) taught geology at Harvard for several decades and was dean of the Lawrence Scientific School. With his colleagues in the new discipline of ecology he well understood that man's relationship with animate nature should not be conducted on a mere piecemeal basis, without concern for the integrity of ecological associations. Although as a recognized resource expert he devoted most of his conservation efforts to satisfying human material needs, in this selection he emphasizes mankind's duty to preserve as much as possible of the whole web of life, both as a matter of self-interest and as a moral obligation implied in our biological roots. That a change in the methods of teaching science—perhaps instituting a broader, ecological study—can be a means of promoting a new environmental ethic has become a common theme since Shaler wrote. Behind this sentiment lurks the fear that science, through intense specialization, will take away with one hand what, through ecology and evolutionary biology, it has given with the other: the possibility for a revolutionary expansion in moral insight based on a wide understanding of man's integral place in nature.

. . . Let us understand that by nature is meant the primitive species of animals and plants and their associations, the physical conditions which give the earth its expression; in fine, the assemblage of objects and actions that make up the wilderness when it is untouched by the hand of man. It is evident that all this is to undergo a great change by that same masterful hand of the supremely wilful creature whose progressive desires are likely to leave little, save with deliberate purpose, of the shapes that the ancient order established. We see, already, vast alterations since those desires began to expand. Half the

SOURCE. Nathaniel Shaler, *Man and the Earth* (New York, 1905), pp. 190–208, 228–233.

land has lost its pristine aspect; many of the greater woods are gone to their remnants; hosts of animals have been destroyed, and other species once wide-ranging and dominant are reduced to scattered bands and are on the verge of extinction. The life of the world has learned of its new master in widespread slaying and subjugation. The question is as to the measure of it that the awakening reason of the tyrant may leave.

First let us note that the organic species of the earth—animals and plants together, including the invisibly small as well as the visible—probably number between two and three million. We know as yet little concerning the microscopic forms, such as the bacteria, save when they are forced on our prying attention by their interference with our affairs. For all we know or are likely soon to learn, the number of these kinds may be as great as those of the other visible forms of life. It is by no means likely that our means of exploring the world of the small are or can be made sufficiently effective to reveal the least of these creatures.

Organic life does not consist, as some think, in a mere huddle of living objects contending with each other for a place in the world. It is rather a group of vast associations in which the species, each representing certain capacities and powers, are united as in a commonwealth. It is true that some prey upon others and most are competing with rivals for a chance to live, as is the case in our human societies; but for all the contention these great combined faunas and floras, these organic hosts of the earth, are effectively balanced organizations, the order of their relations having been determined by endless trials through the geological ages in which they have been developed.

We may see a little of this adjustment of species to species in an organic host when we consider the history of what we may term weeds, be they plant or animal. It is characteristic of all these excessively successful species that they are newcomers in the fields they infest, brought in from some other province where they are so adjusted to the species with which they have long been in contact that there they have no more than a fair chance to develop. In the region where they are weeds or pests they are not checked by their ancient rivals and enemies, species educated to contend with them, and so they run riot in their new-found freedom. This is the case not only with a host of plants, but many animals as well. The hares brought to Australia from Europe were in their native country kept in check by several carnivorous animals, foxes, weasels, etc., but the immigrants, not finding any effective enemies in their new country, became weeds—species with a measure of freedom none have in an adjusted assemblage of life. These weeds usually have their success in the tilled fields and not in the wildernesses; there they are apt to be beaten off by the well-organized forces of the natural life.

Now and then, in the natural order, there enters into these temporarily balanced organic hosts some species developed in its midst or introduced from some other field, a species which disturbs the original order. Usually, however, as above noted, the original occupants of the fauna and flora hold their ground so well that the solitary invaders have no chance to establish themselves: the changes are likely to occur not by haphazard immigration of species, but by the movement of the organic host as a whole under conditions of climatal or geographic change, which permit or compel assemblages to move this way or that over the surface of the land or the floor of the seas. The one exception to this general truth is in the case of man. He alone by his militant and progressive desires has become the successful invader of all the organic provinces—the supremely successful weed.

In his primitive state before he become in any considerable extent a toolmaker, man appears to have been limited in his distribution, much as are the lower animals; but in proportion as he became endowed with fire, clothing, weapons, and other tools, his capacity to invade increased and his efficiency in destroying the inherited order of organic life rapidly augmented. We see the stage to which this has attained; we clearly foresee that it is as yet in its mere beginning, and that the original complexion of life is to remain only so far as man desires to leave it as nature made it. On the supposition that man is soon to begin to manage the life of the planet, not, as at present, in an accidental and generally destructive manner, but rationally and with a view to keeping and leaving it in a shape to be good for his successors, let us see what we can forecast as to the direction and results of his endeavors.

We may assume that the progress of man in the subjugation of the planet will eventually lead to the further disturbance of the ancient organic order. In fact these overturnings will be inevitable, as was the destruction of the North American bison, because most wild species of large size cannot maintain themselves save in large numbers and with a measure of freedom not possible where the land is to serve the needs of man. In part the destruction will be due to the fact that the creatures are on the natural way to extermination, as was the case with the dodo and the great auk, the hand of man giving no more than the last touch in the series of actions that brought the end. In some part the elimination of species will be due to the fact that the creatures are directly harmful to man. The tiger and its kindred among the mammals, sundry venomous serpents, and, perhaps, a few other vertebrates, will on this account have to be eliminated. Yet in this great group of backboned animals there is certainly not one percent of the forms that by their habits warrant extermination.

In the life below the vertebrates we find the groups of animals and plants where the interests of mankind demand extensive destruction; yet there are only three of the many classes where such work is seriously called for. These are the bacteria, certain plasmodiums, and certain limited families of insects. The bacteria have a bad name, but of the vast host of their species there may be no more than a few score, possibly less, that harm man or his domesticated animals and plants. The greater number do work which from our point of view is beneficent, in some cases absolutely necessary for the maintenance of organic life. Of the plasmodiums we know that some forms are harmful, as they are the source of fevers. As a whole, these lowly organisms are to man by far the most inimical of all organisms: certainly more than half, probably more than three-fourths of the deaths in his species are due to their action; all the other agents of death save old age are of relatively trifling importance. His largest and most difficult task is to eradicate these mighty, though invisible, enemies.

From the protozoa to the insects it is interesting to note that there is not a species which can be regarded as a serious enemy of man or of his domesticated animals. Some few, as the slugs, prey upon his gardens, the sea-nettles may sting him or, in the tropics, the land-crabs may become a nuisance, and certain worms are the source of serious diseases, but from this great field of life he experiences at most but limited ills. When we come to the group of insects we find quite other conditions: there is a host of species which directly or indirectly bring us calamities. As is now well known, in the mosquitoes and the flies they transmit the bacteria and plasmodiums which produce malarial, typhoid, and yellow fever, and probably other maladies. The servants of man, the domesticated animals and plants, suffer even as much as their master from insect scourges; in fact, agriculture and herding have from the beginning had to war with these creatures which, by their adaptability to the conditions of other life, their marvelous energy and swift increase, are able to assail as no other creatures can.

The history of the ravages of the locusts in North Africa and elsewhere shows that it is possible for an insect profoundly to affect or even to exterminate a civilization. We are just now on the way of a momentous experiment of this nature in America. A species known as the gypsy moth, long and unhappily known as a pest in Europe, has recently been introduced in eastern Massachusetts. In its new environment, where the few enemies that in the old world contend against it are lacking, the species is spreading steadfastly and certainly. Where it is allowed freely to increase for a few years, it develops in such multitudes that it devours all kinds of vegetation, that of the forests as well as of the tilled ground. So far, in its spread it has come to occupy only a few hundred square miles of territory, and the efforts to supress it, though miserably irresolute, have served to restrain its depredations. There seems, however, to be a certain and very grave danger that when it becomes firmly implanted in the forests its assaults will be practicably irresistible. It is in the power of this creature, that a touch will slay, by its numbers to endanger our culture. This it will certainly do if its increase is not in some way arrested.

In general, we may trust to the arrest of the multiplication of any species of insect developing in its ancient associations with other life to the development of some inimical insect or some of the mould-breeding forms of life competent to destroy it. For a few years these plagues may increase after the manner of the army worm until their devastations are startling, then some ichneumon fly, which has the habit of laying its eggs in their grubs, avails itself of the extended opportunity and becomes in turn so plentiful that it destroys the host. But when, as in the case of the gypsy moth, the pest is an invader from another host and does not have to meet enemies trained for combat with it, the danger of its ravages is vastly enhanced. It is likely to be long before species competent to restrain them are brought to efficiency, and in the meantime the destruction goes on.

As before noted, the organic hosts are generally so well organized that their closed ranks usually defy the efforts of would-be invaders of their realm. It commonly requires the assistance of man, intentionally or unintentionally given, to effect the naturalization of a foreign form. Thus none of our weeds from the old world would have had a chance to obtain a foothold in this country, save for the fact that they have entered by the ways of commerce and have been first implanted on our cultivated fields. From that lodgment and nursery they can have a chance to spread to the less hospitable wildernesses. A good example of how this works in insects is again well illustrated by the history of the gypsy moth in America. This insect has the habit of laying its eggs whenever it finds a chance to deposit them; where the creatures abound they are very often found on timber, furniture, casks, etc., so that it may be assumed as certain that for centuries they have been plentifully imported into this country. We have to believe that in thousands of instances these pests have hatched and the young had the chance to develop, but in no case did the species establish itself until in the latter part of the last century, when some of the kind were brought to eastern Massachusetts for purposes of experiment and reared in cages: by accident a considerable number of them in the grown state were released, and thereby the implantation was effected.

We see by the facts above noted that man's relation to the organic life about him will in part consist in two series of actions: in the suppression of the creatures noxious to him because of their assault on his health or comfort, and in the restriction of the wanderings of species which are kept in control in their native realms but become weeds when they are implanted elsewhere. Another part of his endeavors should go to the limitation of his destructive work within the narrowest possible bounds, so that the body of life of which he is to be the master shall suffer as little as may be from his control. That it is inevitably to suffer much from his innovations has to be accepted as the price to be paid for the humanization of the earth, a process which is but at its beginning and is to go on until the quality of the sphere is to be vastly changed. But the measure of the alteration and its essential results are for his determination, and their effect will be in large measure to determine his station.

It is evident that so far as the land-life is concerned the increase of numbers of mankind will inevitably break up many of the ancient organic hosts. The creatures of the sea, except those that afford food, are not likely to be disturbed, but with all the serviceable land occupied by the few plants and animals that are of use to civilization, and with the forests that remain after this selection devoted to the growth of those trees only that have value as timber, there will remain but the deserts and the untillable fields of high latitude where there will be a chance for nature to be maintained. Europe is already near to this state of complete subjugation: it seems pretty certain that in another century its wildernesses will all have disappeared. Not long after, the same conditions of utter domestication will come upon the fields of our own continent, and soon thereafter, even in the sense of human time, all the lands will be brought to the same state. It is, therefore, not too early to consider what losses this change will entail and what we of our time should do to minimize them.

First, we shall note that, manage the situation as best we may, this humanizing of the earth will necessarily entail a great loss of its organic species, for while only a few hundred, or at most a few thousand, kinds, need be sacrificed for the betterment of man's estate, a host will pass away because of the general disturbance which his civilized life brings about. It may be said that in the history of the earth the passing away of species is as common an event as the death of their individuals in our own times, and that human interference will but add a few score thousand to the hundreds of millions that have departed in their time. Yet we have to remember that this life of the earth is the record of the greatest work of the world and that, precious as it is to the science of today, it is to be vastly more so to the science of the time to come. Each of these kinds we destroy is absolutely irreplaceable; no record we can make of it will be satisfactory to the learning of a thousand years hence. When a species dies it goes forever; for its like will never come into existence again. Moreover, we have to consider that, in the lame and impotent fragments of nature that man is to leave, the processes that make new forms of wild land-life are in general to lapse, so that the places of those to be swept away are not likely to be filled. The question to which we are led by the points above noted is as to the groups of wild animals and plants which should be especially cared for, and the means by which they may most effectively be preserved.

While we cannot clearly foresee what animals will be most important to the science of future centuries, certain points of their interest we may fairly conjecture. We may presume that they will need to have types or examples of each group retained and, above all, those animals which belong to the more intelligent species: for the questions of mind in the lower creatures, interesting as they are to us, are to be far more so to our successors, who will be better able to approach the problems of psychology. We can see clearly enough that they have a right to demand from us the utmost care in preserving those forms that, even with our limited view, are clearly enough seen to be of singular psychologic value.

Leaving out of view the marine species where the advance of man is not likely to have much disturbing effect, and those in which we discern nothing of extraordinary importance, we still find very many groups that demand protection. Among the invertebrates there are no species below the grade of the insects that are in danger of passing away because of man's action, but in that class there are sundry forms of remarkable mental quality that are likely to be exterminated before they have told their story to the students of the future. These are limited to those groups in which there are few kinds that need to be extirpated because of the damage they do. These groups are the ants, the bees, and the termites. In them we find the highest development of that form of mental action we term instinct. In the ants there are probably some hundreds of social species that show in a great variety of peculiar accomplishments the development of instincts. The same is the case in the groups of bees and wasps where the species, if less limited, are even richer in variety of mental actions. In these series of the hymenoptera there are few species in any measure harmful to man, while on the whole they afford the richest and most varied conditions of mentality existing in the invertebrates. The termites, commonly reckoned with the ants, but belonging to a very different order of insects, are a small and peculiarly interesting group: though occasionally harmful to man, they are not likely to be exterminated by him. As a whole, the insects most important to the psychologist are not likely to be exterminated or, if in danger of passing away, the passage will not come about for many centuries.

It is in the invertebrates above the level of the fishes that all the great losses arising from the domestication of the earth are to be expected. In the reptiles and batrachians, the lower classes of the type, the groups are already far advanced in their decline from the richness of their development in the middle age of organic history: there is little among them to preserve that seems specially important from the point of view of psychology. They may well be left to their chance of survival, good for a long time to come, except in the case of the larger saurians, the kindred of the crocodiles, and the more venomous serpents. The humbler and harmless forms are pretty sure to keep their place beside man.

It is otherwise with the superior classes of the vertebrates, the mammals and the birds. In these groups the species are generally so active in their habits and so entangled in their environment that any considerable change in the conditions of their life is likely to lead, as it has in many instances led, to their speedy destruction. Among the birds it is probable that a dozen species have been extirpated by man within a thousand years, and many others are on the verge of extinction. Some of these were recently most abundant. Thus the passenger pigeon, which the present writer remembers only about half a century ago as the most numerous land-vertebrate of this or perhaps any other continent, is now a rare bird not readily to be found in any part of the field where it then superabounded. Another instance from the same field is afforded by a species of parrot of the kind known as paroquets, which when Kentucky was first settled ranged as far north as the Ohio river. This interesting form has now been driven to the far south: the species is perhaps lost. In every part of the world the bird life appears to be far more disturbed by the advance of civilization than that of any other class. There are scores if not hundreds of species which are on the verge of extinction. It is indeed probable that, except for peculiar care, the most of those forms, which do not in a way adopt man and his works in the manner of the British sparrow, will be swept from the earth. This fate is particularly likely to overtake the migratory species, for in their wanderings they are exposed to a great variety of environing conditions, all of which are likely to be changed by the alterations that man is to make. It behooves us to take especial care of these creatures, for they are in many ways the noblest products of life.

It is in the mammalia that we find the species which the students of the future will most desire to explore, for they are our nearest kindred and from them we learn the most as to the history of our own minds. Of the several thousand kinds of wild, suck-giving animals, none but a few score of the smaller sort, and some of the marine species which do not resort to the shores, will be safely housed when the earth is completely subjugated, save they be kept in selected wildernesses protected from the depredations of the monumental slayer. It is not too much to say that nearly all the larger forms already have been brought to the danger line, and that the greater number of them will, in one or two hundred years if they be not well cared for, utterly disappear. Within fifty years, several of the large mammals of Africa and America have been exterminated or brought so near to extinction that their end is certain.

It is not likely that any practicable measure of care will serve to protect the whole of our kindred mammalian species from death. The larger carnivora, the lion, tiger, etc., are too inconvenient to be spared. Certain of the herbivora, such as the African buffalo, are too ineradicably fierce to submit to the domestication of preserves. Of these unsavable forms there are not many; perhaps not more than a twentieth part of the whole number are beyond salvation. The remainder can be preserved, provided their master is willing to be a providence to them. Some of these, perhaps thirty species, need speedy care; the most can wait for a century or so before they are in imminent danger of extinction. On the whole the herbivorous mammals of Africa are the most endangered of all their kindred. That continent, by far the richest in large species of the class, remained until the last century practically untrodden by the sportsman. The human assault on the life of this land was made for food, or, in the case of the elephant and the hippopotamus, for ivory, and with ineffective arms; now the land is the favorite range of that mighty beast, the big-game hunter, who, with tools vastly more effective than the native's spear or the flint-lock gun, kills not for profit but as a dog in a sheepfold for the mere love of killing. The African elephant, several of the antelopes of that country, and other very interesting species have been brought to the verge of extinction. In the opinion of those competent to judge, certain forms plentiful a hundred years ago have already passed away. The Indian elephant, because of his large place as a domesticated beast, although he does not breed freely in captivity, is apparently safe from extinction until supplanted by some kind of engine, but his African kinsman being much less domesticable, hardly fit, indeed, for the service of man, is doomed to certain and speedy extinction unless sedulously guarded from the sportsman; like most other large herbivora, it cannot maintain itself as a solitary paired form: it needs the conditions of the herd for its survival. As soon as it becomes rare it will speedily pass away.

On many accounts the elephants are likely to prove the most interesting of the lower mammalia to the psychologists of the centuries to come. They belong to a branch from the stem whence man came, that separated from the main stem at an early stage of its history and has departed further than almost any other of the herbivora. The most of these aberrant groups, such as the whales, the bats, the armadillos, etc., have low-grade mental powers, but the elephants, for reasons which cannot here be discussed, reasons still doubtful, are mentally the ablest and most humanlike of all the brutes, with the possible exception of the anthropoid apes. Those apes have indeed the brutal qualities of man in startling perfection, but the elephants, at least those of the Asiatic group, share with us many of the better human attributes as do no other of the lower mammalian species. It is a most interesting question in the history of mind how these creatures came by their intellectual, and we may fairly add their moral, capacities. As the nearest of our spiritual kinsmen except the domesticated dogs, they demand our care; they should have it also for their scientific value. From this point of view the African species is needed for comparison with its diverse Asiatic kinsman.

From the point of view of the natural history of man, of which we yet know very little, it is particularly important that all those species which lie near the path through which he came from the lower life should be preserved for future enquiry. It is unhappily certain that there is no infra-human species or genus now existing through which we can trace our descent. Yet the gorilla is a near collateral, so near, indeed, that it may fairly be claimed that he is in the same family as man, or even that as animals are usually classified in the same sub-family or tribe. It is likely enough that he is as near to us in the genealogical tree as is the sheep to the goat, the lion to the tiger, or the bison to the buffalo. So, too, with all the creatures commonly termed apes; they lie about the place of the parent stem of our life, representing in a hundred or so living examples the marvelous history of that age-long up-climbing that brought, in the end, our kind. The greatest of all science problems is this of the coming of man; so far as we shall solve it the work will have to be done from the study of the life nearest to the path on which he won his way. If these monuments be destroyed before they are surely interpreted the riddle may never be read.

It is always difficult to foresee the needs of the generations to come, and nowhere more so than in the field—we may indeed say the wide realm—of enquiry; yet it is safe to anticipate the needs of handing on to our successors all we can of our and their heritage of the earth as little impaired as we can contrive it to be. We may be sure that they will more readily pardon the waste we may make of its physical resources, its coal and ores, or even of the precious soil, than any unnecessary or avoidable destruction of its organic species. They will require these creatures not only for the advance of knowledge in general, but for much they have to learn concerning the safety and development of the mind and body of mankind. It is, for instance, evident that, in studies yet to be made as to the nature and modes of prevention of human diseases, many species of animals are to contribute largely to knowledge as to their nature as well as to the means of prevention. Two out of the limited number of our domesticated animals, by their physiological characteristics, now preserve us from two of the most fatal maladies. The cow has by the method of vaccination effectively relieved us of smallpox, and the horse is the only available creature for producing the antitoxin of diphtheria. Thus we see that, with the next beast swept away, there may go the possibilities of help to life as well as to learning.

In another chapter some of the ways in which we and our heritors may best deal with this difficult problem of making over the surface of the earth with the least possible destruction of its indigenous life will be noted. The arrangements to attain this end cannot be made at once, they must be gradually developed, as required by the advancing needs. What is, however, needed at once is a sense of the situation, a clearing away of the primitive childish notion that the marvelous life of this world is fitly to be taken as a toy for man, to be carelessly rent away with his plough, or slain for his diversion. The establishment of a truly civilized state of mind, as regards man's duty by those creatures of all degree who share life with him, is the necessary foundation for such conduct as will keep our race and time from shame in the age to come. . . .

Those who have read the preceding pages of this book must have perceived that so far as the matter they contain has other purpose than to be interesting, that purpose is meant to awaken a sense of the nobility and dignity of the relation man bears to this wonderful planet and the duty that comes therefrom. In this closing chapter I propose to assemble certain of these considerations in an effort to show the need of another than the old way of looking at the world about us as a mere toy or, at most, a useful mechanism, and to consider the obligations which it lays upon us.

There is a school of philosophers, like the most of such schools ancient and rather out of date, whose followers hold to the interesting notion that the universe is but an extension of the individual man:

that all in the realm is but an enlargement of him who cognizes it—having its existence altogether from his appreciation. Like many another philosophy, this of the solipsists (i.e., *only himself-ists*), it is good to entertain its views at least for a time, because they serve, even if not strictly true, to enlarge our conceptions. As the naturalist sees it, this paradoxical statement of man's relation to the universe needs but a change of form to fit the facts better than any other theoretical interpretation. If we say that the universe is an extension of man because he has come forth from it and embodies in a way all in himself, we have a form of solipsism that suits the student of nature—apparently the new mode of phrasing reverses the tenet—but it retains the essential point of the ingenious philosophy, for it acknowledges the identity of man and the realm in which he dwells.

There is good reason to believe that the main idea embodied in the philosophy which regards the world as essentially kin to ourselves is to be that held by the men of the hereafter. The whole trend of the understanding as to the relation of man to the realm leads to the conclusion that whatever else he may be, he is the sum of a series of actions linked with all that has gone on upon this earth. Already the more discerning see that our kind have come to the beginning of their mastery of this world by penetrating into its meanings, and further knowledge can only increase the clearness and sufficiency of this vision. We may assume that our successors will, generation by generation, be more and more inspired by this understanding: that they will come to see the world as a wider aspect of themselves.

If the above suggested view as to the trend of thought of men as to their relations with nature be true, then we have not long to wait until the care for the economical resources of the earth which has been advocated in the first chapters of this book, and for which people are already prepared, will be merged in a larger care for the sphere as a part of man from which he has been alienated by ignorance, but with which he is to be reconciled by knowledge. Seeing, as he must, for it is written on earth and sky, the oneness of nature and intelligence as its master, man is sure to go forward unto the higher life of understanding out of which will come a sense, of which we see barely the traces in our time, of his duty by the earth. At present, the conception as to our place in the realm is so new, so confused with the ancient misunderstandings, that it is difficult to see how we can do the first part of our task by cooperating with the conditions which have made for the advance which has brought us to the gates of the new life. Certain directions for our endeavors are, however, plain.

To bring men to an appreciation of their station as masters of the earth it is necessary that they be effectively taught the nature of that relation. This is, indeed, the part of modern science, but we are as yet far from its accomplishment. So far as science is now passing to the body of the people, it is in the form of special, though elementary, knowledge of this or that group of the facts. Of such, men may have an endless amount and yet not be nearer to the understanding of the important truth; the need is to have this truth taught as a gospel. It has to go to men with the quality of religion, by the way of imagination and the emotions with which it is conjoined. There is reason to hope that we are at the beginning of the process which is surely to require generations for its accomplishment. At best this enlargement will be slowly brought about and it cannot be expected immediately to affect the common folk. Unless the world of men should become philosophers, we must look in the future as in the past for the leading spirits, the rare men, to be guides to the new dispensation, the masses following in the ancient dumb way—taking their light not directly from nature, but in the good old way, mediately through their prophets.

Something may be done to hasten the growth of a better state of mind as to man's relation to nature by a much-needed change in our methods of teaching science. We now present the realm to beginners as a group of fragments labeled astronomy, geology, chemistry, physics, and biology, each, as set forth, appearing to him as a little world in itself, with its own separate life, having little to do with its neighbors. It is rare, indeed, in a very considerable experience with youths to find one who has gained any inkling as to the complete unity of nature. Seldom it is, even with those who attain mastery in some one of these learnings, that we find a true sense as to the absolute oneness of the realm, or the place of man as the highest product of its work. This is the inevitable position of those whose task it is to advance the frontiers of knowledge. The mass of their knowledge required to make way in any field is so great that little can be known of any other domain. But this situation of the investigator need not be that of the ordinary man. Save for the merest trifle of knowledge which he gains by the simplest individual inquiries, he must take this nature on faith in his teachers. So far from trying to compass the learning of the smallest bit of the realm, he needs [to] be limited to the little of it that will best serve to enlarge his understandings of the world as a part of himself.

In the revision of our project concerning the share of natural science in our scheme of popular education—a revision long overdue and now sorely requiring action—we need [to] begin by determining, first of all, what of its truths have cardinal value from the point of view of conduct; what of them, in a word, help to dutifulness by ennobling the conception of man's place in nature. Other matters may be taught for other purposes, for their purely intellectual values, or for their economic uses; but the great gain we are to have from the modern knowledge of the world is in the change of attitude it is to bring about: in the sense of kinship with the anciently alien realm and of duty by the great inheritance of life. To the making of this new spirit no great body of learning need go; it will depend for its development far more on the way of approach than on the mass of the knowledge that is gained. So soon as men come to feel themselves as really the children of the world, the tides of affection that instinctively tend toward it, but have been sorely hindered by ancient misunderstandings, will help in the good work, and give us souls reconciled to their great house and eager to help its order.

5
NATURAL KINSHIP AND THE LAND ETHIC

Liberty Hyde Bailey
THE HOLY EARTH

In Liberty Hyde Bailey (1858–1954), the old pastoralism and the new may be seen in clear genetic relationship. A professor of horticulture at Cornell most of his life, Bailey wrote extensively on gardening and agriculture. In 1901 he became editor of Country Life in America, *a new publication organized by Doubleday and Page; in 1908 President Roosevelt asked him to chair his Country Life Commission. Bailey was also a biologist interested in the problem of evolution since his days of apprenticeship under Asa Gray at Harvard. As much as he extolled the life of the small farmer, he understood that in an urban age new affinities between man and nature had to be defined—and evolution offered itself as the doctrine of natural kinship. Through the study of evolution and the practice of a broader conservation, he believed, men in the city might discover their responsibilities to the earth and its tissue of life. A vaporous and cryptic prose style obscured the full implications of his "biocentric" message until the 1930s when Aldo Leopold drew directly from Bailey the materials for his own "ecological ethic." Insofar as the pastoral dream traditionally had been the chief expression of man's desire to live in peace within the order of nature, the new land ethic recovered that ideal and gave it scientific footing. Moreover, as Bailey illustrates, the presence of science in the pastoral garden was not necessarily incompatible with more ancient, even archaic, modes of consciousness.*

We hear much about man being at the mercy of nature, and the literalist will contend that there can be no holy relation under such conditions. But so is man at the mercy of God.

It is a blasphemous practice that speaks of the hostility of the earth, as if the earth were full of menaces and cataclysms. The old fear of nature, that peopled the earth and sky with imps and demons, and that gave a future state to Satan, yet possesses the minds of men, only that we may have ceased to personify and to demonize our fears,

SOURCE. Liberty Hyde Bailey, *The Holy Earth* (New York, 1915), pp. 10–31.

although we still persistently contrast what we call the evil and the good. Still do we attempt to propitiate and appease the adversaries. Still do we carry the ban of the early philosophy that assumed materials and "the flesh" to be evil, and that found a way of escape only in renunciation and asceticism.

Nature cannot be antagonistic to man, seeing that man is a product of nature. We should find vast joy in the fellowship, something like the joy of Pan. We should feel the relief when we no longer apologize for the creator because of the things that are made.

It is true that there are devastations of flood and fire and frost, scourge of disease, and appalling convulsions of earthquake and eruption. But man prospers; and we know that the catastrophes are greatly fewer than the accepted bounties. We have no choice but to abide. No growth comes from hostility. It would undoubtedly be a poor human race if all the pathway had been plain and easy.

The contest with nature is wholesome, particularly when pursued in sympathy and for mastery. It is worthy a being created in God's image. The earth is perhaps a stern earth, but it is a kindly earth.

Most of our difficulty with the earth lies in the effort to do what perhaps ought not to be done. Not even all the land is fit to be farmed. A good part of agriculture is to learn how to adapt one's work to nature, to fit the crop scheme to the climate and to the soil and the facilities. To live in right relation with his natural conditions is one of the first lessons that a wise farmer or any other wise man learns. We are at pains to stress the importance of conduct; very well: conduct toward the earth is an essential part of it.

Nor need we be afraid of any fact that makes one fact more or less in the sum of contacts between the earth and the earth-born children. All "higher criticism" adds to the faith rather than subtracts from it, and strengthens the bond between. The earth and its products are very real.

Our outlook has been drawn very largely from the abstract. Not being yet prepared to understand the conditions of nature, man considered the earth to be inhospitable, and he looked to the supernatural for relief; and relief was heaven. Our pictures of heaven are of the opposites of daily experience—of release, of peace, of joy uninterrupted. The hunting grounds are happy and the satisfaction has no end. The habit of thought has been set by this conception, and it colors our dealings with the human questions and to much extent it controls our practice.

But we begin to understand that the best dealing with problems on earth is to found it on the facts of earth. This is the contribution of natural science, however abstract, to human welfare. Heaven is to be a real consequence of life on earth; and we do not lessen the hope of heaven by increasing our affection for the earth, but rather do we strengthen it. Men now forget the old images of heaven, that they are mere sojourners and wanderers lingering for deliverance, pilgrims in a strange land. Waiting for this rescue, with posture and formula and phrase, we have overlooked the essential goodness and quickness of the earth and the immanence of God.

This feeling that we are pilgrims in a vale of tears has been enhanced by the widespread belief in the sudden ending of the world, by collision or some other impending disaster, and in the common apprehension of doom; and lately by speculations as to the aridation and death of the planet, to which all of us have given more or less credence. But most of these notions are now considered to be fantastic, and we are increasingly confident that the earth is not growing old in a human sense, that its atmosphere and its water are held by the attraction of its mass, and that the sphere is at all events so permanent as to make little difference in our philosophy and no difference in our good behavior. . . .

The earth is divine, because man did not make it. We are under obligation to take part and to do our best, living with each other and with all the creatures. We may not know the full plan, but that does not alter the relation. When once we set ourselves to the pleasure of our dominion, reverently and hopefully, and assume all its responsibilities, we shall have a new hold on life.

We shall put our dominion into the realm of morals. It is now in the realm of trade. This will be very personal morals, but it will also be national and racial morals. More iniquity follows the improper and greedy division of the resources and privileges of the earth than any other form of sinfulness.

If God created the earth, so is the earth hallowed; and if it is hallowed, so must we deal with it devotedly and with care that we do not despoil it, and mindful of our relations to all beings that live on it. We are to consider it religiously: put off thy shoes from thy feet, for the place whereon thou standest is holy ground.

The sacredness to us of the earth is intrinsic and inherent. It lies in our necessary relationship and in the duty imposed upon us to have dominion, and to exercise ourselves even against our own interests. We may not waste that which is not ours. To live in sincere relations with the company of created things and with conscious regard for the support of all men now and yet to come, must be of the essence of righteousness.

This is a larger and more original relation than the modern attitude of appreciation and admiration of nature. In the days of the patriarchs and prophets, nature and man shared in the condemnation and likewise in the redemption. The ground was cursed for Adam's sin. Paul wrote that the whole creation groaneth and travaileth in pain, and that it waiteth for the revealing. Isaiah proclaimed the redemption of the wilderness and the solitary place with the redemption of man, when they shall rejoice and blossom as the rose, and when the glowing sand shall become a pool and the thirsty ground springs of water. . . .

The first observation that must be apparent to all men is that our dominion has been mostly destructive.

We have been greatly engaged in digging up the stored resources, and in destroying vast products of the earth for some small kernel that we can apply to our necessities or add to our enjoyments. We excavate the best of the coal and cast away the remainder; blast the minerals and metals from underneath the crust, and leave the earth raw and sore; we box the pines for turpentine and abandon the growths of limitless years to fire and devastation; sweep the forests with the besom of destruction; pull the fish from the rivers and ponds without making any adequate provision for renewal; exterminate whole races of animals; choke the streams with refuse and dross; rob the land of its available stores, denuding the surface, exposing great areas to erosion.

Nor do we exercise the care and thrift of good housekeepers. We do not clean up our work or leave the earth in order. The remnants and accumulation of mining camps are left to ruin and decay; the deserted phosphate excavations are ragged, barren, and unfilled; vast areas of forested lands are left in brush and waste, unthoughtful of the future, unmindful of the years that must be consumed to reduce the refuse to mould and to cover the surface respectably, uncharitable to those who must clear away the wastes and put the place in order; and so thoughtless are we with these natural resources that even the establishments that manufacture them—the mills, the factories of many kinds—are likely to be offensive objects in the landscape, unclean, unkempt, displaying the unconcern of the owners to the obligation that the use of the materials imposes and to the sensibilities of the community for the way in which they handle them. The burden of proof seems always to have been rested on those who partake little in the benefits, although we know that these nonpartakers have been real owners of the resources; and yet so undeveloped has been the public conscience in these matters that the blame—if blame there be—cannot be laid on one group more than on the other. Strange it is, however, that we should not have insisted at least that those who appropriate the accumulations of the earth should complete their work, cleaning up the remainders, leaving the areas wholesome, inoffensive, and safe. How many and many are the years required to grow a forest and to fill the pockets of the rocks, and how satisfying are the landscapes, and yet how desperately soon may men reduce it all to ruin and to emptiness, and how slatternly may they violate the scenery!

All this habit of destructiveness is uneconomic in the best sense, unsocial, unmoral.

Society now begins to demand a constructive process. With care and with regard for other men, we must produce the food and the other supplies in regularity and sufficiency; and we must clean up after our work, that the earth may not be depleted, scarred, or repulsive.

Yet there is even a more defenseless devastation than all this. It is the organized destructiveness of those who would make military domination the major premise in the constitution of society, accompanying desolation with viciousness and violence, ravaging the holy earth, disrespecting the works of the creator, looking toward extirpation, confessing thereby that they do not know how to live in cooperation with their fellows; in such situations, every new implement of destruction adds to the guilt.

In times past we were moved by religious fanaticism, even to the point of waging wars. Today we are moved by impulses of trade, and we find ourselves plunged into a war of commercial frenzy; and as it has behind it vaster resources and more command of natural forces, so is it the most ferocious and wasteful that the race has experienced, exceeding in its havoc the cataclysms of earthquake and volcano. Certainly we have not yet learned how to withstand the prosperity and the privileges that we have gained by the discoveries of science; and certainly the morals of commerce have not given us freedom or mastery. Rivalry that leads to arms is a natural fruit of unrestrained rivalry in trade.

Man has dominion, but he has no commission to devastate: And the Lord God took the man, and put him into the garden of Eden to dress it and to keep it.

Verily, so bountiful hath been the earth and so securely have we drawn from it our substance, that we have taken it all for granted as if it were only a gift, and with little care or conscious thought of the consequences of our use of it.

We may distinguish three stages in our relation to the planet—the collecting stage, the mining stage, and the producing stage. These overlap and perhaps are nowhere distinct, and yet it serves a purpose to contrast them.

At first man sweeps the earth to see what he may gather—game, wood, fruits, fish, fur, feathers, shells on the shore. A certain social and moral life arises out of this relation, seen well in the woodsmen and the fishers—in whom it best persists to the present day—strong, dogmatic, superstitious folk. Then man begins to go beneath the surface to see what he can find—iron and precious stones, the gold of Ophir, coal and many curious treasures. This develops the exploiting faculties, and leads men into the uttermost parts. In both these stages the elements of waste and disregard have been heavy.

Finally, we begin to enter the productive stage, whereby we secure supplies by controlling the conditions under which they grow, wasting little, harming not. Farming has been very much a mining process, the utilizing of fertility easily at hand and the moving-on to lands unspoiled of quick potash and nitrogen. Now it begins to be really productive and constructive, with a range of responsible and permanent morals. We rear the domestic animals with precision. We raise crops, when we will, almost to a nicety. We plant fish in lakes and streams to some extent but chiefly to provide more game rather than more human food, for in this range we are yet mostly in the collecting or hunter stage. If the older stages were strongly expressed in the character of the people, so will this new stage be expressed; and so is it that we are escaping the primitive and should be coming into a new character. We shall find our rootage in the soil.

This new character, this clearer sense of relationship with the earth, should express itself in all the people and not exclusively in farming people and their like. It should be a popular character—or a national character if we would limit the discussion to one people—and not a class character. Now, here lies a difficulty and here is a reason for writing this book: the population of the earth is increasing, the relative population of farmers is decreasing, people are herding in cities, we have a city mind, and relatively fewer people are brought into touch with the earth in any real way. So it is incumbent on us to take special pains—now that we see the new time—that all the people, or as many of them as possible, shall have contact with the earth and that the earth righteousness shall be abundantly taught.

I hasten to say that I am not thinking of any back-to-the-farm movement to bring about the results we seek. Necessarily, the proportion of farmers will decrease. Not so many are needed relatively, for a man's power to produce has been multiplied. Agriculture makes a great contribution to human progress by releasing men for the manufactures and the trades. In proportion as the ratio of farmers decreases is it important that we provide them the best of opportunities and encouragement: they must be better and better men. And if we are to secure our moral connection with the planet to a large extent through them, we can see that they bear a relation to society in general that we have overlooked.

Even the farming itself is changing radically in character. It ceases to be an occupation to gain sustenance and becomes a business. We apply to it the general attitudes of commerce. We must be alert to see that it does not lose its capacity for spiritual contact.

How we may achieve a more widespread contact with the earth on the part of all the people without making them farmers, I shall endeavor to suggest as I proceed; in fact, this is my theme. Dominion means mastery; we may make the surface of the earth much what we will; we can govern the way in which we shall contemplate it. We are probably near something like a stable occupancy. It is not to be expected that there will be vast shifting of cities as the contest for the mastery of the earth proceeds—probably nothing like the loss of Tyre and Carthage, and of the commercial glory of Venice. In fact, we shall have a progressive occupancy. The greater the population, the greater will be the demands on the planet; and, moreover, every new man will make more demands than his father made, for he will want more to satisfy him. We are to take from the earth much more than we have ever taken before, but it will be taken in a new way and with better intentions. It will be seen, therefore, that we are not here dealing narrowly with an occupation but with something very fundamental to our life on the planet.

We are not to look for our permanent civilization to rest on any species of robber-economy. No flurry of coal mining, or gold-fever, or rubber-collecting in the tropics, or excitement of prospecting for new finds or even locating new lands, no ravishing of the earth or monopolistic control of its bounties, will build a stable society. So is much of our economic and social fabric transitory. It is not by accident that a very distinct form of society is developing in the great farming regions of the Mississippi Valley and in other comparable places; the exploiting and promoting occupancy of those lands is passing and a stable progressive development appears. We have been obsessed of the passion to cover everything at once, to skin the earth, to pass on, even when there was no necessity for so doing. It is a vast pity that this should ever have been the policy of government in giving away great tracts of land by lottery, as if our fingers would burn if we held the lands inviolate until needed by the natural process of settlement. The people should be kept on their lands long enough to learn how to use them. But very well: we have run with the wind, we have staked the lands; now we shall be real farmers and real conquerors. Not all lands are equally good for farming, and some lands will never be good for farming; but whether in Iowa, or New England, or old Asia, farming land may develop character in the people.

My reader must not infer that we have arrived at a permanent agriculture, although we begin now to see the importance of a permanent land occupancy. Probably we have not yet evolved a satisfying husbandry that will maintain itself century by century, without loss and without the ransacking of the ends of the earth for fertilizer materials to make good our deficiencies. All the more is it important that the problem be elevated into the realm of statesmanship and of morals. Neither must he infer that the resources of the earth are to be locked up beyond contact and use (for the contact and use will be morally regulated). But no system of brilliant exploitation, and no accidental scratching of the surface of the earth, and no easy appropriation of stored materials can suffice us in the good days to come. City, country, this class and that class, all fall and merge before the common necessity.

It is often said that the farmer is our financial mainstay; so in the good process of time will he be a moral mainstay, for ultimately finance and social morals must coincide.

The gifts are to be used for service and for satisfaction, and not for wealth. Very great wealth introduces too many intermediaries, too great indirectness, too much that is extrinsic, too frequent hindrances and superficialities. It builds a wall about the man, and too often does he receive his impressions of the needs of the world from satellites and sycophants. It is significant that great wealth, if it contributes much to social service, usually accomplishes the result by endowing others to work. The gift of the products of the earth was "for meat": nothing was said about riches.

Yet the very appropriation or use of natural resources may be the means of directing the mind of the people back to the native situations. We have the opportunity to make the forthcoming development of water-power, for example, such an agency for wholesome training. Whenever we can appropriate without despoliation or loss, or without a damaging monopoly, we tie the people to the backgrounds. . . .

I am not thinking merely of instructing the young in the names and habits of birds and flowers and other pleasant knowledge, although this works strongly toward the desired end; nor of any movement merely to have gardens, or to own farms, although this is desirable provided one is qualified to own a farm; nor of rhapsodies on the beauties of nature. Nor am I thinking of any new plan or any novel kind of institution or any new agency; rather shall we do better to escape some of the excessive institutionalism and organization. We are so accustomed to think in terms of organized polities and education and religion and philanthropies that when we detach ourselves we are said to lack definiteness. It is the personal satisfaction in the earth to which we are born, and the quickened responsibility, the whole relation, broadly developed, of the man and of all men—it is this attitude that we are to discuss.

The years pass and they grow into centuries. We see more clearly. We are to take a new hold.

A constructive and careful handling of the resources of the earth is impossible except on a basis of large cooperation and of association for mutual welfare. The great inventions and discoveries of recent time have extensive social significance.

Yet we have other relations than with the physical and static materials. We are parts in a living sensitive creation. The theme of evolution has overturned our attitude toward this creation. The living creation is not exclusively man-centered: it is biocentric. We perceive the essential continuity in nature, arising from within rather than from without, the forms of life proceeding upwardly and onwardly in something very like a mighty plan of sequence, man being one part in the process. We have genetic relation with all living things, and our aristocracy is the aristocracy of nature. We can claim no gross superiority and no isolated self-importance. The creation, and not man, is the norm. Even now do we begin to guide our practices and our speech by our studies of what we still call the lower creation. We gain a good perspective on ourselves.

If we are parts in the evolution, and if the universe, or even the earth, is not made merely as a footstool, or as a theater for man, so do we lose our cosmic selfishness and we find our place in the plan of things. We are emancipated from ignorance and superstition and small philosophies. The present widespread growth of the feeling of brotherhood would have been impossible in a self-centered creation: the way has been prepared by the discussion of evolution, which is the major biological contribution to human welfare and progress. This is the philosophy of the oneness in nature and the unity in living things.

SUGGESTIONS FOR FURTHER READING

The best point of departure is Leo Marx, *The Machine in the Garden: Technology and the Pastoral Ideal in America* (New York, 1964). Another classic in American environmental studies is Henry Nash Smith, *Virgin Land: The American West as Symbol and Myth* (Cambridge, Mass., 1950). For a broad and consistently provocative survey of environmental thought see Paul Shepard, *Man in the Landscape* (New York, 1967). Hans Huth, *Nature and the Americans* (Berkeley, Calif., 1957) is especially informative on the subject of popular culture, as are Roderick Nash, *Wilderness and the American Mind* (New Haven, Conn., 1967), and Peter Schmitt, *Back to Nature: The Arcadian Myth in Urban America* (New York, 1969). An old but still exciting study of nineteenth-century figures such as Muir and Burroughs is Norman Foerster, *Nature in American Literature* (New York, 1927). For a general introduction to the intellectual history of the period consult Richard Hofstadter, *Social Darwinism in America* (revised edition, Boston, 1955). Finally, though its interpretative scheme is not wholly successful, Lewis Mumford, *The Brown Decades: A Study of the Arts in America, 1865-1895* (New York, 1931), is essential; its sections on Marsh and Olmsted are particularly relevant.

On the subject of conservation the unexcelled account is Samuel Hays, *Conservation and the Gospel of Efficiency: The Progressive Conservation Movement, 1890-1920* (Cambridge, Mass., 1959). Also useful are John Ise, *The United States Forest Policy* (New Haven, Conn., 1920), and Roy Robbins, *Our Landed Heritage: The Public Domain, 1776–1936* (Princeton, N. J., 1942). For the major political issues see Elmo R. Richardson, *The Politics of Conservation: Crusades and Controversies, 1897–1913* (Berkeley, Calif., 1962). In his *Science and the Federal Government* (Cambridge, Mass., 1957), A. Hunter Dupree includes a brief but helpful chapter on conservation. The best studies of cultural attitudes toward wild species are Robert Welker, *Birds and Men: American Birds in Science, Art, Literature, and Conservation* (Cambridge, Mass., 1955), and Peter Matthiessen, *Wildlife in America* (New York, 1959). Among biographies of individuals the following are representative: Wallace Stegner, *Beyond the Hundredth Meridian: John Wesley Powell and the Second Opening of the West* (Boston, 1954): Linnie Marsh Wolfe, *Son of the Wilderness: The Life of John Muir* (New York, 1945); M. Nelson McGeary, *Gifford Pinchot: Forester-Politician* (Princeton, N. J., 1960); and S. B. Sutton, *Charles Sprague Sargent and the Arnold Arboretum* (Cambridge,

Mass., 1970). For guidance to further materials, see Gordon B. Dodds, "The Historiography of American Conservation: Past and Prospects," *Pacific Northwest Quarterly*, 56 (1965), pp. 75–81, and the excellent bibliography in Roderick Nash, ed., *The American Environment: Readings in the History of Conservation* (Reading, Mass., 1968).

For the history of the urban environment during this period a valuable work is Arthur M. Schlesinger, *The Rise of the City, 1878–1898* (New York, 1933). Perhaps the most fruitful approach to the subject is visual; two imaginative studies of this type are John Kouwenhoven, *The Columbia Historical Portrait of New York* (Garden City, N.Y., 1953), and Harold Mayer and Richard Wade, *Chicago: The Making of a Metropolis* (Chicago, 1969). The city as a physical structure is also the theme of *Streetcar Suburbs: The Process of Growth in Boston, 1870–1900* (Cambridge, Mass., 1962) by Sam B. Warner, Jr. Contemporary portraits, often wonderfully opaque, of several cities and towns are given in Henry James, *The American Scene* (New York, 1907). Another and quite different view of the urban landscape is found in Jacob Riis, *How the Other Half Lives* (New York, 1890), which introduced many Americans to the environment of poverty. On this subject see also Roy Lubove, *The Progressives and the Slums: Tenement House Reform in New York, 1890–1917* (Pittsburgh, 1962). As an introduction to the history of environmental health an excellent biography is available in James H. Cassedy, *Charles V. Chapin and the Public Health Movement* (Cambridge, Mass., 1962). On Olmsted's career there are three recent works of note: Albert Fein, ed., *Landscape into Cityscape: Frederick Law Olmsted's Plans for a Greater New York* (Ithaca, N. Y., 1967); Albert Fein, *Frederick Law Olmsted and the American Environmental Tradition* (New York, 1972); and S. B. Sutton, ed., *Civilizing American Cities: A Selection of Frederick Law Olmsted's Writings on City Landscapes* (Cambridge, Mass., 1971).

To give coherent focus to this collection of source materials many important developments in architecture and city design had to be omitted. The interested student can find outstanding studies of these related matters in Vincent Scully, *American Architecture and Urbanism* (New York, 1969); John W. Reps, *The Making of Urban America: A History of City Planning in the United States* (Princeton, N. J., 1965); and Don Gifford, ed., *The Literature of Architecture: The Evolution of Architectural Theory and Practice in Nineteenth-Century America* (New York, 1966). Finally, a one-sided but stimulating work is Morton and Lucia White, *The Intellectual Versus the City: From Thomas Jefferson to Frank Lloyd Wright* (Cambridge, Mass., 1962).